Assessment in
secondary schools

Assessment in secondary schools

The new teacher's guide to monitoring, assessment, recording, reporting and accountability

Val Brooks

Open University Press
Buckingham · Philadelphia

Open University Press
Celtic Court
22 Ballmoor
Buckingham
MK18 1XW

email: enquiries@openup.co.uk
world wide web: www.openup.co.uk

and
325 Chestnut Street
Philadelphia, PA 19106, USA

First Published 2002

A catalogue record of this book is available from the British Library

ISBN   0 335 20638 7 (hb)   0 335 20637 9 (pb)

Library of Congress Cataloging-in-Publication Data
Brooks, Val, 1954–
    Assessment in secondary schools : the new teacher's guide to monitoring, assessment, recording, reporting, and accountability / Val Brooks.
        p. cm.
    Includes bibliographical references (p.) and index.
    ISBN 0-335-20638-7 – ISBN 0-335-20637-9 (pbk.)
    1. Education, Secondary–Great Britain–Evaluation–Handbooks, manuals, etc.   2. Educational tests and measurements–Great Britain–Handbooks, manuals, etc.   3. First year teachers–Great Britain–Handbooks, manuals, etc. I. Title.

LB3056.G7 B78   2001
373.41–dc21   2001036208

Typeset by Graphicraft Limited, Hong Kong
Printed in Great Britain by St Edmundsbury Press Limited,
Bury St Edmunds, Suffolk

For my late father, Frederick Isaacs
(1918–2000)

Contents

Acknowledgements

Many people gave me assistance of various kinds while writing this book. In particular, I should like to thank Chris Husbands for his thoughtful comments and for suggesting some helpful references. I am also grateful to all the teachers who talked to me about their assessment work and provided copies of school documentation for use in the book. Thanks are also due to Hodder and Stoughton for their agreement that I should use material previously published in Sutton, C. (1981) *Communicating in the Classroom*.

Acronyms and abbreviations

AEA	Advanced Extension Award
A level	Advanced level
ALIS	Advanced Level Information System
AQA	Assessment and Qualifications Alliance
AS level	Advanced Subsidiary level
AT	attainment target
CAT	Cognitive Abilities Test
CPD	continuing professional development
CSE	Certificate of Secondary Education
DES	Department for Education and Science
DfE	Department for Education
DfEE	Department for Education and Employment
FSM	free school meals
GCE	General Certificate of Education
GCSE	General Certificate of Secondary Education
GNVQ	General National Vocational Qualification
HMI	Her Majesty's Inspectorate
HoD	head of department
ICT	Information and Communications Technology
IEP	Individual Education Plan
IRF	Initiation Response Feedback
IT	information technology
ITT	initial teacher training
KS	key stage
LEA	local education authority
LQ	lower quartile
MARRA	monitoring, assessment, recording, reporting and accountability
MFL	modern foreign languages
MIDYIS	Middle Years Information System

NC	National Curriculum
NCET	National Council for Educational Technology
NFER	National Foundation for Educational Research
NQT	newly qualified teacher
NRA	National Record of Achievement
NVQ	National Vocational Qualification
OCR	Oxford, Cambridge and the Royal Society of Arts
Ofsted	Office for Standards in Education
O level	Ordinary level
PANDA	performance and assessment
PE	physical education
PF	Progress File
PI	performance indicator
P-I-P	Private-Intimate-Public
PoS	Programme of Study
PS	points score
PSHE	personal, social and health education
QCA	Qualifications and Curriculum Authority
QTS	Qualified Teacher Status
RE	religious education
SAT	standard assessment task
SCAA	School Curriculum and Assessment Authority
SEN	special educational needs
SENCO	special educational needs coordinator
SIMS	Schools Information Management System
S level	Special level
SMART	specific, measurable, achievable, realistic, time-related
SMT	senior management team
TA	teacher assessment
TES	*Times Educational Supplement*
TGAT	Task Group on Assessment and Testing
UQ	upper quartile
WYTIWYG	what you test is what you get!
YELLIS	Year Eleven Information System

Introduction

1.1 Background

Students enrolled on initial teacher training (ITT) courses are required to meet an exacting set of assessment standards (Department for Education and Employment (DfEE) 1998a). One of the four areas into which these standards are divided is monitoring, assessment, recording, reporting and accountability (MARRA). Each year, the students with whom I work are asked to evaluate their course of study. These evaluations suggest that MARRA is one of the most inaccessible elements of the training programme. It is unsurprising, therefore, that when I visit students during placement, I find little evidence that they are making an informed and systematic use of assessment to support their teaching or their pupils' learning. There are scant references to assessment in their planning, evaluations and conversations with me. When I focus our discussions on assessment, two things are noticeable. First, many students have a partial and unhelpful view of assessment as an appendage to their teaching. Competent teaching is the goal to which they aspire and assessment is seen as an adjunct to this. Consequently, if the role of assessment is considered at all, it is seen as a bolt-on activity. Second, they tend to think in terms of terminal assessment events: an end-of-topic test or the piece of homework which marks the culmination of a class's work on a topic. The notion that assessment should be an integral element of teaching and learning – taking place informally as well as formally and in fleeting assessment incidents as well as in organized events – is at odds with their traditional view of assessment. The concept of assessment *for* learning as well as *of* learning is one which students find difficult to internalize and translate into practice. Nevertheless, when their classroom practice is observed, there is evidence of an *intuitive* use of formative assessment (Section 1.2). But only if these students can make it a systematic element of their conscious practice will they be able to harness the potential of formative assessment to enhance their teaching and their pupils' learning.

Findings from research and from inspections of ITT suggest that my experiences are not atypical. Traditionally, ITT courses have paid limited attention to assessment and, although the situation has improved recently, the Office for Standards in Education's (Ofsted) (1999: para. 78) most recent overview report on secondary ITT still concluded that: 'The relative weakness of trainees in this area of the standards is striking, and it affects trainees in almost every subject.' One study of the training provided by mentors as part of school-based ITT found that mentors were chary of addressing the subject: 'a small, and in most cases very small, percentage of time was used in this way' (Butterfield *et al.* 1999: 230). In fact, mentors often circumvented students' attempts to raise the topic. When assessment was discussed, mentors presented it as 'an interference, an irrelevance or just something that had to be done' (Butterfield *et al.* 1999: 241). There is no guarantee that newly qualified teachers (NQTs) for whom assessment is a weakness will go on to become capable exponents. On the contrary, teachers have received few incentives to develop a distinctive style of formative teacher assessment (TA) because 'the major resource has gone into the production, administration, analysis and reporting of more and more tests' (James 2000: 353). Tests and examinations exercise a powerful influence over teachers' thinking and practices (Black and Wiliam 1998a). In contrast: 'formative assessment is not well understood by teachers and is weak in practice' (Black and Wiliam 1998a: 20). Nor does assessment feature strongly in teachers' priorities for continuing professional development (CPD). A national survey found that only 4 per cent of a sample of over 1000 teachers had identified assessment as a priority for personal development as part of teacher appraisal (Wragg *et al.* 1996).

This, then, provides the context for this book which takes a Cinderella aspect of teaching – neglected, poorly understood and often despised by teachers – and examines it from the perspective of beginning teachers. There are powerful reasons why student teachers should seek to develop a better appreciation of assessment. First, the tests, examinations and other statutory requirements which punctuate the different stages of secondary education will inevitably form a key element of their work. Moreover, assessment – particularly summative assessment – has become an important feature of successive governments' educational policies which is used in an attempt to monitor and raise educational standards and to increase the accountability of different sectors of the educational service. Teachers, who are required to implement policy, need a sound understanding of assessment's possibilities and potential, as well as of its defects and shortcomings. Perhaps the most powerful incentive for new teachers to develop expertise in this area of their work comes from research which suggests that *formative* assessment has the capacity to produce learning gains which exceed those derived from other educational interventions designed to raise attainment (Black and Wiliam 1998a). This important finding raises the profile of formative assessment, making it a key tool in new teachers' repertoire of skills. NQTs need, therefore, to be 'assessment literate' (Gipps 1994: 160) if they are to derive full benefit from formative assessment as well as countering some of the worst effects that certain types of assessment are known to have on teaching and learning.

That, however, may be easier said than done for as Claxton observed:

> All students when they arrive at a teacher-training course have a personal theory about education, schools, children, teaching and learning; what is important and what is not . . . They have their own intuitive, largely tacit, largely unexamined set of beliefs, attitudes and values that are variously idiosyncratic, partial, simplistic, archaic and rigid.
>
> (Claxton 1984, quoted in Smith and Alred 1994: 105)

These underlying attitudes and values are important because they determine students' preferred classroom approaches and their willingness to experiment with others. The challenge for a book such as this, therefore, is to help students to recognize their own predispositions so that they may reach a better understanding of what underlies their preferred approaches to assessment. By exposing beliefs to scrutiny, an individual may ascertain whether they are well founded or amount to little more than prejudices. For instance, consider where you stand in relation to the dichotomy illustrated in Figure I.1.

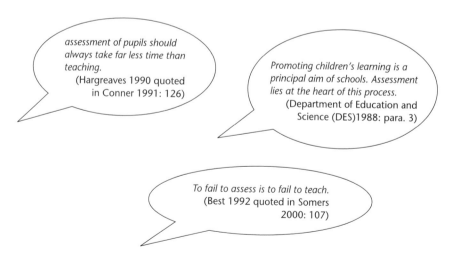

Figure I.1 Contrasting views of the relationship between teaching, learning and assessment

Here we have opposing views of the relationship between learning and assessment. The first implies a disjunction between the two processes with assessment interrupting learning. It is, therefore, important to limit the time spent on assessment. The alternative view sees assessment as a life force at the core of the learning process and inseparable from it. You will quickly realize that although this book acknowledges the negative potential of certain types and uses of assessment, it nevertheless sympathizes strongly with the latter view.

What pre-existing beliefs and attitudes towards assessment do you bring to reading this book? Whatever they are, they will inevitably influence the way you receive the material presented here. The following activity is intended to help you to start examining your own ideas about assessment – ideas which may have been internalized to the point where they are no longer part of your conscious thinking on the subject (that is, they have become tacit).

Task I.1

Write two brief paragraphs about your own experiences of assessment. In the first, describe a positive experience where assessment was beneficial and in the other relate a negative experience where assessment was counter-productive. The experiences may come from any area of life: school; further and higher education; the workplace; hobbies; skills or qualifications gained in a non-academic context such as learning to drive. Use these accounts as a basis for producing two lists:

- ways in which assessment helps learners
- ways in which assessment hinders learners.

When you have read the book, reconsider your lists.

I.2 Organization and content

The content and organization of this book have been determined by its attempt to meet the needs of beginning teachers. The text is organized into three broad parts which are intended to mirror stages in the experience and concerns of student teachers. Each part places assessment in a context.

Part 1 Assessment and learning: the classroom context

For beginning teachers, the most immediate context is the classroom and so Part 1 examines issues which exercise students in the early stages of their course when experiences of assessment are limited to informal, class-based activities. It contains four chapters, each dealing with different aspects of classroom practice: how assessment contributes to teaching and learning (Chapter 1); its role in planning (Chapter 2); classroom approaches (Chapter 3); and ways of responding to pupils' written and practical work (Chapter 4). Its main goal is to alert beginning teachers to the 'paradigm shift' (Gipps 1994: 1) which ideas about assessment have undergone:

> Traditional assessment cast the teacher as the assessor who set summative examinations, marked them in private and wrote a report about the student's success or failure in private, to be delivered to the student's parents or guardian. The student was largely kept out of the assessment.
>
> (Cohen *et al.* 1996: 424–5)

This quotation highlights the extent to which traditional ideas about assessment have been challenged in recent years. There is no longer widespread acceptance that assessment

- is a terminal activity which serves mainly summative purposes
- is the prerogative of teachers
- is conducted in private
- is principally concerned with measuring success and failure
- produces results which are used mostly for reporting to others.

Ideas and approaches described in Part 1 show how far thinking and practices have shifted.

Part 1 presents assessment as a classroom concern. In this context, although students may be required to follow departmental schemes of work and use set assessment tasks, they will nevertheless work on their own initiative and enjoy discretion over the detail of what they do. However, practising teachers are not simply collections of individuals working independently in their own classes. They are also members of departmental/faculty teams and of a school's staff. Collectively, they are subject to requirements and responsibilities, some of which are developed at departmental or school level while others are externally imposed and may be legally binding. Therefore, although teaching is still a profession where there is scope for choice and creativity, there are aspects of their work where schools have found it helpful or necessary to work in a coordinated way based on a consensus about what is required and how it should be accomplished. These aspects are the focus of Part 2.

Part 2 Managing assessment: the school context

The chapters in this part adopt a broad perspective to consider aspects of MARRA which are 'whole-school' or departmental concerns. They consider the development of policies and systems for managing and making use of assessment data and meeting various statutory requirements. Chapter 5 outlines the main areas of monitoring, assessment and accountability where there are collective interests and responsibilities and Chapter 6 focuses on record-keeping and reporting.

Part 3 Assessment: the wider context

As their training progresses, students are introduced to formal, public aspects of assessment such as government policy and school-leaving qualifications. Although managing assessment remains the focus of attention in this section, the context is broadened further to encompass the political and statutory frameworks. Chapter 7 examines the use of assessment for accountability purposes and for monitoring and raising standards of attainment nationally. Chapter 8 considers trends and developments in testing and public examinations, providing an overview of the current framework for summative assessment. The text, therefore, places assessment in varying contexts, moving from the most immediate to the most remote, in an attempt to address issues in the order in which students are likely to prioritize them.

The content has a practical orientation because beginning teachers have only a limited fund of experiences on which to draw in developing their ideas about assessment. The intention is not to produce a comprehensive guide to the theory of assessment which simply re-covers ground which has been given expert treatment elsewhere. Rather, the text seeks to provide an in-depth consideration of fundamental elements of practice which exercise teachers at the beginning of their careers such as the role of assessment in planning or how to mark pupils' work. Concrete examples are used and copies of school documentation are reproduced for readers to consider. This helps to make abstract ideas meaningful by showing what they might look like in practice. However, the examples are not intended to be copied slavishly. Indeed, while most exemplify good practice, occasionally they illustrate shortcomings too. This material is intended as a stimulus, to encourage novices to develop and refine their own practices. There are also suggestions for further reading at the end of two chapters and tasks designed to help readers to deepen their insight into assessment issues.

Although the text has a practical orientation, it is not simply a collection of hints and tips, characterized by simple, formulaic recommendations for practice. It is aimed at a developing professional audience and is intended to promote a thoughtful approach and a critical awareness of issues which arise out of practice. It aims to inform readers and to enable them to make an intelligent use of assessment. Frequent references to research findings, to the theory of assessment and to the complex issues which dog assessment are, therefore, embedded in the commentary. This is not a contradiction of the previous claim for the practical orientation of this text for, rather than forming the focus of the book, these matters will be used to elucidate practice and reference will be made to them as appropriate.

Although most chapters deal with topics one might expect to find in a book on assessment, the first two focus on subjects which are more commonly dealt with in their own right or as part of a general introduction to teaching ('learning' and 'planning'). It is important to understand that the intention in these chapters is *not* to provide a comprehensive, general introduction to these topics but to highlight the contribution which assessment can make. Therefore, Chapter 2 does not provide a guide to planning *per se*. Likewise, although Chapter 1 explores the relationship between assessment and learning, it does not provide an introduction to the various theories of learning. However, where there is a reference to a particular theory of learning, the relevant part of that theory will be explained briefly. Suggestions for further reading are provided at the end of both these chapters for those who require general introductions.

1.3 Terminology

Assessment has its own technical language comprising terms that have a specialized meaning distinct from their everyday use. Most technical terms are explained at their first mention in the text. Readers are referred to the relevant section for those which are defined subsequently. Abbreviations and acronyms are given in full at their first mention, with the abbreviation used thereafter. There is a list of acronyms and abbreviations at the front of the book.

There are many terms in use to describe those who are learning to teach: student teachers, beginning teachers, associates, interns and so on. Government circulars have also been influential. Although those preparing to teach were described as 'students' by Circular 9/92 (Department for Education (DfE) 1992), Circular 4/98 (DfEE 1998a) replaced this with 'trainees', which is currently the preferred term in DfEE/Ofsted publications. I prefer the term students, finding it a more dignified term and one which is better suited to the exacting professional standards which recruits to teaching must meet. This, therefore, is the chosen nomenclature on most occasions. To distinguish learner teachers from learners who they teach, I avoid referring to school pupils as 'students' in this text.

Part 1 | Assessment and learning: the classroom context

The role of assessment in teaching and learning

1.1 Introduction

This chapter examines the relationship between teaching, learning and assessment.

Objectives

By the end, you should have developed your understanding of two key ideas:

- the dual potential of assessment to enhance or inhibit meaningful learning
- assessment can be both a tool for teaching and a straitjacket restricting it.

Task 1.1

What lessons does the following account contain about the relationship between teaching and learning? How might assessment be used to improve that relationship?

John, Matt and Jennifer are American high school pupils who were filmed during a study of how children develop scientific concepts. The study involved pupils being interviewed by a researcher to ascertain what they already knew about a topic prior to being taught about it. They were reinterviewed following lessons, which were delivered by their regular teacher, to establish how their understanding of the topic had been altered by teaching. Bob teaches John and Jim teaches Matt and Jennifer. Both are experienced science teachers. They are shown recordings of the pre-teaching interviews with their pupils before they start to teach. Afterwards, they are shown the post-teaching interviews for comparative purposes. Their reactions to the pupil interviews are also recorded.

Lesson 1: the composition of wood

John is about to be taught how trees grow and of what they are made. In the pre-teaching interview, we learn that John, like other children, has used common sense to interpret the world around him. Common sense has led him to believe that everything that trees are made of comes out of the ground. When asked to specify the composition of wood, he answers thus:

60% – water
0% – sunlight
40% – soil

Bob grimaces when he is shown the tape. He is bemused by his pupil's belief that wood is made of soil and jokes to the researcher that back yards would look different if trees really did consume soil! He is amused by the idea of householders having to import truckloads of soil to replace that absorbed by their trees. His lesson is intended to elucidate how trees actually grow and the role of carbon dioxide from the air resulting in wood being composed almost entirely of carbon.

The post-teaching interview starts well. John now knows that trees grow by absorbing sunlight through their leaves and converting it into the food needed to grow. Bob smiles to the researcher and nods approvingly at this point when viewing the tape. The researcher then reminds John of his previous analysis of the composition of wood and asks him whether his ideas have changed. On reflection, John revises his answer thus:

70–75% – water
25–30% – the rest

When questioned about 'the rest', he answers hesitantly and dismissively: 'The rest . . . the bark, all the minerals and soil and stuff like that'.

Lesson 2: electrical circuits

Jim is about to teach his class about electrical circuitry. Before teaching, the researcher asks members of the group whether you can light a bulb using just a battery and some wire. Matt and Jennifer say 'yes', the correct answer and, while the circuit diagrams which they produce are not perfect, they are reasonably accurate. After the lesson, Matt's revised circuit diagram suggests that he has lost his understanding and he explains to the researcher: 'We didn't use batteries to power the light bulbs'. Jennifer, on the other hand, can now draw a perfect circuit diagram, the sort which would command full marks in an examination, but when the researcher questions her closely, it emerges that she no longer believes that battery and wire alone are sufficient to light the bulb. During the experiment, the light bulbs had been held upright in sockets. Jim assumed that his pupils would realize that the sockets were there for convenience but Jennifer developed a misconception which was overlooked during teaching. She now believes that it is impossible to light a bulb without a socket and tells the researcher that she will fall off her stool if he manages to light the bulb using only the battery and wire!

These snapshots of pupils learning reveal that it is dangerous to assume a simple, straightforward relationship between what teachers teach and what pupils *actually* learn. They convey something of the subtle, complex and equivocal relationship between teaching and learning. Although science provides a particularly striking illustration of the difficulties which may arise, because scientific principles are often at variance with what common-sense reasoning tells us, similar problems occur in the teaching of many subjects.

Pupils inevitably bring their prior learning and personal theories to bear when tackling new topics. This is consistent with constructivist theories of learning which stress that each of us actively constructs a personal world view by creating links between existing knowledge and understanding and new information. Constructivists suggest that we develop our understanding by relating new material to our existing mental schema, a process which Ausubel (1987) described as 'anchoring' new information. But as the incidents above show, the efficacy of this process depends on the status of existing ideas about a new topic. Sometimes, as John demonstrates, pupils already have misconceptions which may be resistant to change (for example that soil is a component of wood). Cognitive theory suggests that firmly rooted misconceptions need to be subjected to some form of cognitive conflict which will force the learner to confront their misconception. This process helps to dislodge well-established but unsound ideas (for example Bob could have challenged John to consider why people were not regularly replacing soil in their gardens). But if a teacher is unaware of a pupil's misconceptions, it is unlikely that this process will take place.

Sometimes, as in the case of Matt and Jennifer, pupils already possess a good level of understanding of a new topic. Ideally, a teacher will build on this. Even here, learning may go awry when pupils develop misconceptions *during* teaching, as in the case of Jennifer. It may be trivial or incidental features of the teaching environment which cause the confusion. Jim assumed that his pupils would realize that the sockets were simply holding the light bulbs in place whereas Jennifer assumed that they played a critical role in lighting the bulbs. Assumptions are dangerous in teaching! Unfortunately, the taken-for-granted nature of assumptions means that neither teacher nor pupils will be conscious of all the assumptions each makes so many will go unchallenged. Indeed, one might have assumed, on the basis of her perfect circuit diagram, that Jennifer had grasped the concept of an electrical circuit. It is only because the researcher probed Jennifer's understanding that her confusion was uncovered. Perhaps the most disconcerting example is Matt, who appears to have *regressed* as a result of teaching despite displaying a promising level of understanding in the pre-teaching interview.

It is not hard to see how a more systematic use of formative assessment might have improved the teaching and learning involved in these incidents. For instance, baseline assessment could have alerted teachers to what pupils already knew – or thought they knew – *before* teaching started. This would have placed both in a better position to build on existing knowledge and understanding. Even more important, misconceptions are easier to confront if they are identified promptly. A learner's knowledge and understanding shift constantly in the light of teaching and interactions with other pupils. Teachers, therefore, need to monitor the development of understanding. Close monitoring of progress *during* teaching – perhaps through a combination of focused observation and probing questions – enables teachers to tap into the learning process. This rapid feedback can be used to adjust teaching. Simpson (1990, quoted in James 1998) compares teachers to marksmen who are trying to perfect their shot. In this analogy, assessment is a means to the end of more effective teaching: attending carefully to its results helps teachers to refine their practice:

> Assessment must therefore extend beyond the simple determination of the extent to which [students] have learned as intended to the discovery of what they have actually learned, right or wrong. Teachers, like marksmen, may have clear objectives, but if they are to improve the quality of their performance then – like marksmen – they will want to know where all their shots went, and not merely how many find their target. Indeed, the patterns of 'wrong' learning, like the distribution of off-target shots, will provide the clearest cues to improvement.
>
> (Simpson 1990, quoted in James 1998: 182)

The idea that learning can be scaffolded was familiarized through the work of Bruner (1983). In its everyday use, the term scaffolding refers to a temporary system of external support for a building during construction which is removed once the building is capable of standing alone. Similar principles have been applied to learning where scaffolding refers to the external framework (for example of ideas and questions) provided by an adult or a more capable peer which enables learners to progress beyond what they could have attained alone. Careful scaffolding is critical in the early stages of learning, supporting the emergence of new knowledge and guiding the development of new understandings, but as learning becomes established, the scaffolding can gradually be withdrawn. Gipps (1994: 27) argues that this notion of scaffolding may be extended to assessment: 'to move beyond static assessment of what is known to . . . a more interactive model looking at learning potential'. She characterizes this type of scaffolded assessment as being 'somewhere between teaching and traditional examination in that the adult gives aid only as needed, allowing the child to show competence when s/he can' (Gipps 1994: 28). A constructive use of verbal questioning which builds on pupils' contributions and channels their thinking into fruitful areas of inquiry thereby extending their learning as well as assessing it exemplifies this approach.

These examples of pupils learning show how unhelpful it is to confine assessment to formal exercises undertaken summatively – end-of-unit tests or homeworks, for instance. For a start, the feedback associated with this kind of assessment is delayed whereas research suggests that learners benefit most from rapid feedback (Black and Wiliam 1998a). Timing is crucial. The longer the time lag between performance and feedback, the less efficacious the feedback is likely to be in correcting errors and enhancing future performance. This is not to suggest that summative assessment has no place in a teacher's repertoire but that a heavy or exclusive reliance on it limits the potential of assessment to enhance teaching and learning.

1.2 Formative assessment

Some of the key features of formative assessment are implicit in the above discussion. Formative assessment entails intervening *during* the learning process to gather feedback which is used to guide subsequent teaching and learning. Genuinely formative assessment, therefore, fulfils a dual function, providing feedback which is then used for feedforward purposes. If feedback is not acted upon – for instance, if a teacher simply makes a record of results or a learner ignores their implications for future performance – then the activity could not be regarded as genuinely formative (Sadler 1989). Constructivist theorists are keen to remind us that learning must be an active process – that teachers cannot do their pupils' learning for them. This does not mean that pupils need to engage in a never-ending circus of practical activities but it does suggest that teachers should help pupils to make personal sense of new material, to construct their own meaning and to integrate new information into their own mental map. The same principles apply to assessment. Sadler's (1989) work emphasizes that feedback must be for both teachers *and* learners. Feedback enables teachers to modify their teaching plans and adjust the curriculum to learners' needs but it should also show pupils how to improve their performance as well as motivating them to do so.

Just because a teacher assesses pupils regularly, it cannot be assumed that the activity is formative. While teachers are the providers of TA, not all TA is formative. It is possible to assess in a routine, mechanical way such as periodically collecting sets of books for marking and relying on ticks, marks and terse, written comments ('Well done! A good effort', 'A scrappy piece of work. You can do better than this!') and setting occasional tests. As the previous paragraph indicates, this approach does not satisfy the criteria for formative assessment.

1.3 The positive potential of assessment

Research has shown that *formative* assessment is associated with significant learning gains – gains, moreover, which exceed those produced by other educational interventions devised to raise attainment. Black and Wiliam's (1998a) international study is a key text. It is based on a survey of almost 700 pieces of research; these were subsequently reduced to 250 focusing on formative assessment which were studied in depth. Black and Wiliam point out that they encountered no research where enhancing formative practices had an adverse effect on attainment. On the contrary, the studies which they reviewed produced effect sizes ranging between 0.4 and 0.7. They translate these statistics into practical equivalences arguing that even the most modest effect sizes of 0.4, if they were replicated in the UK, would produce an improvement in candidates' General Certificate of Secondary Education (GCSE) performances of between one and two grades. England's position in an international comparative study of performance in mathematics was used to calculate an equivalence for the largest effect size of 0.7. Although England was actually ranked somewhere in the middle of the 41 countries involved in the study, an effect size of 0.7 would have raised England into the top five nations.

Another important finding concerns the impact of formative assessment on the *spread* of performances. A disconcerting feature of educational attainment in the UK is what has been described as a 'long tail' of underachieving pupils. However, Black and Wiliam (1998a) found that formative assessment helps low achievers more than the rest thus reducing the spread of attainment while raising it overall. Black and Wiliam adopt a cautious approach, qualifying their findings and conclusions. For instance, they concede that much of the work on which their claims are based took the form of specially devised experiments rather than deriving from everyday, classroom experience. These qualifications deserve to be taken seriously. There is no guarantee that results produced under experimental conditions could be replicated in ordinary classrooms. On the other hand, the messages about the potential of formative assessment come so consistently from so many different studies involving so many different types of learners – pupils in special education as well as those in the mainstream, infants in nursery schools, children in primary and secondary phases of education and adults in higher education – that they deserve to be taken with equal seriousness.

So far, this chapter has focused on the positive impact which assessment can have on teaching and learning and this may be taken to imply that it is never associated with negative consequences. This would be misleading, for assessment is a double-edged sword, capable of cutting both ways.

1.4 The negative potential of assessment

1.4a Teaching

It has long been recognized that what teachers teach and the ways in which they teach are heavily influenced by particular types of assessment

– especially external tests and examinations such as GCSEs and the National Curriculum's (NC) end-of-key-stage tests. When pupils are being prepared for these tests, the principle that assessment should complement the curriculum tends to be reversed so that the curriculum becomes assessment driven. Whether this influence is a force for good or ill depends on what is assessed but, more often than not, the backwash effect of examinations has adverse effects on the curriculum. Examinations tend to dictate what pupils are taught, narrowing it to what it is possible to assess in brief, written examinations. Many abilities, especially practical ones, are not amenable to assessment in this way. Traditionally, examinations have also acted as a disincentive to change and experimentation by teachers thereby preserving an externally imposed status quo. For instance, as long ago as 1939, the Spens Report concluded that the School Certificate, a forerunner of GCSE, had become a straitjacket for the secondary curriculum: 'Most of our witnesses seemed unable to think of the curriculum except in terms of the examination, while some defined the curriculum entirely in such terms' (Board of Education 1939: 142). Valentine (1932: 16) provides a striking example of what this might mean in practice: 'One of my students told me that in her own school the pupils studied the Hanoverian period of English history for four consecutive years . . . because that was to be the period selected for their School Certificate examination'.

Problems associated with the backwash effects of external tests have not gone away in the intervening years and, as the following quotation shows, they are not confined to the preparation of mature candidates for formal qualifications:

> Good early years practice was quickly replaced by an assessment-led curriculum. In many classes children were ricocheting from one unrelated activity to another to ensure all attainment targets were covered; there was no time for children to learn in any meaningful way, things were just being 'taught' . . . The idea, too, that the Programmes of Study guided what was to be taught was quickly replaced by teaching the 'attainment targets'.
>
> (Pidgeon 1992: 136–7)

Here, Pidgeon (1992) describes her experience of observing Year 2 infant teachers implementing recently introduced NC requirements. This tendency of tests and examinations is epitomized in the acronym, WYTIWYG (what you test is what you get!) American researchers have elaborated the theory of 'high stakes' assessments, identifying a number of principles associated with 'high stakes': 'If important decisions are presumed to relate to test results, then teachers will teach to the test' (Madaus 1988 quoted in Stobart and Gipps 1997: 6). If test results are the sole or even partial arbiter of a candidate's future educational or life choices, then the stakes are raised further. Thus, the more important the consequences of the test result, the higher the stakes and the more powerful the influence on what is taught.

Very occasionally, innovations in examination practice have been responsible for promoting curriculum reform. This applies especially to subjects/skills which have struggled to gain a place in the curriculum. Examining a subject or a skill helps to confer status, making acceptance onto examination syllabuses a way of raising the profile of certain subjects. The teaching of oral English is a case in point. Although 'Speaking and Listening' is now firmly established as one of the attainment targets (ATs) in the NC's English Programmes of Study (PoS), this was not always the case. When General Certificate of Education Ordinary levels (GCE O levels) were introduced in 1951, attempts to incorporate spoken English into O level English language were resisted and the examination tested only candidates' written skills. Consequently, there was little incentive for secondary teachers to develop pupils' speaking and listening skills during the final years of secondary schooling. The status of oracy started to rise only with the advent of the Certificate of Secondary Education (CSE) in 1965. This new qualification was designed to be innovative and it introduced oral tests into its English examinations from the outset.

Examples like these, where innovations in examination practice have had a positive effect on the curriculum, are few and far between. High stakes tests and examinations not only determine the content of the curriculum, but also can dictate how it is taught, offering a disincentive to certain styles of teaching and assessment while favouring others. Consequently, teachers have received little encouragement to develop a distinctive style of TA in a system dominated by high stakes tests and examinations. Rather, they have become inured to summative approaches which they imitate in the classroom. Black and Wiliam (1998a) enumerate some important pedagogical consequences:

- over-reliance on summative tests with little attention to the feedback/feedforward potential of formative assessment
- an emphasis on the ability to recall knowledge, usually of isolated facts and fragments of information, which might be required in an examination
- a preference for closed questions (Section 3.8) which call for lower order thinking skills rather than exploratory, open questions which promote higher order thinking
- little attention paid to improving the quality of assessments – assessment questions are not reviewed or discussed critically with other teachers so there is little reflection on what is being assessed
- teachers are mostly ignorant of the assessment work of colleagues and distrust their own results
- current practices do not usually tell teachers what they need to know about their pupils' learning because the grading function is overemphasized at the expense of the learning function
- even among teachers who take assessment seriously, little use is made of innovative strategies such as self-assessment and peer assessment.

To sum up, the deleterious effects which assessment has on curriculum and pedagogy are usually associated with high stakes assessments which invariably take the form of external tests and examinations. As far as the curriculum is concerned, they have the capacity to limit what is taught to that part of the examination syllabus on which a teacher predicts that classes will be examined. Teaching content is thus narrowed and externally prescribed. The content of examination syllabuses display a tendency to lag behind and inhibit curriculum innovations, offering little incentive to the kind of professionally led experimentation and examination reform which characterized the period when CSE was available (1965–87) (Brooks 1993). Teachers, anxious to cover the syllabus, are reluctant to follow up an interest which a class may have developed if that interest is not consistent with their aim of preparing pupils for examination. Getting through the syllabus achieves an overriding – and ultimately counter-productive – significance as experience with the original NC (pre-1994) demonstrates. Individual PoS were seriously overloaded and teachers reported feeling obliged to rush through topics and move onto the next irrespective of whether pupils had grasped the work in hand. Thus, the quality of pupils' learning was sacrificed to programme completion. Learning is affected in other ways by the powerful backwash effects of high stakes summative assessments.

1.4b Learning

Although all learners have preferred learning styles (Honey and Mumford 1992), the approach which learners actually adopt is itself learnt and may or may not coincide with preference. Values and beliefs, previous experiences, social and power relationships and gender are but some of the factors which influence approach to learning. Assessment is a particularly potent determinant of approach at secondary school level because so much assessment at this stage is summative and involves high stakes.

Research (for example Gipps 1994) has distinguished two types of learning: deep and meaningful or surface. The latter may involve passive acceptance of information without a true grasp of its meaning whereas the former is characterized by an ability to apply learning to novel or challenging tasks. An associated distinction is often drawn between the acquisition of higher order skills such as the abilities to analyse, to reason, to speculate and to evaluate, and lower order abilities such as the capacity to memorize the curriculum as received and to reproduce faithfully pre-packaged facts, ideas and opinions in response to appropriate triggers for example examination questions which follow a familiar formula. (Remember that, after teaching, Jennifer could draw a perfect circuit diagram, the sort which would earn her full marks in an examination, but that the researcher's searching questions quickly revealed flaws in her understanding.) Although deep learning and the development of higher order skills are of greater value to pupils than the shallow learning which promotes lower order thinking, the type of assessment to which they are exposed is critical, exercising a powerful influence on what pupils learn and how they learn it. Thus, Stobart and Gipps (1997: 16) observe that: 'It is a reflection on much of our classroom and examination assessment that even "deep learners" will opt for last-minute surface-learning approaches as the most effective, since little more than the regurgitation of information is required'.

Table 1.1 is based on Gipps (1994) and Black and Wiliam (1998a). Alongside common approaches to TA, their consequences for pupils' learning are described.

This section has suggested that the negative effects of assessment are closely associated with an emphasis on summative functions such as grading. Should we, therefore, assume that formative assessment is free from unwanted effects? Just as we cannot assume a straightforward relationship

Table 1.1 Approaches to teacher assessment and their consequences for learning

Approach to assessment	*Effect on learning*
Focus on low level aims, such as the ability to recall isolated items of information	The ability to memorize and reproduce information is placed at a premium; pupils resort to superficial and rote learning; fragments of information learnt in isolation are quickly forgotten.
Focus on closed questions	Pupils' focus on discovering the answer required by the teacher; meaningful learning becomes 'incidental rather than . . . intentional' (Gipps 1994: 23) as pupils concentrate on gaining teacher approval by providing desired responses.
Insufficient attention to assessment techniques which promote deep learning, such as self- and peer assessment	Higher order skills such as critical reflection and speculation are not encouraged; more risky cognitive activities are avoided.
Focus on norm-referencing (Section 3.4)	Pupils encouraged to compete against one another rather than focusing on personal improvement; teaches weak pupils that they lack the ability to succeed so they lose confidence in their own abilities and become demotivated; able pupils prone to become complacent.

between what teachers teach and what pupils actually learn, neither should we assume that assessment which is formative in intent is always positive in its impact on pupils. This is the conclusion reached by Torrance and Pryor (1998) as a result of investigating the formative assessment of children aged 4–7. Although this study focused on the assessment of infants, its salient messages are important for all teachers. For Torrance and Pryor (1998: 10), formative assessment is essentially 'a social interaction between teacher and pupil which is intended to have a positive impact on pupil learning but may not'. Although this description makes no mention of peers or self-assessment, it usefully alerts us to key features of formative assessment. First, formative assessment is not simply a matter of employing certain techniques with benefits to learning accruing automatically. Rather, most assessment is mediated through a social interaction with an adult in authority and this interaction: 'might have negative as well as positive consequences for learning, despite the teacher's best intentions' (Torrance and Pryor 1998: 83–4). Even in ordinary social situations, it is difficult for us to judge the impact of our words and deeds on others. Sometimes we make the unwelcome discovery that the impression created was the opposite of that intended and we are genuinely surprised by the reaction of others. The same degree of complexity and potential for a mismatch between intention and effect are implicit in assessment interactions, according to Torrance and Pryor. However, a body of research has identified types of feedback and feedforward which are most likely to have a positive impact on pupils' motivation to learn and their images of themselves as learners. Thus, by attending to research, it is possible for new teachers to make an informed and intelligent use of formative assessment and to reduce the randomness of its impact on learners. Various subtle but potent influences on learning will be examined in subsequent chapters. For now, it is important to note that learning is not simply a cognitive (thinking) activity. There are equally important emotional and social dimensions to learning. One's beliefs about one's own capacity to learn are shaped by previous experiences of learning which translate into positive or negative motivation and poor or high self-esteem. Social pressures from the peer group, school and family also play a part in enhancing or inhibiting one's capacity to learn. Well-judged feedback and feedforward attend, therefore, not only to the cognitive aspects of learning but also to these more elusive social and emotional elements.

Task 1.2

When you have read Parts 1 and 2 of this book, set yourself some assessment targets for personal development.

1.5 Further reading

Theories of learning are discussed in the following books.

Child, D. (1997) *Psychology and the Teacher*. London: Cassell.
Kolb, D. (1984) *Experiential Learning: Experience as the Source of Learning and Development*. Englewood Cliffs, NJ: Prentice Hall.
Riding, R. (1998) *Cognitive Styles and Learning Strategies*. London: David Fulton.
Wood, D. (1998) *How Children Think and Learn*. Oxford: Blackwell.

2 | Assessment and planning

2.1 Introduction

Students are likely to be involved in two of the types of planning which schools undertake – planning for the medium and the short term. This chapter examines the contribution of assessment to both. Medium-term planning is an aspect of teaching where practice varies considerably from school to school and from subject to subject and this is reflected in texts which offer an introduction to planning (Section 2.6). For instance, medium-term planning is variously described as scheme of work, unit of work, module, programme of work and so on. The time scale for medium-term planning is equally variable – several weeks, half a term, a term or even longer. Recommended planning proformae also look different and their organization and contents vary. Therefore, it is important to familiarize yourself with the approaches of schools/departments in which you complete placements.

Since the introduction of the NC (1989) and the inspection of schools by Ofsted (1994), schools have adopted a more collaborative approach to planning than was typical before. Therefore, although you may be able to contribute to your department's medium-term plans and may also be required to write your own, especially on a longer placement, you may well find that schemes have already been written and are handed to you as a fait accompli. It may be, therefore, that the individual lesson plan will form the bulk of your planning activity as a student teacher.

Objectives

By the end of this chapter, you should have developed your understanding of key ways in which planning which is informed by formative assessment differs from conventional approaches by offering

- heightened responsiveness to feedback
- more flexibility
- greater use of differentiation.

2.2 The neglected relationship between planning and assessment

If, as Chapter 1 argued, assessment is at the heart of teaching and learning, it follows that it requires careful consideration at the planning stage. This may sound like a platitude but I frequently encounter planning models which make no reference to assessment among the headings under which students are advised to plan. Items which feature routinely on planning templates convey a message that relatively incidental features of a lesson, such as the room in which it will take place or the date, are worthy of inclusion in the planning process whereas assessment is not. I am not, of course, suggesting that the physical setting for a lesson or the time of day are unimportant considerations which may safely be ignored in planning a lesson. Nevertheless, simply recording these items on a plan provides no guarantee that serious thought will be given to their implications for lesson content and it does, in comparison, seem extraordinary that assessment is not even mentioned. This omission provides the strongest clue to the fact that, traditionally, the role of assessment in planning has been either marginalized or ignored. It also creates a 'chicken and egg' situation when it comes to explaining why the formative potential of assessment has so rarely been realized. Is this caused by insufficient attention to assessment at the planning stage or is the neglect of assessment in planning a symptom of a wider problem rather than its cause? Either way, it is clear that the contribution of assessment to planning requires greater attention than it conventionally receives. For instance, the most recent Ofsted (1999: para. 21) overview report on ITT notes that: 'Trainers do not always give sufficient attention to planning, especially planning for progression, and to the assessment and recording of pupils' progress.' As a consequence: 'Trainees are more likely to have weaknesses in planning than in classroom management ... Trainees in all subjects find difficulty with planning for progression and the monitoring of progress, and need more guidance' (Ofsted 1999: paras 76 and 49).

As was noted in the Introduction, when systemic weaknesses are identified at the initial training stage, there is no guarantee that NQTs will subsequently become capable exponents of a skill. Therefore, it is unsurprising that James (1998) produced similar findings in her survey of the work of practising teachers which uncovered 'clear, recurring themes and issues' in a sample of Ofsted reports: 'Perhaps the most serious criticism was that there was very little evidence that assessment, recording and reporting was being used to monitor students' progress and to inform planning of teaching and learning. This undermined the suggestion that the formative potential of assessment should be paramount' (James 1998: 10–11).

It is easy to talk about these ideas in the abstract but more difficult to construe what this type of planning might actually look like. As part of their inquiry into formative assessment at Key Stage 1 (KS1), Torrance and Pryor (1998: 27–8) asked teachers to describe their own, or their team's, approach to planning. Some of their responses are reproduced in Task 2.1.

These brief quotations may not, of course, provide comprehensive accounts of the relationship between planning and assessment in the work of these teachers. Nevertheless, they do provide useful illustrations of the types of failings identified by Ofsted (1999) and James (1998). The first quotation depicts a linear, fragmented approach to planning in which assessment features as a terminal activity: plan → teach → assess/plan → teach → assess. Teaching units seem to be treated as discrete entities with

---

Task 2.1

What do these quotations tell you about ways in which teachers were using assessment? What role did it appear to play in their planning?

'What we would do in our planning meeting beforehand, we would say okay we're doing this learning intention, or these learning intentions this week. What are we going to do? How are we going to check that the children know or have learnt something?'

'We have weekly planning meetings and in those meetings we define the area of assessment which had already been defined by the topic anyway and we formally decide what we are going to do for that assessment . . . if we decide to use questions we have a specific question, if we're going to do worksheets then one person makes the worksheet and it's given to every teacher.'

'I'll set up for example a Maths activity then I will be looking for specific things within that activity and noting them down, so from the beginning I'll have quite a clearly defined criteria for what I'm looking for in each child and I'll be noting that down. With every activity I carry out with my children I am looking for things and I'm noting them down.'

'I'm much more um, do it retrospectively, look at what I've done . . . you've planned out what attainment targets are meant to be covered so really I suppose that is what is really what you're assessing as well . . . I'll be sitting in the next week or so with last term's topic books and looking through them and doing my assessment from those. Other than that it's generally what I remember.'

assessment being used ritualistically to mark the closure of a unit. There is no mention of information about children's development and progress gathered during one phase being utilized at the next so that assessment forms a thread weaving its way through units of work, helping to pro-vide cohesive learning experiences. It entails assessment *of* learning, not assessment *for* learning. The use of assessment to produce records emerges as an important purpose in the third quotation. What does not emerge from any of these quotations is a sense of assessment and planning interacting with one another or the information provided by assessment being fed forward into planning for future teaching and learning. In-deed, the final quotation provides an example of summative assessment being used retrospectively which completely eliminates any formative potential. Although teachers may have been monitoring the progress of individuals in some instances (quotations 1 and 3), it is by no means clear that this formative purpose was actively pursued alongside the compilation of records and the making of summative judgements.

Another feature of current practice which may be counterproductive is the way in which assessment activities are framed as 'opportunities'. For instance, among the qualities of 'Good lesson planning' identified by Ofsted (1998a: 78) there is a reference to 'any assessment opportunity'. Presenting assessment in this way may encourage teachers to regard it as an opportunistic activity which takes place rather haphazardly, in re-sponse to fortuitous conditions. Indeed, when Torrance and Pryor (1998: 26) asked infant school teachers to describe their approach to planning, they spoke in similar terms: 'assessment opportunities were planned, or were meant to be planned'. This approach threatens to consign assess-ment to the status of a chance activity. Another pitfall, according to Sutton (1992: 30), is that it may lead to an indiscriminate pursuit of opportunities: 'you should have some assessment objectives for the topic under consideration. These will always be fewer in number than the full set of assessment opportunities that the topic could provide ... "Assess less better" seems to be the motto here'.

This book contends that assessment should be a more deliberate and systematic part of the planning process than the phrase 'assessment opportunity' suggests. This is not to deny that good teachers exploit assessment opportunities in the same way that they exploit other oppor-tunities as they arise but to redress the balance by stressing the import-ance of planning *actively* for an organized use of assessment.

Task 2.2

Consider your own approach to planning.

What use(s) do you make of assessment? Does it play a part in your planning?

2.3 Student teachers and planning

Planning is one of the areas of competence specified in the Standards for Qualified Teacher Status (QTS) (DfEE 1998a). A student's plans, therefore, fulfil a dual role. On the one hand, they are working documents and completing them helps students to 'translate ideas about what they would like to happen into *guidelines for action in the classroom*' (Husbands 1999: 44). Written plans also provide *evidence* which will be used for formal assessment purposes. They are the means by which students demonstrate that planning standards in Circular 4/98 have been met (DfEE 1998a). This means that students' plans are likely to be more detailed and explicit than those used by qualified teachers for whom some of the detail may have become internalized and tacit. Therefore, the planning which suits an experienced teacher may not serve the purposes of a student.

Those at the beginning of their careers usually have their own peculiar concerns when it comes to developing the ability to plan. Often, the mechanics of planning and its surface features preoccupy them: 'Does it look OK?', 'Does it matter that I've adapted the model which was introduced on the course?' Although it is understandable that novices are preoccupied with the nuts and bolts of planning, the fact remains that too often their concern misses the point. Their focus on planning as a mechanism can distract students from real issues which separate good from inferior planning. Thus, it is uncommon for students to raise questions about the clarity of their objectives or the appropriateness of the cognitive demands that a lesson will make on pupils or how to gather evidence about the extent to which objectives have been achieved.

Learner teachers need to move beyond the stage of 'planning as a mechanism' to focus on it as one of the processes which helps to make teaching purposeful and intelligent. The different elements of a plan are there as an aid to thinking constructively about the different constituents of a lesson which need to be melded if effective learning experiences are to ensue. Central to this is the need to think systematically about assessment.

- What are the implications of previous assessment data for your current plans? Which elements of your plan will need to be modified in the light of feedback?
- What are its implications for pupils? How can you ensure that they will understand and act upon its implications for them?
- What information do you need to gather next? About which pupils?
- How will you go about collecting and recording it?

These are complex issues that require careful forethought. Furthermore, they relate only to one dimension of the planning process. It is, therefore, unsurprising that planning to teach has been described as being as 'complex and cognitively demanding as the practice of medicine, law or architecture' (Clark 1989 quoted in John 1993: 2). This point applies particularly to planning which is informed by formative assessment.

Teachers who develop their use of formative assessment are often surprised by the extent to which their teaching is altered. Even quite minor alterations to assessment practice can have an impact on pedagogy, supporting Black and Wiliam's (1998a: 17) assertion that: 'It is hard to see how any innovation in formative assessment can be treated as a marginal change in classroom work'. Planning is not exempt from this effect because planning which is responsive to feedback differs in important respects from more conventional approaches to planning. The distinctiveness of this approach forms the focus for the rest of this chapter.

2.4 Medium-term planning

2.4a The need for flexible planning

According to Torrance and Pryor (1998: 155), a distinctive feature of the planning associated with formative assessment is its flexibility. In fact, formative assessment simply cannot function if teachers plan too far ahead in too much detail and are unwilling to modify their plans. Adaptability is thus at the heart of formative planning which is alert to feedback and responds sensitively to its messages. Sutton's (1995: 12) notion of the 'loose/ tight dilemma' is pertinent here although neither of these extremes is compatible with formative assessment. Planning which is too tight is rigid, making it incapable of responding to feedback whereas planning which is too loose is inclined to 'drift aimlessly' (Sutton 1995: 13).

It is important to consider how flexibility can be built into medium-term planning. Black and Wiliam (1998a) suggest that:

> the problem of acting on assessment results is tackled by constructing the work on a particular module or topic in such a way that the basic ideas have been covered by about two-thirds of the way through the course; assessment evidence is reviewed at this stage, so that in the remaining time differentiated work can proceed according to the needs of different pupils.
>
> (Black and Wiliam 1998a: 43)

An alternative approach is described below.

2.4b Using assessment to finalize initial teaching plans

Ausubel (1968: 36) argued that: 'The most important single factor influencing learning is what the learner already knows; ascertain this and teach him [her] accordingly'. This suggests the need to plan for some form of baseline assessment to identify the point that a learner is at in relation to new work *before* teaching commences. Baseline assessment can range from structured activities such as quizzes and question/answer sessions to unstructured approaches involving brainstorming or pupils' diary entries about a topic. Either way, achieving a match between teaching and pupils' needs and starting points is critical. Is the prior learning needed to tackle the new topic secure? Do pupils need to prepare by revising previous work or undertaking preparatory reading? Do pupils already have ideas and information which they have picked up outside formal schooling? Have they formed any misconceptions?

Most people have vivid memories of occasions when teaching was incorrectly pitched, either going over their heads because the starting point was too advanced or quickly losing their interest because there was too much overlap with what they already knew. In such circumstances, it is not only learning which suffers. Teachers are more likely to encounter behavioural problems if pupils are bored, confused or demoralized. Two key concepts for planning, therefore, are *continuity* and *progression* and it is useful to think in terms of two types of work: that which is pitched at the same level and is being used for practice and reinforcement, and that which aims at development by setting work at a slightly higher level. Teaching needs this dual emphasis to enable it to engage smoothly with what pupils already know, understand and can do as well as taking their learning forward in a way that is motivating. Without assessment, this kind of careful matching is left to chance.

Baseline assessment can help to finalize teaching plans in various ways. You may find, for instance, that new items need to be added to the list of key concepts that you were planning to introduce or that your explication requires adapting in the light of pupils' ideas on a topic. For instance, a student teacher discovered through baseline assessment that the technical term 'program' had an everyday meaning for her Year 7 pupils which was quite different from the subject specialist use to which she would be putting it. She realized that it was important to clarify this discrepancy during her introduction to the topic. You may decide that you need to start your introduction to a topic a stage further back or forward. For instance, a scientific investigation may be more successful if you first reinforce earlier work on 'lines of best fit'. It may be that a practical activity will illustrate a point better than the verbal explanation you had originally planned to use. In fact, the ways in which teaching may be refined in response to initial feedback are almost limitless.

This approach is not as radical as it may at first appear. You are unlikely to find yourself jettisoning your original plans and starting again from scratch but you may be able to make subtle but important adjustments which will fine tune teaching to a group's needs and interests. As Simpson argued (in James 1998: 182), teachers who use assessment formatively are like marksmen using target practice to improve their shot. This makes their planning more fluid and dynamic than is typical of conventional planning, which is less receptive to feedback. It entails an openness to the possibility of adjustments being needed, emphases being shifted and approaches being modified. Most important of all, the detail of teaching plans can be finalized only when assessment data have been considered.

2.4c Using assessment to monitor progress

Once teaching is underway, both teacher and learners must monitor progress. A prerequisite for this is that learning objectives and assessment criteria are clearly articulated so that both parties understand them well enough to make informed judgements about the gap between perform-ance and requirements. This topic is dealt with in detail in relation to lesson planning (Section 2.5). In the context of medium-term planning, it requires the identification of regular points at which progress can be reviewed. The transition points in a scheme represent natural breaks in the flow of work, providing useful opportunities for checking under-standing. These progress reviews may suggest further modifications so you need to be prepared to adapt and fine tune plans not only at the outset of a unit of work but also at interim stages. This requires teachers to plan actively for assessment and to build in the necessary *time* for it to become an organic part of teaching. The attempt to graft assessment onto a plan once it has been finalized is unlikely to prove satisfactory. Sutton (1995: 16) argues the case for creating small spaces in every scheme 'to allow for the unexpected, to give time for remediation or consolidation if necessary, to allow challenging extension work to be offered to those learners who need it . . . It gives us the opportunity to customise the plan without jeopardising it'.

Many teachers are reluctant to use time in this way. Assessment is viewed as an activity which takes hard-pressed time away from teaching. It is either a luxury or a distraction which teachers can ill afford. Although it is unwise to underestimate the demands on teaching time, if we genu-inely embrace the view that assessment is part of learning rather than a distraction from it – and that it can enhance learning – the force of the argument for safeguarding teaching time is undermined.

2.4d Selecting assessment strategies

It is important to consider the concept of 'match', choosing approaches which are well adapted to their purpose. Thus, if your concern is the extent to which a class has grasped the assessment criteria which will be applied to their work, a peer assessment exercise, by requiring them to apply the criteria, may provide the best test of their ability to understand them. For instance, an English teacher may want an Advanced level (A level) literature group to appreciate the distinction between analysing a text and simply describing what happens in it. A peer assessment exercise in which pupils mark each other's assignments using A level grading criteria is an example of this kind of matching. It also exemplifies scaffolded assessment because completing the marking and then discussing it with their teacher may *further* pupils' understanding of the distinction between analysing and describing as well as telling their teacher how well they have understood the distinction. Assessment tasks must be well matched to the knowledge, skill or understanding being taught to provide valid (Section 8.7) results.

Medium-term planning provides a useful opportunity to take an *overview* of what is being required of pupils and the opportunities they are offered. For instance, teachers can check whether there is a satisfactory balance between assessment activities which encourage deep and surface learning. They can also consider whether the range of assessment activities is sufficiently diverse rather than being over-reliant on one or two approaches. For instance, it is known that certain assessment techniques favour one sex over the other. Girls have been found to do better than boys on sustained tasks which are open-ended, process-based and related to realistic situations whereas boys fare better on traditional tasks which required the ability to memorize abstract, unambiguous facts and rules that have to be acquired quickly (Arnot *et al.* 1998). Girls tend to perform less well on multiple choice tests whereas boys do less well on extended writing tasks (Gipps and Murphy 1994). Likewise, over-reliance on one assessment format will disadvantage pupils who prefer working in a different medium. For instance, the older pupils become, the more likely teachers are to rely on the written medium for assessment (Stobart and Gipps 1997: 18). This requires a facility for reading and writing which is unhelpful to pupils in whom these skills are less well developed but who might, nevertheless, perform well on practical exercises or in a verbal medium or through the use of information and communications technology (ICT). Teachers should avoid hampering certain pupils' ability to demonstrate knowledge, skill or understanding by always opting for particular assessment strategies or the same performance medium. A conscious attempt to vary assessment strategy and medium should give all pupils, over a period of time, an opportunity to work in ways which best suit them.

Research into the nature of intelligence is relevant here. The notion that intelligence is a single, global attribute has been challenged, most notably by the work of Gardner (1983, 1993). Gardner's studies in neurology showed that individuals with specific conditions may be impaired in many aspects of their mental functioning, but unusually talented in a particular area, for example savants with special educational needs (SEN) who possess special gifts in music, art or mathematics. Gardner's theory of multiple intelligences is based on the identification of at least seven separate intelligences (or learning preferences): verbal-linguistic; logical-mathematical; visual-spatial; bodily-kinaesthetic; musical; interpersonal and intrapersonal. Although people with certain mental conditions may display extreme differences in these attributes, most of us have uneven profiles with strengths in some areas offset by weaknesses in others. Although Gardner's theory is by no means universally accepted, his work adds weight to the body of evidence which challenges teachers to embrace diversity and to avoid the tendency to become over-reliant on one or two tried and tested approaches to assessment.

To sum up, a formative approach to medium-term planning is characterized by its dynamism and its ability to fine tune plans to messages from feedback. It involves a systematic overview of a scheme of work, monitoring assessment approaches for diversity and balance, validity and equity. It is possible to explore the role of formative assessment in medium-term planning even if you have no opportunity to write your own schemes of work.

Task 2.3

Examine an existing scheme of work.

Has the role of assessment been considered? For what purpose(s) is assessment used?

Could the scheme be modified to make a more formative use of assessment?

2.5 Lesson planning

2.5a Clarifying lesson objectives

Subject-specific differences cause subjects to favour different types of objectives. The possibilities include content, teaching or learning objectives and behavioural or non-behavioural. Learning objectives indicate what pupils should know, understand or be able to do as a result of teaching or how their attitudes should be affected (for example describe how frictional forces, including air resistance, affect motion). Given that pupils' learning is prioritized throughout this book, the favoured approach to setting objectives is learning objectives. Whatever the preferences in your subject, the key assessment considerations are whether objectives are sufficiently well defined to

- guide your teaching
- be accessible to pupils
- allow judgements to be made about the success of a lesson in attaining objectives.

2.5b The relationship between objectives and assessment

Student teachers often fail to appreciate the interrelatedness of objectives setting and assessment. Without a clear specification of what they are aiming to achieve in a lesson (their objectives) formative assessment cannot take place (how will they know when they have arrived if they were not sure where they were going?) Viewed the other way round, a key issue from an assessment perspective is the extent to which object-ives have been attained. Assessment is one of the principal means by which a teacher can judge the success of a lesson in attaining objectives. Teachers can, of course, rely on evaluations (Section 2.5f) but these may be partial and impressionistic sources of information. Assessment is an additional source of evidence which will either corroborate or question judgements formed during evaluation. So, clearly defined objectives facilitate assessment which, in turn, helps to determine the objectives for future lessons. This close relationship is the reason why it is odd that lesson planning models often omit any reference to assessment. In fact, it is helpful to place learning objectives and assessment criteria/strategies in close proximity to one another on a plan. The positioning of assess-ment at the core of the plan, rather than as an appendage to it, has more than symbolic significance. It helps to reinforce the relationship between setting objectives and collecting appropriate assessment data.

2.5c Sharing objectives with pupils

Sometimes formative assessment is presented as a tool for teachers which enables them to plan 'next steps' in pupils' learning. An alternative view is that if the formative potential of assessment is to be properly harnessed, pupils must become active participants in the process (for example Sadler 1989). This book shares the latter view that pupils need to be fully involved in responding to feedback and acting upon its feedforward implications. This is particularly important for secondary pupils whose growing inde-pendence makes it less and less tenable to treat them as passive subjects of assessment.

The need to involve pupils applies particularly to the formulation of objectives which are capable of being shared with and understood by them. It has been shown that when teachers invest time in clarifying objectives for their classes, pupils develop a more positive attitude to learning, working with increased self-confidence and a greater sense of pur-pose (for example Her Majesty's Inspectorate (HMI) 1992). At the primary level, teachers who have adopted this approach:

> often report dramatic changes in the culture of the classroom and in children's application and attitude to their work . . .
> - Children are more focused on the task.
> - Children will persevere for longer.
> - The quality of children's work improves.
> - Behaviour, especially time-wasting tactics at the beginnings of lessons, improves.
>
> (Clarke 1998: 55)

In the mid-1990s, I was involved in the evaluation of a local education authority (LEA) project designed to raise achievement in the authority's schools (Brooks and Little 1995, 1997). Several of the project's initiatives involved formative assessment. Teachers were trained to share the 'learning purposes' of lessons with pupils. This entailed translating PoS and examination syllabuses into pupil-friendly language so that objectives could be made transparent for pupils. Learning purposes were sometimes written on a board at the beginning of a lesson and remained there throughout or pupils recorded them on their work. In that way, they remained visible, acting as a constant reminder to the class of what they were trying to achieve. Sometimes, learning purposes were converted into a series of questions to encourage pupils to adopt a critical and inquiring approach to their learning. When performing tasks, pupils were encouraged to think about assessment criteria, and occasionally to devise their own, to give them a clear idea of what constituted success and what successful pieces of work might look like. Lessons ended with a review of progress or, alternatively, the review stage was part of homework or was picked up in subsequent lessons. The project was disseminated through a range of the LEA's schools and covered all age phases. It was found that even infants could be successfully introduced to metacognition (thinking about the quality of their own learning) using imaginative approaches suited to the immaturity of these learners. Teachers involved in the project were positive about ways in which the approach had enhanced pupils' thinking skills and improved their motivation and rates of work. Shared goals helped to engender a sense of purpose. Pupils worked in a more focused way when they knew not simply what they were doing but why they were doing it, how it fitted in with previous learning and how it related to future work.

2.5d Differentiation

Close and continued attention to feedback provides a clear picture of how groups and individuals within a group are progressing. Even when groups are setted, it is unlikely that all pupils will be making the same progress at a similar rate. It is also unlikely that they will share preferred learning styles or perform equally well on the same assessment tasks using the same performance medium. Therefore, a second consequence of formative assessment is a greater use of differentiation. This, again, contrasts with conventional practice: 'More commonly, teachers pitch their teaching largely to the middle of the ability range in the class but provide some additional support for those who might otherwise struggle' (Ofsted 1998a: 85).

There are various methods of differentiating (for example see Dickinson and Wright 1993; National Foundation for Educational Research (NFER) 1998). Approaches include differentiation by task, by resource, by pace, by support and by outcome, the most commonly used being differentiation by outcome and by task. It is also useful to consider differentiating learning objectives. The notion of a global set of objectives which apply to all members of a group, in exactly the same way, is a planning convention which may prove incompatible with a heightened sensitivity to feedback. The tailoring of objectives to groups and individuals offers a sensible alternative. However, the extent to which this is feasible may depend on subject specialism. In subjects where teachers meet a limited number of classes several times a week and get to know them well, it is practicable but in subjects where a teacher is responsible for a large number of classes and sees each once a week or less frequently, differentiating objectives is challenging.

2.5e The flexible lesson plan

Section 2.4 dealt with the kind of feedback which can be planned for in the medium term. Responding to this kind of feedback is a comparatively leisured and deliberate business. It certainly does not require instant responses. There is, however, a more immediate type of feedback which teachers receive while lessons are in progress (Gipps 1994: 130). Whether this comes solicited or unsolicited, pupils will nevertheless provide teachers with ongoing feedback on how their teaching is being received. Body language and facial expressions may be the most immediate indicators of how learning is progressing and it is important to attend carefully to these. Pupils' responses to the teacher's questions and instructions, as well as their own questions, are further sources of feedback.

If you already have classroom experience, you will know that lessons do not always go according to plan even for experienced teachers! You may also be gaining a sense of the contingencies which frequently exercise inexperienced teachers. Although the detail of every plan which goes awry in the classroom is unique, underlying causes of difficulty are often assessment related. They include timing activities inaccurately and pitching content inappropriately. Pitching work at an inappropriate level is often the root cause of subsequent problems when work turns out to be unexpectedly hard or easy. When pupils are ready to move on much more quickly or slowly than anticipated, problems with timing can have knock-on effects on other aspects of a lesson. Therefore, the ability to respond flexibly is just as important in the short term as it is in the medium term. However, it requires a much more rapid reaction.

This may be unrealistic for those who are at the very beginning of their career. Research into the stages of development through which student teachers pass has suggested that, in the earliest stages, students are particularly reliant on highly structured, 'tight' (Sutton 1995) plans from which they are either unable or unwilling to deviate. For instance, Furlong and Maynard (1995) report that:

> Students often appeared frightened to deviate from what they had planned. One class teacher commented that she had noticed that

student teachers, in their first few weeks in the classroom, would pursue discussions, explanations and activities even when it was painfully obvious to all concerned that it was heading for disaster – rather like 'holding onto the back of a runaway horse'.

(Furlong and Maynard 1995: 81)

At the start of a course, then, with little or no prior experience on which to draw, it is probably wisest to accept that you may be obliged to deliver lessons as planned even though occasionally these may turn out to be more of a learning experience for you than for a class! However, as you accumulate experience, your ability to respond to feedback will develop. For instance, when novices use verbal question and answer, they are often 'response-seeking' (Black and Wiliam 1998a) and will simply reject 'wrong' answers, preferring to carry on fishing until they obtain the desired response. However, with growing experience and confidence, it is possible to treat inaccurate answers as a learning resource. They may provide valuable clues about what and how pupils are learning which can be used diagnostically to tackle difficulties and enhance the class's understanding. This 'information-seeking' approach (Black and Wiliam 1998a) is consistent with formative assessment.

Experienced teachers appear to improvise as a matter of course. You may have marvelled at an experienced teacher's ability to switch activities mid-lesson, moving, for instance, from requiring pupils to work independently to whole-class interactive teaching when it has become apparent that a class is struggling with its work. However, what may appear like improvisation may actually be the teacher's capacity to draw on a fund of previous teaching experiences. It is this memory bank of previous lessons which enables experienced teachers to adapt quickly but this may prove disastrous if attempted too early in a career. If this sounds unnerving, it is worth remembering that the more use you make of assessment information from previous lessons to plan the next, the less likely you are to have to deviate significantly from your plan. Thus, formative assessment may be the novice's best safeguard against the need for improvisation in the face of the unexpected.

As you acquire basic planning skills, you will gradually be able to think more flexibly about lesson plans. Thus, although it is impossible to plan for every eventuality, it is useful to have anticipated some of the more common occurrences and to have contingency plans ready for problems associated with mistiming and mispitching content. For instance, pupils may find new concepts or skills more difficult to master than you, as a specialist in the subject, had imagined possible. It is, therefore, helpful to have extra demonstration or practice examples ready in the wings should these prove necessary. It is also helpful to have decided in advance which element of a lesson may be postponed or jettisoned if you are obliged to take longer than anticipated over an earlier stage. Alternatively, you need to be prepared to curtail the explication stage of a lesson if pupils demonstrate familiarity with a topic, or a quick grasp of it. Student teachers who neglect baseline assessment run the risk of discovering that pupils are already familiar with what they had planned to teach and consequently race through what is, in effect, revision of previous work. This is a particular problem when students are unfamiliar with PoS from previous key stages and is best addressed by acquainting yourself with relevant programmes. It is also helpful to have identified alternative scenarios in case a particular stage in the lesson is accomplished very quickly or proves unnecessary. For instance, it is helpful to have extension or enrichment work available for those who race through a task. It is also worth building up a stock of topic-related puzzles, challenges and games which provide scaffolded assessments to cater for those occasions when a class finishes early.

2.5f The relationship between assessment and lesson evaluation

Evaluation is a weakness in the work of many trainee teachers (Ofsted 1999: para 57). Some are confused by the distinction between assessment and evaluation, treating these terms as if they are interchangeable. It is helpful to recognize that each activity has a different focus. Assessment is the process of gathering information about *pupils'* performances and attainments. Evaluation judges the efficacy of the *teacher's* contribution to this through lesson content, style of delivery and so on. Thus, although these activities are closely related, they are not the same. Students are also inclined to see evaluation as a chore, completing it in a routine, superficial manner in too many instances. It is the element of the plan → teach → evaluate cycle which is most likely to slip off a student teacher's agenda as a placement progresses and the workload increases. The ability to use evaluation as an aid to self-improvement is one of the standards against which fitness for the award of QTS is assessed. Therefore, you need to provide written evidence that the necessary reflection is taking place on a regular basis.

There are various reasons why some students find evaluation an unedifying experience. Poor lesson evaluations often provide descriptive accounts of what happened during lessons rather than attempting to judge their efficacy. This contributes little to deepening insight into the relationship between teaching and learning. Although many students adopt a more constructive approach, too often they depend on a sense of how the lesson 'went'. Evaluations are strongly influenced by an impression of the extent to which pupils were engaged by and enjoyed a lesson. It would, of course, be foolish to deny the importance of enjoyment and active engagement with a lesson to the quality of a learning experience and experienced teachers do take these factors into account (McIntyre and Cooper 1996). Nevertheless, it is easy for a vicious circle of poorly focused lesson objectives reinforced by a neglect of assessment and superficial evaluations to become established. The 'feel good factor' engendered by a lesson should not become the be-all and end-all of evaluation since not all pleasurable activities result in high-quality learning. It is possible for a lesson to work well and for pupils to enjoy it while little or nothing is achieved in terms of learning. Likewise, it would be wrong to assume that, because overt enjoyment did not feature strongly in pupils' responses to a lesson, effective learning did not take place. Therefore, just as learning is the key to formulating objectives so too is it the key to rigorous evaluation. The efficacy of a lesson as a learning experience is best judged by using assessment to corroborate (or question) judgements (Section 2.5b).

Pupils should be involved in the evaluation process from time to time. Various studies have emphasized the degree of insight of which pupils are capable and the value of taking their views seriously (for example Lucas 1995; Rudduck *et al.* 1996). Indeed, Clarke (1998: 55) notes that when primary teachers routinely share learning intentions with pupils, they 'become automatically self-evaluative, subconsciously or consciously weighing up how well they are doing against the learning intention'. In fact, the more teachers share responsibility for learning with pupils, the more they will take ownership of their learning, even questioning the appropriateness of a teacher's choices for themselves:

> Some children also begin to negotiate the appropriateness of the activity to fulfil the learning intention! This usually takes the form of changing resources or ways of working (for example '*I think I'd do that better if I worked on my own/with someone else*').
>
> (Clarke 1998: 55)

However, Furlong and Maynard's (1995: 187) study of the growth of student teachers' professional knowledge found that initially students are 'primarily focused on developing their own *performance* as teachers' and that they 'showed little appreciation of the relationship between teaching and how children learn' (Furlong and Maynard 1995: 89). In fact, viewing teaching in this way 'represented an enormous challenge and was met with varying degrees of resistance . . . One student described it as being asked to "think of a lesson for them [the pupils] rather than a lesson for me"' (1995: 94). Furlong and Maynard argue that a key challenge for trainers is to help students to make the transition from focusing inward on their own performance to decentring so that teaching is recognized as a process which facilitates learning. They suggest that the re-evaluation of lesson plans has a crucial role to play in this and that, as their course progresses, students should be urged to revisit early attempts at planning with a rigorous focus on the quality of the plans as an aid to pupils' learning.

Task 2.4

Use one of your own early lesson plans or the account of a lesson below to complete Tasks 2.4 and 2.5. The account below features a biology lesson taught by a student during her first placement to a top set of Year 11 pupils. The pupils were preparing for a GCSE examination in which they could expect to encounter population graphs which they would be required to analyse and interpret. On her plan, the objective for the lesson was recorded as 'Population – increase and decrease'.

Evaluate the lesson, using two blank columns to identify: (1) the teaching approaches that are employed at different stages, (2) the cognitive demands that are made on pupils. For example are they required to memorize, to hypothesize, to reproduce, to analyse and so on?

What are your conclusions about the quality of the lesson as a learning experience?

The lesson	*Teaching approaches*	*Cognitive demands on Pupils*
The lesson opened with a 10-minute exposition.		
Various concepts associated with population were covered: population increase and population decline. Ms C. described how various population statistics are calculated such as birth rates and death rates.		
Ms C. asked a series of closed questions (Chapter 3) about concepts which had been introduced, with each question addressed to an individual pupil. This section of the lesson lasted less than 5 minutes.		
Ms C. used an overhead projector (OHP) to display a graph for a bacterium which had increased its population. She then showed a contrasting graph for a second bacterium which had experienced a brief period of population growth followed by decline. Ms C. interpreted each graph in turn, explaining that different species compete for space and that the most successful increase their populations by competing successfully. This stage lasted 7 minutes.		

The final stage of the lesson, occupying
25 minutes, was spent by pupils working
independently. They were asked to copy the two
graphs into their files while the teacher placed
a written account of what the graphs showed
on a board. They were then instructed to copy
the written account into their files below
the graphs.

Task 2.5

Produce an alternative plan for the lesson focusing on

1 improving the quality of the learning experiences offered to pupils
2 using assessment to enhance teaching and learning.

Notes

1 It is helpful to think carefully about the efficacy of the lesson objective.
2 Replanning this lesson will inevitably raise questions such as 'which elements
  of pupils' prior learning were relevant to the lesson?' Where the information is not available in the account, make your own assumptions.

2.6 Further reading

Chapters which deal with medium-term and lesson planning may be
found in the following books.

Capel, S., Leask, M. and Turner, T. (1999) *Learning to Teach in the Secondary
  School: A Companion to School Experience*. London: Routledge.
Cohen, L., Manion, L. and Morrison, K. (1996) *A Guide to Teaching Practice*.
  London: Routledge.
John, P. (1993) *Lesson Planning for Teachers*. London: Cassell.
Kyriacou, C. (1992) *Essential Teaching Skills*. Hemel Hempstead: Simon and
  Schuster.

3 | Assessment in the classroom

3.1 Introduction

Assessment in the classroom takes many forms ranging from formal 'assessment events', such as end-of-topic tests, to fleeting, informal 'assessment moments' such as when a pupil provides an incorrect response to a question and the teacher uses the answer diagnostically to probe the pupil's misunderstanding. A great deal of classroom assessment tends towards the informal, spontaneous end of the spectrum. It may provide positive examples of the 'assessment opportunism' discussed in Chapter 2, for when an unplanned but nevertheless constructive assessment opportunity arises, a teacher should be prepared to exploit it. Unfortunately, while students are familiar with big assessment events, much of the assessment activity which takes place towards the informal end of the spectrum goes unrecognized. A student who was observed introducing a topic in mathematics illustrates the point. Having finished his explanation, he set the class to work on problems and started to circulate. After a few minutes, he focused on a pupil who he expected to struggle with the task and observed his work. When the pupil performed a wrong action, the student intervened and asked him to explain it. The pupil explained his thinking and the conversation continued for several minutes with the student using questions to scaffold the pupil's learning and correct errors. The student then continued to circulate, checking individuals' progress and dealing with questions. During post-lesson feedback, I focused the discussion on assessment. The student replied defensively that assessment wasn't appropriate in this lesson because he had only just introduced the topic and, anyway, he planned to set homework on it later which he would take in and mark. When I pointed out that formative/diagnostic assessment had been a prominent feature of the lesson, the student was taken aback, claiming that he had not planned to undertake any assessment! However, by setting pupils to work on problems testing their understanding of his exposition and then using focused observation and close questioning to monitor individuals' progress, this student had made extensive use of formative/diagnostic assessment! Indeed, Black (1998: 25) points out that all formative assessment 'is to a degree diagnostic'.

This incident illustrates why assessment is a 'blind spot' in their practice for many student teachers. Formative assessment is often so organic to the teaching/learning process that it blends seamlessly with it. Although it could be argued that it is an artificial exercise to single it out, this chapter seeks to address the fact that so much assessment practice is unconscious practice. When assessment is a tacit process conducted in an unknowing manner, teachers are not in a position to exploit systematically its formative potential. One aim of this chapter is to raise awareness of the range of activities which should be recognized as having assessment potential. It also considers empirical research on the efficacy of various approaches with the intention of helping new teachers to maximize the learning potential of assessment by making informed choices between strategies and manipulating them skilfully.

Objectives

By the end of this chapter, you should have developed your understanding of two key ideas:

- although conventional classroom assessment is norm-referenced, ipsative and criterion-referenced approaches are more beneficial (see pp. 45–8)
- the need to attend to social and emotional aspects of assessment as well as the cognitive dimension.

It is impossible, within the scope of a chapter, to provide an exhaustive account of techniques suitable for classroom use. In keeping with the focus of this book, this chapter concentrates on approaches which have the capacity to enhance learning. First, though, it is important to establish some general principles about the role of assessment in the classroom.

3.2 The role of assessment in establishing classroom climate

As Chapter 1 noted, learning does not take place in a cognitive vacuum but is subject to a range of powerful influences associated with factors as diverse as gender, race, social class, peer group culture, prior learning, personality, expectations from home and school and so on. Some of these factors are largely outside teachers' spheres of influence. One variable which they are in a position to influence is the atmosphere inside the classroom. If pupils are to thrive, teachers need to create a positive classroom climate in which pupils feel secure and motivated to learn, free from fear of humiliation or failure. Assessment plays a key role in creating classroom climate because 'all the assessment processes are, at heart, social processes, taking place in social settings' (Black and Wiliam 1998a: 56). Kyriacou (1992: 65 and 66) argues that the salient features of a positive classroom climate include it being 'relaxed, warm [and] supportive', reminding us that: 'Learning is an emotionally high-risk activity and failure is often extremely painful. Prolonged experience of failure or deprecating remarks by a teacher about pupils' low attainment can have devastating consequences'.

I remember an experience which illustrates this point. I was teaching a GCSE course at a time when it was possible for final grades to be based entirely on marks achieved in coursework. Written assignments were completed regularly so that pupils would have a good range of pieces from which to compile the coursework folder that would be submitted for examination. I taught in a mobile unit where the dividing walls were so thin that lessons in adjacent classrooms were clearly audible. Each week, my group and I became conscious of a 'coursework returning ceremony' taking place with a parallel GCSE class in the adjoining room. We could hear pupils being summoned to the front of the class, one by one, to take receipt of their work. The mark for each piece was announced along with some explanation of why it had been awarded. As this was a re-sit group, its members were striving to reach C grades. Their marks were low and the teacher's comments critical. It is possible to speculate on the impact which this ritual had on the classroom climate from the deathly hush which descended on the group and remained until the end of the lesson. Pupils seemed subdued, rarely volunteering comments to interrupt the drone of the teacher's voice. From the other side of the wall, it seemed that this repeated public grading of pupils was damaging the ethos of the class. This contrasts starkly with the findings of a study which sought to identify the characteristics of two teachers recognized as outstandingly able practitioners (Black and Wiliam 1998a: 31). Both were found to monitor the development of pupils' understanding closely and their classes were characterized by a high frequency of questioning. Interestingly, 60 per cent of all the questions posed were asked by pupils. It seems that part of the success of these teachers stemmed from their ability to use assessment to create a climate of inquiry in which pupils felt free to contribute and to ask questions. In the lessons you have observed, who does most of the questioning: teachers or pupils? Empirical research (Section 3.10) suggests that teachers dominate classroom talk, exercising a virtual monopoly over higher order questions associated with teaching and learning whereas pupils' questions are connected with low level, procedural issues (for example 'Can I use a calculator to work it out?', 'Do I have to produce a draft first?') This chapter focuses on approaches to assessment which exert a positive influence on classroom climate.

3.3 Assessment and pupils' self-esteem and motivation to learn

Just as a positive climate is necessary for learning at the macrocosmic level of the class, so too positive self-esteem and motivation are essential at the microcosmic level of the individual. Through the process of education, everyone develops beliefs about their own capacity to learn and the likelihood that they will succeed on given tasks. Black (1998: 133) notes that: 'These feelings are built up steadily from ... earliest experiences of schooling' and Gipps (1994) points to research which suggests that serious differences in self-esteem start to open up at about the age of 10 – just as pupils are about to embark on secondary education. Thus, self-esteem is learnt, with children quickly gaining a sense of their position in the class pecking order. Assessment, in particular the quality of the feedback they receive, plays a decisive role in this.

Children's images of themselves as learners and their belief in their own capacity to succeed have an impact on their approach to learning. Research (for example Gipps 1994; Black and Wiliam 1998a; Torrance and Pryor 1998) has distinguished two broad categories of learners and, although it would be foolish to suggest that all pupils fit neatly into one category or the other, it is nevertheless helpful to be aware of these broad types. Those with positive self-esteem tend to be strongly motivated to learn and display a willingness to take intellectual risks and tackle difficult tasks. They see success as within their grasp providing they are prepared to try hard enough and do not regard their intelligence as fixed but as capable of improvement. When tasks prove difficult, they do not give up easily but persist, working in flexible and reflective ways. Their confidence is not undermined by failures which they do not attribute to lack of intelligence.

Children with low self-esteem form a negative motivation to learning. Previous experiences of failure may have conditioned them to expect to fail and so learning is perceived as threatening to the self. Consequently, children shrink from it in an attempt at self-protection. Failure avoidance leads them to reject risks and challenges where possible or give up easily when they encounter difficulties. They have a feeling of powerlessness, attributing difficulties to their own inability to learn, and believing there is nothing they can do to improve their intelligence or their likelihood of success. They are reluctant to seek help as this would expose their weaknesses to teachers and peers. Consequently, they become adept at avoiding notice by cultivating the appearance of working well whenever the teacher is close by. The help which is proffered may be shunned as it would signal their difficulties to others.

Perhaps the most important point to note about these two categories of pupils is that those with high self-esteem stack the odds in their own favour by behaving in ways which are conducive to success whereas those with low self-esteem court failure by indulging in counter-productive behaviours. Thus, the expectation of failure encourages failure-inducing behaviour which further reinforces the expectation thereby trapping these pupils into a hard-to-break vicious circle of under-performance. The factors involved in reinforcing the two groups' mind-sets vary and intelligence is not the critical factor in determining group membership. Thus, able children may also display low self-esteem. The quality of the feedback they have received over the years is one of the factors which plays a key part in shaping pupils' images of themselves as learners.

More optimistically, it is important to note that motivation and performance are not fixed attributes which are incapable of change or variety. Pupils can, in fact, perform quite differently in different lessons which is why many ITT courses require students to shadow a pupil over a period of time to alert them to this variation. Many factors influence motivation and performance. For instance, students who were placed in a challenging school where there were high levels of pupil disaffection were stunned by the impact which the introduction of General National Vocational Qualifications (GNVQs) had on the motivation and behaviour of truculent adolescents jaded by conventional academic courses. GNVQ's innovative style of learning/assessment proved to be highly motivating. The following sections consider ways in which assessment may contribute to motivation and self-esteem.

3.4 Norm-referencing and criterion-referencing

Assessment literacy involves becoming familiar with different ways of referencing assessments. Assessment is not a 'standalone' activity which takes place in a standards vacuum. It requires a reference point or scale against which individual assessments can be set.

Criterion-referencing is a member of the formative/ipsative assessment 'family'. Indeed, Black (1998: 63) argues that formative assessment 'requires criterion-referencing'. Criterion-referencing involves specifying the knowledge, skills, concepts or other qualities required to achieve a particular level, grade or qualification. All those who meet requirements are awarded accordingly. For instance, the example shown in Figure 3.1, from a unit

PROBLEM SOLVING, LEVEL 3		Key Skills Reference
When students are:	They should be able to develop the following Key Skills evidence:	
• analysing a given financial problem	PS3.1 Explore a complex problem, come up with **three** options for solving it and justify the option selected for taking forward	S

Figure 3.1 An example of criterion-referencing

in financial accounting in the business vocational A level (Section 8.5b), details what candidates must do to achieve Key Skills level 3 when performing a given task.

However, conventional classroom practice is characterized by 'a tendency to use a normative rather than a criterion approach' (Black and Wiliam 1998a: 18). Whereas criterion-referencing assesses performances against relevant criteria, norm-referencing compares them with one another. It is designed to produce results that conform to a normal bell-shaped curve of distribution. By discriminating between different levels of performance, it aims to spread performances across the curve. Therefore, test items which prove to be very easy or exceptionally hard so that almost all or hardly any candidates can do them may be eliminated from norm-referenced tests on the grounds that they do not discriminate well.

Widely used in traditional examinations, norm-referencing has been the subject of much criticism. The main concern is that candidates' results are not based solely on their own performance but depend, to some extent, on how well other candidates in a cohort perform. The 11-plus test illustrates the problem. It was used to allocate places in secondary schools following the 1944 Education Act's introduction of a tripartite system of secondary education based on grammar, technical and secondary modern schools. LEAs provided anywhere between 10 and 40 per cent of secondary places in grammar schools, making competition for these places intense. The 11-plus was used to produce a rank order of candidates so that selection decisions could be made. Therefore, securing a grammar school place depended not only on a child's performance in the test, and on the generosity of a LEA, but also on the performance of the entire cohort. This was widely regarded as an arbitrary and unfair method of allocating children to secondary schools. Many other high stakes tests and examinations display similar characteristics in that they are designed to spread performances, producing a rank order of candidates which allows grade boundaries to be fixed.

Criterion-referencing is regarded as superior for various reasons. For example, specifying criteria for success is a cardinal principle of formative assessment. Criterion-referencing conforms to this by publishing requirements, providing teachers and pupils with clear goals for which to aim. In contrast with the transparency of criterion-referencing, norm-referencing has been described as a 'hidden' process (Gipps 1994: 145). Criterion-referencing is also more egalitarian, giving everyone the potential to succeed if they satisfy performance criteria. It does not require performances to be ranked and it does not compare them with one another. If something is considered educationally important, it will be incorporated into a criterion-referenced assessment irrespective of its discriminatory powers, making for a success-orientated approach. However, it would be misleading to draw an absolute distinction between these two types of assessment, suggesting that there is no common ground between them. There are, in fact, elements of norm-referencing in any criterion-referenced system and vice versa. This is because when standards are set for a criterion-referenced system, they are inevitably informed by relevant performance norms. Imagine, for instance, setting a criterion-referenced test for 11-year-olds based on A level standards. A similar point applies to norm-referencing. Many awarding bodies distance themselves from norm-referencing, insisting that their qualifications provide a consistently used measure of absolute standards. Although an underlying principle of many public examinations is the need to spread and grade performances, awarding bodies do nevertheless make a determined effort to apply consistent standards based on grade-related criteria. It is in the difficult area of establishing grade boundaries that normative considerations may come into play.

This is a complex area of assessment theory which it would be inappropriate for this chapter to explore further. The main point to note is that while strict criterion-referencing has proved problematic in the context of public examining (Chapter 8), it has a valuable part to play in the classroom contributing usefully to a formative/ipsative assessment regime. A normative approach on the other hand, although commonplace in the classroom, has many drawbacks. According to Gipps (1994):

> Competition is central to norm-referencing, which is a form of social comparison. This can lead to severe discouragement for students who have few academic successes in competition with their peers. It also discourages students from helping each other with their academic work and encourages the covering up of misunderstandings. It threatens peer relationships and tends to segregate groups into higher and lower achieving pupils. Neither does it encourage intrinsic motivation. It also tends to encourage students to attribute success and failure to ability, rather than to effort, which is especially harmful for low-achieving students.
>
> (Gipps 1994: 41)

3.5 The challenge of ipsative assessment

Research suggests that a radically different approach to assessment is more efficacious for all pupils, but especially for low achievers. Ipsative assessment is self-referenced, encouraging pupils to pit themselves against their own former achievements rather than comparing themselves with others. This makes it a form of *self-competition* which places the emphasis firmly on self-improvement regardless of the progress of others. Ipsative assessment is, in fact, a logical complement to the formative approach to planning recommended in Chapter 2 because it individualizes assessment in the same way that formative planning is differentiated. It is unhelpful to think of ipsative assessment as a specific strategy – like, for instance, focused observation or a standardized test – which can be selected for use on a particular occasion. It is more meaningful to think of it as an approach to assessment which can be promoted by employing certain methods including

- criterion-referenced assessments in which performance standards are clearly specified (as opposed to norm-referenced assessments)
- task-focused feedback which provides clear guidance on how to improve (as opposed to performance-focused feedback which usually involves unhelpful comparisons with the attainment of peers)
- SMART learning targets (Section 3.7) (as opposed to a general aim to improve)
- active involvement of pupils in self-assessment (as opposed to the passive exercise of self-marking)
- allowing pupils some choice in the way they go about achieving learning objectives.

Before examining some of these approaches, it is important to acknowledge that ipsative assessment is not always feasible. In a school system dominated by external testing where the 'grading function is over-emphasised' (Black and Wiliam 1998a: 18), there will inevitably be occasions when you will be required to assign pupils to levels/grades using the wider standards embodied in the NC or other public examinations. You may also meet considerable resistance to ipsative assessment from pupils who are familiar with norm-referencing and have developed an understandable pre-occupation with their position in the class pecking order. These forces may combine to squeeze ipsative assessment out of the classroom altogether if teachers do not make a concerted effort to use it whenever possible. Although teachers need to be determined to foster ipsative assessment among pupils, the effort is repaid by a more healthy and productive approach to learning, especially among the lowest achievers who find few incentives in norm-referenced systems.

3.6 Providing oral feedback

Whether it is done consciously or unconsciously, formally or informally and in written form or verbally, teachers provide feedback to pupils as a routine feature of classroom interactions. Pupils are in regular receipt of comments about their work, progress, potential and attitude, and of corrections to their errors. A number of studies have identified feedback as the largest single influence on subsequent performance (Black and Wiliam 1998a). Whether this is a productive or counter-productive experience depends on the *quality* of the feedback. One large-scale review reported that about two in every five feedback effects were negative (Black and Wiliam 1998a: 48), suggesting that incomplete or poor quality feedback may be as unhelpful as providing none at all. Because feedback is a core activity in formative assessment, it is considered twice. Oral feedback is dealt with here and written feedback is examined in Chapter 4. As well as reading each chapter in turn, it is helpful to read the two sections on feedback in conjunction with one another because many of the points made in each are pertinent to both.

Some research suggests that oral feedback is more effective than written (James 1998: 99). Indeed, Black and Wiliam (1998a: 52) found that: 'the quality of dialogue in a feedback intervention is important . . . and can, in fact, be more significant than prior ability and personality factors combined'. There are various reasons why oral feedback is so important. First, feedback works best when it is given regularly and while it is still relevant. This favours oral feedback which generally has greater immediacy than written. For instance, a modern foreign languages (MFL) teacher can instantly correct errors of pronunciation or grammar in a pupil's use of the target language. In contrast, there is usually a delay in the provision of written feedback. Various features of spoken communication can be used to clarify oral feedback which would be lost in written communication. For instance, the potential for a two-way exchange allows pupils to respond and ask questions. A teacher can elucidate a difficult concept by repeating or rephrasing it. Stress or pauses can be used to emphasize important points and so on. Written feedback also has distinct advantages that should not be overlooked. For instance, it provides a permanent record which can be used for future reference and reflection whereas oral feedback is ephemeral and relies upon memory. Clearly, both approaches have strengths and both have drawbacks so a balanced approach ensures that pupils receive plenty of both.

Oral feedback can be given on a group or individual basis. For instance, going over a piece of marked work together in class, 'postmortem style', offers a powerful learning experience because pupils' work provides excellent teaching material. It is more authentic than a teacher's contrived examples and allows common misunderstandings to be targeted. It is, of course, important to protect the anonymity of individuals and to stress that, if their work is used to illustrate difficulties, it is because many pupils made the same mistake. Alternatively, good work can be a source of ideas or a model for others to emulate.

Oral feedback can be given individually while the rest of the class are working independently. In this way, it can become an ongoing part of classroom dialogue, lessening the need for formal progress reviews (Section 3.10). It can be used for going over previous work or for a negotiated assessment of work in progress. Teachers who assess pupils' *current* work with them are the embodiment of formative assessment. Assessing work in progress, in collaboration with its author, is a powerful alternative to 'cold marking' (Headington 2000: 67) which is completed after the event away from the child. It is the most immediate form of teacher feedback a child can receive and allows improvements to be made *before* the work is finalized.

Although the ability to provide constructive oral feedback is an essential teaching skill, Pryor and Torrance (1996) remind us of the complex, subtle nature of oral feedback and its hidden pitfalls. In a verbal exchange, pupil and teacher respond spontaneously and, under the pressure of the moment, well-intentioned remarks may have unintended consequences. Much of this classroom discourse functions at a subliminal level, making it difficult for either party to appreciate fully the impact its words are having. Some teachers were found to operate on the assumption that assessment was rather a nasty business from which pupils needed protection. Teachers who obeyed this instinct to protect pupils from the 'negative' impact of assessment also deprived them of the learning potential of feedback. New teachers need to beware of these issues so that they can proceed with care, alert to their own attitudes to feedback as well as to the impact it may be having on pupils.

3.7 Target-setting

An important means of exploiting the feedforward potential of assessment is target-setting. Target-setting is a current educational vogue with entire books devoted to offering guidance on best practice (for example Lawley 1999). It takes place at many levels ranging from the national targets set by government through to those set at LEA, school, department, teacher and individual pupil level. Indeed, Gann's (1999: 32) description of 'the current blizzard of target-setting' conveys something of the volume and intensity of this activity at present. Clearly, target-setting in the classroom represents the lowest echelon on the target-setting hierarchy so it is inevitably influenced by decisions taken at other levels. However, decision-making at higher levels cannot ignore what is realistic for individual teachers and pupils. Chapter 7 examines target-setting at school and national level but in this chapter the focus is on short-term, individual learning targets set as part of regular classroom work.

It is important to clarify the distinction between learning targets and learning objectives. In some instances, the differences are obvious. For instance, one of the national targets set by the Conservative government in 1995 was that by 2000 85 per cent of 19-year-olds should achieve five GCSEs at grade C or above, an intermediate GNVQ or a National Vocational Qualification (NVQ) level 2 (Ofsted 1996a). There is an obvious difference between the scope and time scale for this national target and the learning objectives which were described in Section 2.5a. However, the distinction between *learning targets* and *learning objectives* may be less obvious. A learning objective is lesson specific, focusing on lesson outcomes. A learning target, on the other hand, relates to a pupil's needs. The need will be associated with an ongoing weakness or gap in their work and hence the target is likely to be relevant to more than one

S	Specific	Specific targets relate to a defined area of competence – perhaps related to NC levels
M	Measurable	Measurable targets are couched in terms which allow the teacher – and pupils – to point to evidence that they have been achieved
A	Achievable	Achievable targets are ones which pupils can achieve – that is, they are do-able rather than vague aspirations
R	Realistic	Realistic targets are defined in relation to the context in which pupils are working and – importantly – the standards to be achieved
T	Time-related	Time-related targets have clear dates for review and monitoring in relation to the time scale available

Figure 3.2   SMART target-setting
Source: adapted from DfEE 1997: 10

lesson. For instance, in working with a class on descriptive writing, an English teacher's learning objective may centre on the development of such descriptive skills as diction and the ability to use language figuratively. However, a pupil who has a long-term difficulty with writing in sentences may be working on a personal writing target which has more to do with technical features of language than its creative use (for example to write in sentences, correctly punctuated). Therefore, although the pupil should be aiming to produce an effective piece of descriptive writing, they should also be striving to achieve this personal target.

Target-setting focuses pupils' efforts on areas earmarked for improvement. It aims to raise standards overall, not through a generalized commitment to improvement, which is known to be ineffectual, but by systematically identifying gaps and weaknesses which are then targeted for development. The key to effective target-setting is to think SMART: see Figure 3.2.

To be genuinely SMART, a target should be specific enough to give a pupil precise guidance on the action needed to improve their work. For instance, concerned about his poor presentation of written work, Joe's science teacher suggested a general target: 'To improve presentation of written assignments'. A SMART target, in contrast, would have helped Joe by diagnosing the problem (for example illegible handwriting, poor layout, inadequate labelling, too many careless errors or too much crossing out) and indicating the actions Joe needed to take to improve. In contrast, when Leah's history teacher was concerned about the lack of detail in her essays, she agreed the following SMART target with Leah: 'To provide an example to illustrate each point that I make and include at least five facts or figures in my next homework assignment'.

The principle that pupils should be actively involved applies to target-setting in the same way that it applies to other aspects of assessment. Pupils are more likely to find targets meaningful, and to be motivated by them, if they have been involved in setting them (Lodge and Watkins 1999). Either pupils could assume responsibility for determining targets, as part of a system of self-assessment, or targets could be negotiated with them. Challenging but realistic targets, coupled with regular progress reviews, can be very effective. Even with very young children, it has been found that:

> Children are highly motivated by their targets and appear to remember them very quickly, even if they cannot read them, probably because they are very personal and clearly relate to them. Children become increasingly able to say what they think their next target should be and when they believe they have fulfilled a target.
>
> (Clarke 1998: 96)

Other research (Black and Wiliam 1998a: 41) shows that pupils' rates of progress can be accelerated by working in this way. It is, however, important not to get carried away, setting so many targets that pupils become overwhelmed. When the process starts to feel unmanageable, pupils are liable to abandon it. The number of targets an individual feels comfortable with will vary and experience is the teacher's best guide but, as a general rule, most pupils should cope with one or two complementary targets at any one time in a subject. However, it is important to recognize that target-setting is not a panacea and not all pupils can be motivated in this way (Lodge and Watkins 1999). Part of the explanation for this may be that different types of targets are not equally effective. Targets which focus on learning lead to higher motivation and achievement than targets which focus on performance (Black and Wiliam 1998a: 14). Performance targets focus on how well individuals should perform – often relative to the performance of others – and make inferences from this about their general ability. They encourage pupils to focus on their own ability, which they tend to regard as fixed, and on outperforming others. It is more constructive to use learning targets which emphasize the knowledge, concepts or skills which should result from engaging in a particular task. Learning targets encourage self-referenced standards and improved competence. Torrance and Pryor (1998) argue that:

> a tendency to adopt performance goals is not in the long-term interest of the learner. Unsuccessful children quickly become demotivated and even successful ones, especially girls, are liable to suffer from low confidence which, if persistent, results in what has been termed 'learned helplessness' . . . it is better to inform pupils specifically of what it is that is causing their lack of success and to create an emphasis on learning goals and personally challenging tasks.
>
> (Torrance and Pryor 1998: 86)

3.8 Oral questions

'Teachers may ask on average one, or even two, questions per minute, which means several hundreds in a day and tens of thousands over a school year' (Wragg 1997: 25). Questioning is a staple feature of classroom communication. In fact, it is such a routine part of human behaviour that it is easy to overlook its importance which would be a mistake for question-asking has been described as 'our most important intellectual tool' (N. Postman, quoted in Morgan and Saxton 1993: 9). It play a vital role in assessment, contributing to the achievement of high standards. Thus, pupils have been found to achieve more when teachers make frequent use of questions to monitor progress and check understanding (Harris 1998: 172). Ofsted (1996b: 23) goes further, identifying questioning as 'the single most important factor in students' achievements of high standards, where questions were used to assess students' knowledge and challenge their thinking'.

There are many reasons why questioning is one of the most powerful tools in a teacher's repertoire of assessment skills. Questioning is versatile, fulfilling a multitude of purposes. It can be used to establish baselines, test recall, reinforce ideas, monitor progress, challenge misconceptions, scaffold learning and so on. The immediacy of oral questioning is also important. A question can be asked as and when necessary. It does not require elaborate planning and preparation, like a test, and pupils do not need advance notice of its use. It can provide teachers with instant feedback, allowing them to monitor the impact of teaching on pupils and intervene rapidly if misunderstandings arise. Although ease of use and immediacy are two of its most important attributes, the interactive nature of questioning is also important. Questioning is a particularly searching form of assessment because each response provides a basis for subsequent questioning, enabling teachers to probe pupils' understanding in depth and from a variety of perspectives. This is important because pupils frequently develop a superficial grasp of a topic without any depth of understanding. Pupils are also adept at guessing the answer a teacher wants to hear and devote a good deal of their energy to doing just that! Therefore, a teacher may attribute a correct answer to genuine learning when, in fact, it owes more to chance. When it is used skilfully, oral questioning avoids these tendencies, probing understanding and taking teachers closer to the core of pupils' thinking than any other technique. To exploit this potential, teachers need to provide pupils with frequent opportunities to make extended responses by using plenty of open questions.

'Open' and 'closed' are two of the basic categories into which questions are divided. Open questions require extended answers and promote higher order thinking, for instance speculation, analysis, problem-solving. Closed questions require short, 'correct' answers and encourage lower order thinking such as learning by rote. For instance, compare the question 'What does Diwali mean?' with 'Why is Diwali important for Hindus?' Open questions are particularly important to formative assessment because 'one of the most potent forms of learning is receiving and giving elaborated explanations' (Gipps 1994: 41). When pupils provide this kind of answer, they are also providing their teacher with important clues about what and how they are learning. Teachers need to attend carefully to the replies so that they can use the information diagnostically. Dialogue based on open questioning is also an example of scaffolded assessment because it can actually extend pupils' thinking, enabling them to 'articulate understandings of which . . . they had not previously been conscious' (McIntyre and Cooper 1996: 66).

Clearly, the flexibility, spontaneity and incisiveness of questioning provide a winning combination. However, it would be misleading to suggest that questioning is an easy skill or that its potential benefits are readily realized. Questioning has been the subject of many empirical studies which paint a more complicated and problematical picture of its use in the classroom. Black and Wiliam (1998a: 17) suggest that questioning is a neglected field of expertise. Teachers do not review their own assessment questions or discuss them critically with other teachers so that there is little reflection on what is being assessed, or improvement of its quality. Research into the types of questions teachers ask has found that they favour closed questions whereas open questions, which promote deep learning, are less commonly used. Gipps *et al.* (1995) found that closed questions were restrictive. Ofsted (1998a: 80) agrees that they 'close pupils down' and 'only allow a limited response'. However, it would be misleading to characterize closed questions as axiomatically inferior to open ones. Every subject requires pupils to master basic facts and items of information and closed questions are a good way of testing these lower order skills of memorizing information and reproducing it accurately. As with any other aspect of teaching, the test of a question is fitness for purpose. Closed questions are not, therefore, a problem *per se* but teachers' over-reliance on them is associated with negative consequences for teaching and learning.

Black and Wiliam (1998a: 56) distinguish between *information-seeking* and *response-seeking* questions. Closed questions fall into the latter category and pupils who are over-exposed to this kind of questioning are conditioned to respond in certain ways. They are encouraged to concentrate on winning teacher approval by providing the desired response rather than developing their own understanding. At its worst, this quest to discover the 'correct' answer degenerates into an unproductive guessing game in which the original learning purpose is obscured. Rote and surface learning are placed at a premium by over-reliance on this type of questioning. Depth of learning is not the only casualty when teachers emphasize pupils' ability to regurgitate faithfully what has been transmitted to them. Teachers may be deceived into regarding accurate answers as evidence of learning which it by no means guarantees. Remember

Jennifer's 'textbook perfect' electrical circuit diagram in Chapter 1 which concealed a fundamental failure in understanding. By the same token, a pupil's failure to supply the response a teacher requires does not necessarily prove that the child lacks the knowledge or skill in question. Torrance and Pryor (1998: 50–2) describe an infant who failed to demonstrate the necessary skills in an activity his teacher had devised to test number recognition and the ability to count to three. However, when a commotion was caused by a classroom assistant removing a group of children from the room, the same child turned round and remarked that there were only five people left in the room! One consequence of response- rather than information-seeking is that teachers' questions 'do not tell them what they need to know about their students' learning' (Black and Wiliam 1998a: 18). In contrast, when the emphasis is placed on information- seeking, 'wrong' answers are as useful as 'correct' ones because they provide diagnostic clues to pupils' thinking processes. Simpson (1990) (in Chapter 1) was making a similar point when she argued that teachers, like marks- men, should be interested in discovering where all their shots go, not merely how many find their target.

Black and Wiliam (1998a: 56) provide an interesting example of the pitfalls inherent in assuming that a correct answer to a closed question signifies meaningful learning. Most pupils were able to solve the equation $3a = 24$ but declared it 'impossible' when it was extended to include $a + b = 16$, arguing that 'b' can't be 8 because 'a' is 8. If all the examples they have previously encountered use a different letter to denote each number, pupils may assume that this is always the case. Once again, we are reminded that pupils can develop all manner of misconceptions during teaching. It is the 'richness' of a teacher's questioning which holds the key to distinguishing between deep, meaningful learning and flawed, surface understanding. Ideas must be probed in different ways for teachers to be confident that pupils really understand (or fail to understand).

Research suggests that 'teachers' questions are as much to do with accomplishing the lesson – making it happen as a piece of social interac- tion – as they are to do with eliciting particular information from par- ticular pupils' (Torrance and Pryor 1998: 17). A common form of classroom discourse which exemplifies this is the IRF cycle (English 1981; Torrance and Pryor 1998), a three-phase verbal cycle which is initiated and con- trolled by teachers. IRF involves *Initiation* (teacher's questions), *Responses* (pupils' replies) and *Feedback* (teacher's evaluation of answers). Many classroom exchanges are of this type. Even though it is pupils who need to use language to organize their thoughts and make sense of lessons, teachers typically 'have "conversational control" over lessons and over the amount and nature of pupils' contributions. Much of what we think of as "teaching" is in fact this monitoring of all the verbal exchanges in the classroom. Pupils have correspondingly few conversational rights' (English 1981: 57).

Although the IRF pattern is a ritualized and controlling form of discourse, it nevertheless allows teachers to conduct lessons, determining their direction and pace, to ensure that learning objectives are met and the curriculum covered within the time available. Imagine, for instance, that classroom interactions regularly followed the conventions of ordinary conversation. Learning would become a haphazard business under such circumstances! Nevertheless, researchers have raised serious concerns about this approach. For instance, Torrance and Pryor (1998: 169) concluded that IRF is 'problematic', producing 'negative consequences for both learning and social development'. They noted that teachers persisted in its use even when they were fairly confident that their questioning was testing levels of knowledge and understanding which were beyond the child. In these instances, didactic teaching would have been more helpful whereas repeated questioning encouraged guessing.

Although an advantage of oral questioning is the possibility of providing immediate feedback, this asset is not always utilized because teachers have a tendency to allow inconvenient contributions to pass without comment. For instance, one study of over a thousand teachers' questions found that over one-third of responses 'attracted a non-verbal reply or no response' (Wragg 1997: 29). As Wragg points out, this has serious implications when a question is directed at a group, for many pupils will be holding suspended in their minds their imagined answer to the question. If teachers provide ambiguous feedback, or withhold it altogether, the status of different answers remains unclear. Another 'common failing' noted by Ofsted (1998a: 80) is a tendency to be 'undemanding or over-sensitive to pupils' feelings, accepting a wrong or partial answer rather than pressing the pupil to reflect and refine or go a stage further'. Torrance and Pryor (1998: 18) reported similar findings. Teachers, anxious to utilize infants' contributions, accepted partial or irrelevant answers and avoided explicit correction of errors, imposing, instead, a subtle reinterpretation on what children had said so that the answer provided suitable teaching material. Avoidance of 'negative' or corrective feedback is clearly intended to encourage pupils but the possibility of misleading them is disturbing.

One characteristic of classroom discourse which has been recognized for many years is its domination by teachers. With teachers doing anywhere between 65 per cent and almost 90 per cent of the talk according to different studies, the principal tasks of pupils, it seems, are to listen and to write. There have been some startling individual case studies which bear out this general conclusion including a 15-year-old who spoke in class for only 12 seconds throughout an entire day, a primary pupil who spoke only to two friends but never to the teacher and a 14-year-old who wrote 3000 words covering 16 sides of paper in a day (English 1981: 49). Even among infants whose writing and listening skills are immature, and who may consequently be expected to talk more, Torrance and Pryor (1998: 106) found: 'A feature of most of the transcripts . . . is that very few words are actually spoken by pupils. The overwhelming quantity of talk comes from the teacher despite the fact that the ostensible purpose of their utterances is to elicit responses from children'. They present this irony as an 'almost inevitable' consequence of IRF interactions.

Not only do teachers dominate the talking, but also they are reluctant to provide the 'wait time' which would enable pupils to think and for-mulate thoughtful answers to questions. Ofsted (1998a: 80) noted that: 'too often teachers seem scared of silence, so that they fail to allow pupils sufficient time to think'. In one study the average wait time after a question was found to be about a second but 'where a longer silence was left – even as short as three seconds – the quality and extent of pupils' responses improved dramatically . . . not only longer but also more thoughtful' (Wood 1998: 176). Teachers' desire for their lessons to have pace may explain this tendency. Nevertheless, an emphasis on the flow of a lesson can have unfortunate consequences. One is for teachers to defeat their object by answering their own questions! The preference for closed questions is also reinforced because open questions are incom-patible with quick-fire responses promoting instead a more tentative approach. When answering questions becomes a competitive scramble, rather than a thoughtful undertaking, many pupils give up, feeling that there is no point in trying when they are incapable of a rapid response and they know that another question or the answer will be forthcoming in a second or two (Black and Wiliam 1998b: 11). Teachers are thereby encouraged to 'focus on a limited group of pupils' (Ofsted 1998a: 80) who keep pace with the flow of a lesson and exclude the rest. Although this enables teachers to 'keep the lesson going', this is at the expense of 'the understanding of most of the class – the question–answer dialogue becomes a ritual, one in which all connive and thoughtful involvement suffers' (Black and Wiliam 1998b: 11).

As well as making a conscious effort to provide the wait time which gives pupils the space to think, there are various strategies which teachers can use to make questioning a more thought-provoking and egalitarian process. Smith (1998: 86) suggests various techniques. For instance, 'Traffic Lights' entails using a large poster depicting traffic lights to monitor pupils' understanding as a lesson proceeds. Pupils are taught to indicate how much they have grasped using red (not yet understood), amber (some uncertainty) and green (fully understood). Husbands (1996: 94–7) recommends a three-stage process: private-intimate-public (P-I-P). Stage 1 (private) entails pupils writing down their response to a question. Stage 2 (intimate) involves comparing responses with a neighbour or small group. Only at Stage 3 does the response become 'public' when groups are invite to report back. Black and Wiliam (1998b: 12) suggest giving pupils a choice between answers and getting them to vote on options or giving them time to write down a response and then reading out a selected few. One way of interrupting the IRF pattern is to hand Stage 3 (evaluation of responses) over to pupils, encouraging them to appraise each other's contributions. This is a useful strategy for challenging pupils to listen actively and think deeply. One consequence of involving pupils at Stages 2 (pupils' responses) and 3 is that they play a more equal part in classroom discourse. These exchanges occasionally develop their own momentum, becoming self-sustaining dialogues in which the quality of thinking is high but they are not orchestrated by a teacher. Clearly, ways of posing and responding to questions are as capable of variety as other elements of teaching and teachers should guard against over-reliance on one approach, for example always directing questions at the whole class and then accepting the answer of the first person to raise their hand or – worse still – to shout the answer out.

Typically, classrooms operate according to tacit rules about who can use certain kinds of talk. This could mean that only teachers evaluate the contributions which are made and that they ask most of the higher order, open questions. Pupils' questions might be confined to low level, procedural issues such as the requirements for a piece of work – length, deadline for completion and so on. In fact, research (for example Black and Wiliam 1998a) has suggested that pupils are reluctant to ask other types of questions – requests for help, for instance, or questions to do with learning, fearful that it may suggest that they are struggling with the work and damage their standing with their peers. But if question-asking really is 'our most important intellectual tool', pupils should be using it as much as teachers.

Creating a supportive classroom climate in which everyone feels free to ask questions is a necessary precondition for meaningful, active learning. As well as modelling this approach by posing lots of thought-provoking questions, teachers need to inculcate helpful attitudes by welcoming pupils' questions and responding enthusiastically to them. For instance, a school science department decided to investigate why middle school pupils were reluctant to study science at a higher level. It discovered that pupils were put off by their difficulty in understanding key concepts, believing that they would struggle with advanced science. The department decided to examine the efficacy of different teachers' approaches to elucidating difficult concepts: 'The opportunity to ask questions during the explanation is particularly valued, especially from the pupils whose teacher split the explanation into smaller sections and checked understanding at each stage' (Wragg 1999: 146). Studies from around the globe (Black and Wiliam 1998a: 29 and 33) have shown that when learners are trained to generate their own thought-provoking questions, and then try to answer them, they outperform groups trained in other study techniques. This suggests that pupils should be encouraged to develop a more inquiring approach to their own learning. Learners are often aware of the gains to be made by working in this way claiming that it encourages them to think more and learn more effectively. When developing a formative test, for instance, pupils could be involved in devising or selecting items for inclusion. They are, after all, best placed to judge which aspects of a topic they have found difficult.

Questioning is most commonly used in conjunction with other teaching strategies. For instance, when introducing a topic, a teacher will often switch back and forth between explication and questioning to check that pupils are following the development of ideas, and to maintain their interest. In this way, assessment is woven into the texture of teaching and learning. An assessment technique which works particularly well in conjunction with questioning is observation.

3.9 Observation

Like questioning, observation is a natural feature of human behaviour which is performed without encouragement or training. However, in a more developed form, observation is a useful assessment technique. Approaches to observation fall into two categories: unfocused, general observation and focused observation. Teachers perform the former as a matter of course. It is done fleetingly and repeatedly throughout a lesson and forms a routine part of classroom encounters. For instance, at the beginning of a lesson a teacher may decide how to proceed by scanning the room to judge the mood of a class. Then, at regular intervals throughout, the teacher may sweep the room to assess pupils' level of engagement with the task in hand. This ability to scan a room has been identified as a skill that is essential to the 'with-it-ness' and the ability to 'overlap' which competent teachers display (Kounin 1970, quoted in Cohen *et al.* 1996: 312). Although it is impossible for a teacher to know everything that is going on in a classroom, with-it teachers are aware of most of what is going on most of the time. Frequent scanning of a class is one of the techniques which helps teachers to maintain with-it-ness. Overlapping means the ability to attend to more than one task at once. Thus, while helping an individual, a teacher should nevertheless be conscious of noise and activity in other parts of the classroom. Novice teachers, however, have a tendency to become involved with individuals to the point where they are oblivious to what other members of a class are doing. They also tend to focus on a restricted segment of a class, usually those in a V-shaped wedge of seating which is in their line of vision (Wragg 1984). Clearly, the ability to undertake frequent, unfocused observations and to use them as a basis for making rapid decisions about how to proceed are essential teaching skills without which classrooms could not function. This type of unfocused observation is, therefore, useful in the context of general class management. However, from an assessment perspective, it does have limitations.

Unfocused observation is necessarily fleeting. Harlen (1977, quoted in Conner 1991: 51) describes it as little more than 'brief glimpses of a passing scene'. This makes it impressionistic. The problem with impressions is that they can mislead. The child who appears to spend too much time gazing idly out of a window may think best that way. Pupils who appear to apply themselves assiduously whenever the teacher looks in their direction may have cultivated this air to avoid drawing attention to themselves. Dean (1990, quoted in Conner 1991: 49) reminds us that teachers need to be very sure of their evidence because 'much depends upon the outcome of your judgements'. It is, therefore, essential to recognize the limitations of unfocused observations and to take steps to offset these by using other techniques to corroborate impressions.

Focused observation is quite different. As the name implies, a particular focus is selected for scrutiny beforehand. As with any assessment activity, the principal task is to achieve a good level of match between strategy and purpose. Nowhere is the need for purposefulness more important than in the context of focused observation. Teachers who have embarked on it without a clear idea of why they are using it or what they are seeking have found focused observation disappointing (Conner 1991: 53). Frequently it is an individual – possibly one with learning or behavioural difficulties – who forms the focus of observation although this technique may also be used with small groups. To be of value, the observation usually has to be sustained over a period of time. Focused observation is, therefore, a labour-intensive activity which makes heavy demands on teachers' time and attention. It also requires considerable forethought and planning (Torrance and Pryor 1998: 162) to identify the precise focus for observation and to decide how information should be recorded: for instance, a tally sheet to record the frequency and conditions under which particular behaviours occur or notes written in longhand? *An Introduction to Classroom Observation* (Wragg 1999) details different observation and recording methods. Teachers also need to ensure that they have created conditions which allow other pupils to work independently while they observe. For all these reasons, subjects make a variable use of focused observation. Certain subjects – for example information technology (IT), physical education (PE) and drama – make a more extensive use because focused observation occurs naturally within subjects which emphasize the acquisition of practical skills and where the concern is with educational processes as well as with end products. Where teachers find that observation is not a natural feature of their work, the advance planning which is required, coupled with the logistical difficulties, may act as disincentives to its use. Whereas unfocused observation is a routine feature of secondary teachers' work, focused observation is used more sparingly.

It is primary teachers, especially early years specialists, who have been most active in developing focused observation as an assessment technique (Gipps *et al.* 1995; Conner 1999). To some extent, these teachers are obliged to observe because young children's written and verbal skills are too immature to provide adequate guides to their learning. Gipps *et al.* (1995) also attribute the development of KS1 teachers' observational skills to the standard assessment tasks (SATs) which were used for end-of-key-stage assessments when the NC was introduced. As children's abilities to express themselves in speech and writing develop, the need for focused observation may decline to the point where some teachers make no use of it. However, Hook (1985, quoted in Conner 1991: 54) argues that observation is an essential skill in any teacher's repertoire. Therefore, there are lessons for all teachers in the insights which primary specialists have gleaned from experiences with focused observation.

Using a single piece of evidence as a basis for judgements is hazardous because the most obvious conclusion is not necessarily the correct one. It is helpful, therefore, to employ a combination of methods to gather a range of evidence before making judgements. Triangulation involves cross-checking inferences based on one set of evidence against other evidence drawn from different sources and it is one measure which can be taken to make the process of reaching judgements more secure. This is one reason why it is useful to combine observation with questioning. For instance, you may be puzzled to observe a pupil's approach to performing a task, making it natural to question the chosen approach. Similarly, a pupil's reply to a question may suggest certain conclusions which you will want to test by observing to see if your impressions are confirmed. Thus, questioning and observation are complementary approaches which work well in tandem. There are other means of triangulation. For instance, impressions formed on the basis of unfocused observation may be tested more rigorously by subjecting them to focused observation. Likewise, an independent observer can act as a critical friend, offering an alternative perspective on observational data. This may be helpful in avoiding the halo effect of seeing only what you expect to see based on prior knowledge of a pupil. As a student, you will be observed regularly by mentors and class teachers as part of your training. You may, therefore, be in a better position to take advantage of this approach to observation than practising teachers. Co-enquiry is a recognized technique for mentoring student teachers (Rudduck and Sigsworth 1985). It entails mentor and student jointly determining a focus for the mentor's observation of a lesson taught by the student. The mentor then provides an evidence-based record of the lesson for joint consideration. Since this should be 'a process of collaborative enquiry in which both might be expected to make discoveries' (Brooks and Sikes 1997: 27), observing in this way allows a student and the regular class teacher to investigate a common cause of concern to their mutual benefit. Clearly, there are several ways in which inferences drawn from one method of assessment can be corroborated or refuted by using the evidence of others. However, questioning is perhaps the most natural complement to observation. Indeed, Torrance and Pryor (1998: 162) conclude that 'observation has to be sustained and accompanied by focused questioning to bring most benefit'.

The principal use of focused observation is as a formative/diagnostic tool where it can be particularly powerful. For instance, Gipps *et al.* (1995: 175) describe how focused observation was a 'revelation' for the

KS1 teachers who were obliged to use it by the introduction of SATs. Although many of them felt unable to sustain this time-consuming approach once SATs had been abandoned, teachers had nevertheless been alerted to the powerful combination that focused observation and questioning provide and attempted to incorporate it into their practice whenever they could. The description of focused observation as a revelatory experience conveys its ability to heighten consciousness. Indeed, those teachers who have taken the trouble to develop their observational skills generally testify to the insightfulness of this approach. For instance, one teacher reflected: 'The fascinating thing is I've begun to see things that I never noticed before' and another noted that: 'It seemed that, the closer I looked . . . the more I saw' (quoted in Conner 1991: 52 and 64). Harlen (quoted in Conner 1991: 63) sums up this aspect of observation thus: 'Observation is the process through which we come to take notice, to become conscious, of things and happenings'. Part of the explanation for this may be that adopting the role of observer allows teachers to become 'semi-detached', distancing themselves mentally from the action even though, physically, they may be close to it. This provides valuable space for reflection which may yield unexpected insights.

Focused observation, therefore, enables teachers to see more intelligently and to make their questioning more incisive. Thus, although observation may not provide direct access to pupils' thinking in the way that questioning does, it does provide firsthand information about *behaviours* and, by focusing on the *processes* which pupils use to complete tasks, it complements questioning by suggesting fruitful areas for inquiry. It also enables teachers to remediate more effectively by intervening precisely at the point when an error occurs to gain instant access to the thinking which triggered the error. Prompt intervention helps to avoid further reinforcement of errors. In contrast, assessment which focuses on end results or products of learning – such as a test paper or a piece of homework – provides a delayed indication of a problem without giving clues to the underlying cause of difficulty.

Focused observation is an effective diagnostic tool which is helpful in working with pupils with SEN to investigate the precise nature of their difficulties. Where pupils find working in a written or verbal medium difficult either because of SEN or because English is not their first language, observation allows them to be assessed on practical exercises. Observation is also important in the identification of certain kinds of SEN such as hearing or sight impairment, which may first become apparent because of the way a pupil tilts their head in straining to hear or narrows their eyes in an attempt to see. Teachers need to be alert to such signs that pupils have experienced a sensory loss.

The systematic and sustained scrutiny which focused observation requires make it unlikely to be a routine assessment strategy for many teachers but that does not justify rejecting it out of hand. There are occasions when focused observation is the most appropriate method for diagnosing difficulties, for gathering evidence and for gaining insight into educational processes and the acquisition of skills. Imaginative use of learning support assistants and team teaching could help to offset the logistical difficulties inherent in using focused observation.

3.10 Finally

Above all, it is important to remember that a classroom is a social environment in which personal relationships are formed. Assessment is part of this fabric of relationships. Therefore, it is essential to create time to speak with individuals on a one-to-one basis – an approach which is most sympathetic to the derivation of the word 'assessment' in the Latin *assidere*, to sit beside. However, finding time for individual consultations may not be easy. Many schools freeze their timetables at key assessment points during the year for this to happen. Outside this whole-school/departmental framework, individual consultations are logistically demanding, requiring lessons that enable pupils to work independently so that tutorial-style interactions may take place in a whole class setting. Although typical class sizes may make it impossible to have a worthwhile dialogue with every member of a group in a single lesson or even over the course of a week, over a longer period of time, it should be possible to plan to spend some time with everyone to check progress with personal targets, discuss current work, go over difficulties with recent work and so on. Although this should form an element of the teaching of all classes, systematic progress reviews are particularly important when pupils are working on self-directed projects of the type which form part of GCSE/GNVQ coursework or tasks involving experiential learning.

Personally, I have found assessment conferences with individual pupils a source of many benefits in terms of consolidating relationships, deepening insight into individuals' learning needs and strengthening their commitment to their work. Most pupils respond well to individual attention and even the most disaffected adolescent may display a marked improvement in attitude to schoolwork if teachers show that they care enough to set time aside to discuss personal progress and difficulties.

Ways of responding
to pupils' written and
practical work

4.1 Introduction

This chapter considers ways of providing feedback on pupils' written and practical work.

Objectives

By the end of it, you should have developed your understanding of two key ideas:

- involving pupils in the feedback process increases its efficacy
- conventional marking procedures encourage a preoccupation with the grading function of assessment and a neglect of its learning potential.

Students who opt for a supplementary course on assessment which I offer indicate that their reason for attending is their concern over marking pupils' work. On closer examination, it emerges that their real concern is the ability to grade or assign work to levels accurately. They want to be confident that if they award B+ or 7/10 or level 6, the score is reliable (Section 8.7a). Their concern is understandable; the ability to rate work appropriately and consistently is a necessary professional skill. However, it is only one – and arguably not the most important – skill which new teachers need to acquire if they are to mark competently. In fact, research casts the beginning teacher's preoccupation with the grading function of marking in a disconcerting light. For instance, Black and Wiliam (1998a: 12–13) cite a study which investigated the effects of three different feedback types on pupils' subsequent achievements and motivation. The pupils were given a series of tasks to complete and at the end of each pair of tasks they were given feedback before embarking on the next pair:

- one-third of the group received individually composed comments on the level of match between their work and the assessment criteria which had been described to all beforehand
- another third were given grades only
- the final group received a grade and a comment.

When asked to predict which feedback type produced the best results in terms of improving pupils' subsequent performances and motivation, most people believe that it is the third (grade + comment) which is the most efficacious. In fact, the only group which managed to raise its performance and then to sustain the improvement over the series of tasks was the 'comments only' group. The 'grades + comments' group showed a steady decline in performance across the tasks whereas the 'grades only' group showed an initial improvement in performance which was not sustained. Pupils' interest in the work followed a similar pattern to their attainment with one exception. The pupils who took part in this marking experiment were drawn from various classes in different schools. However, they were selected on the basis of ability, either because they were among the highest achievers in their class or because they were among the lowest attainers. It was found that high achievers maintained a high level of interest in the tasks irrespective of the type of feedback they received. However, both feedback systems which entailed giving grades undermined the original level of interest displayed by low achievers.

Several qualifications need to be borne in mind when considering the implications of these findings. They are derived from a single study based on a marking experiment which was not related to pupils' normal curriculum and was not carried out by their regular teachers. This raises questions about the extent to which the findings can be generalized to ordinary classrooms. However, these reservations have to be set against the equally serious questions about conventional marking practices which this study raises in its findings that:

- different feedback types had a differential impact on subsequent performance (grading was associated with a decline in performance for both groups who were exposed to it)
- different feedback types affected motivation differently for high and low achievers (grading was associated with a loss of interest in work among low attainers)
- the effects of grading were more potent than the effects of constructive written feedback (even when feedback tailored to individuals' needs was provided, its formative potential appeared to be undermined by the presence of grades).

Most people find these results disconcerting because they conflict with established wisdom about good professional practice. This may result in the findings being dismissed out of hand, just as pupils have difficulty in accepting new concepts which clash with existing ideas (for example

John's belief in Chapter 1 that everything that trees are made of comes out of the ground). However, these findings should at least give us pause for thought and cause us to question the prominence attributed to scoring in conventional marking procedures. There is other evidence which points to a similar conclusion: that *conventional marking practices simply don't work!*

> even when teachers provide students with valid and reliable judgments about the quality of their work, improvement does not necessarily follow. Students often show little or no growth or development despite regular, accurate feedback.
>
> (Sadler 1989: 119)

> Even when teachers' comments on work are thorough and point the way to improvement, pupils often do not engage with or respond to them. Corrections are frequently not made. Inadequate work is seldom improved. Even when pupils attempt to respond to comments, teachers do not sufficiently acknowledge this when next marking their books. The full potential of marking to support progress is rarely capitalised upon.
>
> (Ofsted 1998a: 93)

When we add to this the tracts of teachers' time and energy that marking absorbs, the conclusion that it is time for a radical rethink of approaches to marking is further reinforced.

Your ability to think and act radically is, of course, constrained by your status as a trainee. If there is an agreed marking policy operating in your placement department/school, you should normally comply with it. If a laissez-faire approach pertains, allowing you discretion, you should resist the temptation simply to adopt the practices with which you are familiar from your own education without subjecting these practices to careful scrutiny. The challenge is to provide the kind of feedback which persuades pupils to engage thoughtfully with its messages and then to translate that engagement into improved performance.

Perhaps the first thing to challenge, however, is the notion of 'marking'. It is a curiously inexact term which may suggest the making of marks on scripts, annotating them with codes and strokes. It may also suggest the process of arriving at a mark. The conventional mark book, full of tiny squares big enough to accommodate only numbers and symbols, reinforces this impression. In contrast, this chapter examines approaches to feedback in which the provision of a mark may have no part to play. This is why the chapter is entitled 'Ways of responding to pupils' written and practical work' not 'Marking . . . work'. Although the term 'marking' is too deeply embedded in teaching culture to be ousted, it is worth acknowledging that it is an imprecise, catch-all term and potentially misleading. Indeed, one study of how mentors presented assessment to student teachers found that: 'More commonly, the term "assessment" was used to mean marking [with an emphasis on its] summative function . . . Homework was most frequently explained as a necessity which teachers set to meet the expectations of others, with the marking fulfilling a policing function' (Butterfield *et al.* 1999: 238 and 232).

The focus of this chapter is the provision of constructive feedback with or without (preferably without) the addition of scores. However, any attack on this problem must be double-fronted because pupils' attitudes to assessment represent equally important obstacles to progress.

4.2 Pupils' attitudes to assessment

When marked work is returned to pupils, they usually have two overriding concerns. The first is to discover their own mark and the second is to compare it with marks awarded to other members of the group. Once this is ascertained, they often display little interest in any other aspect of the feedback. Research suggests that this is an almost inevitable consequence of feedback systems based on norm-referencing. These systems encourage a preoccupation with competition and with comparing oneself with others. One of the most important confounding variables in any attempt to use feedback formatively, therefore, is attitudes to assessment which pupils have acquired. Most pupils have an unhelpful view of assessment as something that is done to them by and for others: teachers, parents and so on. The idea that it could serve their own interests, helping them to learn more effectively, is alien: 'Most pupils see assessment results as summary indicators of their success; they do not . . . look for feedback about how to improve the way they work' (Black 1998: 135). Clearly, any attempt to increase the efficacy of marking cannot afford to ignore pupils' perceptions because pupils are the ones who must transform feedback into improved performances.

Sadler (1989: 130) argues that pupils' detachment from assessment not only is a matter of unfavourable attitudes but also derives from ignorance. He examines the complex processes involved when teachers make 'multicriterion judgements', pointing out that much of the underlying knowledge about which assessment criteria to apply and when and how to apply them are ' "caught" through experience . . . "the apprentice unconsciously picks up the rules of the art [which are] . . . communicated only by example not by precept" ' (Sadler 1989: 135). Thus, much of a teacher's assessment knowledge is tacit knowledge acquired through experience and by sharing judgements with other assessors during moderation exercises. In this way, teachers are inducted into 'the guild of people who are able to determine quality using multiple criteria' (Sadler 1989: 135). Traditionally this has been teachers' 'prerogative' (1989: 141) and it has set them apart from pupils and the rest of society. Small wonder then that although pupils are the subjects of assessment, they actually see themselves as outsiders looking in on an obscure process which is part of the art and mystery of teaching. Ofsted (1998a: 93) agrees that pupils see marking as 'done ... to them and that they are not greatly aware of, or involved in, that process'. Sadler (1989: 135) argues that pupils must be transformed into 'insiders rather than consumers' of assessment. This suggests that the concept of assessment literacy needs to be expanded to embrace pupils as well as teachers. As well as examining ways of making teachers' feedback constructive, this chapter explores ways of inducting pupils into 'the guild knowledge of teachers' (Sadler 1989: 141) so that assessment ceases to be a 'black box' (Black and Wiliam 1998b). It is direct experience, above all, which converts outsiders into insiders. Therefore, this chapter gives prominence to strategies which employ self- and peer assessment as well as examining ways of improving conventional teacher assessment.

4.3 Self-assessment

Effective self-assessment helps pupils to become better learners, heightening self-awareness and deepening their insight into the assessment process. Pupils cease to be passive recipients of a process which they barely comprehend and develop the ability to monitor and correct their own performance. Self-assessment is any activity which entails the learner, rather than the teacher, taking the lead. For instance, Chapter 3 noted that target-setting can be a teacher-led, pupil-led or negotiated activity. The distinguishing characteristic of self-assessment, therefore, is not the form which it takes but who assumes the lead in its conduct. Sutton (1995: 136) reminds us that in moving towards a greater involvement of pupils in their own assessment we need to be mindful of our 'own starting point as well as theirs and probably take things one step at a time'.

The notion of involving pupils in self-assessment has a mixed reception among student teachers. Occasionally their own schooling has involved negative experiences, making students reluctant to employ an approach which they found personally unhelpful. Others are attracted by an approach which appears to offer a means of lightening heavy marking loads. Others still are appalled by the idea of pupils grading their own work, arguing that it is impossible for adolescents to provide accurate judgements of quality. Each of these reactions is worth examining.

It is unsurprising that some students arrive on training courses with negative views on self-assessment. This innovation is 'still in its early stages' and 'has neither been researched, nor explored and developed in practice to any significant extent' (Black 1998: 133 and 135). Nevertheless, the extant literature suggests that those pupils who have been exposed to self-assessment find it difficult. The idea that assessment is something they could undertake for themselves, to support their own learning, is a radical one which pupils have difficulty grasping. For instance, a study by Broadfoot *et al.* (1988) reported that, because pupils had little or no insight into assessment criteria or how teachers reached assessment judgements, they tried to second guess what would be acceptable to their teachers, thereby defeating the purpose of the exercise. Pupils also down-graded their work and their reasons remind us, once again, that assessment is essentially a social activity. They were anxious not to appear immodest in front of their peers or to lose face if teachers' judgements of their work compared unfavourably with their own. Finally, pupils seemed unable to break free from the normative approach which they had been conditioned to expect by years of schooling. This encouraged them to compare their performances with the range of achievement in the teaching groups with which they were familiar even when they were given criteria against which to rate their own work. All of this undermines the purpose of self-assessment and negates its most important benefit – its learning potential. Black (1998: 128) notes the commitment which a class and its teacher may have to show if they are to get self-assessment to work productively, pointing to a study where it took almost a year for pupils to learn to use it effectively.

Getting self-assessment to work well is a challenge for pupils and teacher alike and students may wonder whether its development is worth the effort. Black and Wiliam (1998b: 19) argue that it is 'essential' rather than 'a luxury'. Black and Wiliam's (1998a) survey identifies studies from around the globe in which self-assessment seems to have been the key to impressive learning gains. For instance, in one study pupils were trained to undertake frequent – usually daily – self-assessment as part of their teachers' participation in an in-service course on assessment in mathematics. Pre- and post-tests of achievement in mathematics were used to establish baselines and measure learning gains (Black and Wiliam's 1998a: 10). At the end of the 20-week course, these pupils showed a mean learning gain which was about *double* that of a control group of pupils whose teachers were following another in-service course on a different topic in mathematics and who consequently received no training in self-assessment. This result is an impressive testimony to the learning potential of self-assessment.

The views of students who regard self-assessment as a way of reducing their marking burden and those who see it as an attack on standards are also worth examining because they illustrate common misconceptions about self-assessment. Authentic self-assessment is possible only if pupils are given access to the assessment criteria associated with the task in hand and then encouraged to become actively self-monitoring. However, students who see self-assessment as a means of increasing their own efficiency usually have something different in mind – the kind of in-class marking exercise which simply requires pupils to apply the teacher's or a textbook mark scheme and then calculate a final score. This practice is more accurately described as 'self-marking' (Freeman and

Lewis 1998: 120), especially when the exercise is undertaken mechanically, with answers ticked or crossed unthinkingly. Ofsted (1998a: 93) found that even practising teachers commonly confuse self-marking with self-assessment. Self-marking is an established technique for speeding up assessment of items which have a single correct answer or where answers can be drawn from a limited range of alternatives but it should not be confused with self-assessment. Therefore, although there is evidence that *genuine* self-assessment can reduce the time which teachers spend on measurement (Black and Wiliam 1998a: 27), that is neither its main purpose nor its main benefit.

Students whose principal concern is the reliability of results are similarly missing the point about self-assessment. Although reliability is a major concern for external assessments, this need not be the case in formative classroom assessment which is primarily concerned with validity (Chapter 8). Even so, it is worth noting that when pupils are trained, they have generally been found to be honest and capable of assessing their own work and that of others with a reasonable level of accuracy (for example Clough *et al.* 1984; Freeman and Lewis 1998). However, the real purpose of self-assessment is not to equip pupils to carry out the grading function which teachers and other assessors normally perform – rather it should enhance the formative potential of assessment.

As has been noted, the distinguishing feature of self-assessment is not what is done but how it is accomplished. Consequently, there are various ways in which conventional TA may be transmuted into self-assessment. They all depend on ensuring that certain prerequisites are in place.

- The rationale of self-assessment should be explained to pupils so that they understand how it is intended to work and how it is capable of helping them.
- Pupils must be trained in the required metacognitive skills by teachers modelling the processes for them. Teachers can do this by sharing marking exercises with classes, using exemplification material to show how criteria are applied and how judgements are reached. Negotiated assessments, involving collaboration with a teacher and the peer group, provide useful staging posts in the journey to independent self-assessment.
- Pupils need practice to hone their assessment skills.
- Pupils must be introduced to relevant assessment criteria (Section 2.5c) such as the relevant awarding body's grading criteria, NC level descriptions or departmental assessment criteria.
- Abstract criteria must be made accessible. Some teachers translate NC criteria into pupil-friendly language. Pupils also find it helpful when teachers itemize criteria, breaking them down into detailed, task-specific checklists against which they can judge their own work (see Figures 4.1 and 4.3 on pp. 71 and 83). Indeed, pupils are generally better able to engage with self-assessment if their responses are guided by the use

---

Roundhill Community College

Assessed Work on USA Leisure Industry

Location

Mark on an outline map the areas important for Tourism. Name the areas. Write a description of the activities and describe where they are.

Climate

Write a general statement for the overall temperature and rainfall for the year for the area you have chosen.
Draw a graph, and use it to describe the climate in more detail.
Write an explanation for the overall temperatures and rainfall pattern.
Write an explanation for seasonal differences/no seasonal differences, and say why these differences occur.

Economic Activities

Show the ways in which people of the region/area make or earn a living. Give a description of these, and identify if they are primary, secondary or tertiary activities.

Explain why the activities take place in this region, mentioning climate, physical features and how important they are to the USA economy.

Describe the facilities that are provided for the visitor and explain how the facilities and activities are linked to the demands of the visitor, and how they reflect the area in which they are found.

Predict how changes in the number of visitors and in the type of facilities might affect the area in the future.

Level 3 – General descriptions for each heading.

Level 4 – Accurate, detailed descriptions for each heading.

Level 5 – Accurate, detailed description with some attempt to give explanation about why it is like it is.

Level 6 – Accurate, detailed description with good explanation.

Level 7 – As for level 6 with information showing how all the information under each heading is inter-related.

Figure 4.1   Task with NC level-related criteria to support pupils' self-assessment

of prompts and questions. Showing pupils' exemplification material is a means of demystifying criteria. When this is carefully chosen, it can model the standards to which pupils should aspire, providing concrete examples of what success might look like. It can also illustrate common failings, providing a more powerful learning experience than simply being exhorted to avoid something by a teacher! Therefore, it is helpful to show pupils work across a range of levels exhibiting strengths and weaknesses. Schools compile portfolios of work which can be used in this way. Alternatively, awarding bodies provide marked scripts at different grade levels with commentaries explaining why grades have been awarded. The School Curriculum and Assessment Authority (SCAA) and later the Qualifications and Curriculum Authority (QCA) have produced 'exemplification of standards' materials.

- Pupils' metacognitive abilities can be sharpened by having to devise their own assessment criteria or to produce tasks or questions suitable for assessing current learning objectives. They are, after all, uniquely placed to judge which questions and tasks they would find most testing! Studies in which learners have been trained to produce their own thought-provoking questions and then attempt to answer them – or use them on their peers – have yielded impressive learning gains when set against the attainment of control groups who have used questions set conventionally by teachers (Black and Wiliam 1998a: 33–4).
- The convention of teacher-initiated, teacher-dominated communication can be countered by initiating an assessment dialogue to which both sides contribute on a more equal footing. For instance, pupils may be invited to request feedback on particular aspects of their work or to record responses to teachers' feedback. Initially, this may serve simply to encourage pupils to engage thoughtfully with feedback but, if a dialogue is sustained, it may provide insights into pupils' learning which can be mutually beneficial. 'The overriding advantage of involving pupils in an assessment dialogue would seem to be that it provides insights into the effects of teaching – insights drawn from a thoroughly obvious and yet largely untapped source' (Clough *et al.* 1984: 64).
- Similar initiatives involve pupils maintaining learning journals or diaries where they keep an open record of their responses to teaching and learning. Self-assessment occurs naturally in such a context. Teachers have access to the material and can add comments. This approach has similar benefits to the assessment dialogue, deepening teachers' insights into what and how pupils are learning.
- Pupils can be encouraged to take some responsibility for determining their own learning targets. Assuming responsibility for deciding when targets have been met, and identifying supporting evidence, encourages pupils to develop critical self-awareness.
- Pupil-maintained assessment records (Section 6.5) help to focus attention on personal progress and can offset the negative effects of norm-referencing.
- When pupils are involved in recording their own progress, it also makes sense to involve them in reporting. Most schools' reporting procedures provide opportunities for pupils to comment and they may also be invited to contribute to meetings where their progress is discussed with parents (Sections 6.10e and 6.11a).
- Self-assessment should be used *during*, rather than at the end of, a unit of work so that pupils have an opportunity to reflect on work while it is in progress and put what they learn into practice while it is still relevant.

4.4 Peer assessment

Peer assessment is a variant of self-assessment. It entails pupils assessing the work of contemporaries rather than their own and is often conducted as a pair or group activity so that pupils can benefit from sharing ideas and insights. Although common sense suggests that peer assessment will promote learning in the same way that self-assessment has been shown to, Black and Wiliam (1998a: 29) point out that research evidence is not clear cut. Peer assessment is mostly used in combination with self-assessment and other innovations, making it difficult to disentangle those effects associated with its use. Nevertheless, benefits do seem to accrue when peer assessment forms one element of a formative assessment regime. For instance, all of the pupils involved in one study 'said that the self- and peer-assessment work made them think more, and 85 per cent said that it made them learn more' (Black and Wiliam 1998a: 29).

In theory, then, peer assessment offers an attractive alternative to self-assessment. It involves working collaboratively and, by adopting the role of critical friend, pupils can support, challenge and extend each other's learning. Examining other people's work can act as a stimulus to developing one's own, providing a source of new ideas. However, this book has emphasized the importance of the social and emotional dimensions to learning and nowhere is the potential for these factors to enhance or inhibit learning more apparent than in the context of peer assessment. This is because peer assessment tends to be carried out in social settings – pairs, small groups or the whole class – and often entails evaluating one's classmates. Hence, the social and personal delicacy of peer assessment is considerable and may be critical to its success. Most pupils are unskilled in the arts of constructive assessment and the potential for insensitive remarks to damage individuals' fragile self-esteem is a constant feature of peer assessment. Students sometimes report that they have been victims of such exercises when jealousy and rivalry have flared and peers have been cruel or unjust in their treatment of individuals. This outcome is particularly likely when pupils have only ever encountered competitive, norm-referenced assessment regimes. Other work (for example Munby *et al.* 1989: 108) has emphasized the importance of group dynamics in peer assessment, suggesting that group members may be intimidated by more dominant individuals. Attitudes are also critical. Unless pupils understand the rationale of peer assessment, they can feel let down by teachers' seeming abdication of their responsibility to mark pupils' work for them. This may lead pupils to question the purpose of completing work if it is not going to be 'properly' marked (Smith 1998: 47). Under such circumstances, peer assessment is undertaken grudgingly and learning gains are unlikely to ensue.

For all these reasons, the ground needs to be prepared with considerable care when embarking on this type of assessment.

- Pupils need to have the rationale of peer assessment explained so that they understand how it is intended to work and how it is capable of helping them.
- Pupils require training in the necessary interpersonal skills such as the ability to listen respectfully, to question sensitively, to suggest tactfully, to negotiate and to criticize constructively.
- Ground-rules need to be established to pre-empt inappropriate behaviour (for example no put-downs).
- The composition of groups needs careful forethought when pupils are assessing each other's work.
- Teachers need to monitor pupil interactions closely, especially in the early stages of working in this way, and intervene to challenge inappropriate behaviour.
- At the outset, it helps if the activity can be depersonalized. Anonymizing work does not always help as pupils recognize each other's handwriting but anonymized work from previous year groups (with authors' permission) or from external sources are useful alternatives. Even after pupils have acquired the necessary skills, this remains a useful way of working. Pupils can enjoy the benefits of peer assessment without it becoming entangled with relationships and feelings within a group.
- Above all, pupils need to be taught to make criterion-referenced judgements. It is unreasonable to expect them to avoid personal comparisons if their own experiences of being assessed have been norm-referenced.

Clearly, firsthand experience is essential if pupils are to become 'assessment insiders'. However, the quality of teachers' written feedback is no less important for the development of pupils' assessment literacy.

4.5 Written feedback by teachers

I often ask students to estimate the amount of individual attention pupils receive on average during a typical lesson. Most students believe that it is less than a minute and this is consistent with research findings on this topic. Of course, averages are misleading and while some pupils demand an inordinate amount of teachers' time, others receive none at all. Sutton (1995: 79) has coined the phrase 'the good, the bad and the missing' to describe this phenomenon. When it is viewed in this light, the written feedback a teacher provides for pupils takes on added significance. For some individuals, written feedback could be the single most important point of contact between the teacher and that child. Its potential for giving guidance tailored to individual needs and for building positive feelings towards the subject is, therefore, of paramount importance.

The feedback mechanism has been anatomized (for example Sadler 1989: 121; Black and Wiliam 1998a: 48) to identify the following components:

- a clear specification of the required standard of performance
- information about a pupil's actual level of performance
- a comparison aimed at generating information about the gap between the two
- use of this information to alter the gap.

The final stage is crucial to formative assessment:

> If the information is simply recorded, passed to a third party who lacks either the knowledge or the power to change the outcome, or is too deeply encoded (for example, as a summary grade given by the teacher) to lead to appropriate action, the control loop cannot be closed and 'dangling data' substitute for effective feedback.
>
> (Sadler 1989: 121)

In essence, then, the feedback mechanism focuses on identifying the gap between actual and desired levels of performance, providing teachers and learners with the information needed to close the gap.

High quality feedback is set against relevant assessment criteria. It is detailed and constructive, providing pupils with information about what they are doing well, suggestions for how they might improve their work and specific guidance on where corrections are needed and how to make them. However, a study where pupils were given a complete solution as soon as they encountered difficulties produced disappointing results. Denied opportunities to work things out for themselves, pupils learnt less effectively and were less able to apply their learning in novel situations. Feedback should provide scaffolding, offering pupils as much help as they need to move forward but no more. The best kind of feedback stimulates the correction of errors through a thoughtful approach to them. One study described this as a state of 'mindfulness' (Black and Wiliam 1998a: 51) with regard to the feedback.

Constructive feedback focuses firmly on the knowledge, skills or concepts which are relevant to the task in hand. This is sometimes described as task-involving feedback and it is contrasted with ego-involving feedback which has been shown to impair subsequent performance in a number of studies. It seems that feedback which draws attention away from the demands of the task and onto self-esteem is liable to have an adverse effect on performance, especially for low achievers. Pupils need to be directed to think about the task – not themselves. Somewhat surprisingly, this finding applies even to feedback involving praise. Here, again, we encounter a research finding which is counterintuitive. It may seem natural to praise as a means of encouraging pupils. This finding may also be at variance with advice received on other parts of a training course (for example positive approaches to behaviour management often recommend the use of praise to reinforce wanted behaviour). In the context of assessment, however, it seems that while praise may increase pupils' interest in a task, it is likely to have little if any positive effect on performance and is particularly likely to be deleterious in the case of low attainers. Black and Wiliam (1998a: 49) suggest that this 'goes some way to explaining why several studies . . . found that the most effective teachers actually praise *less* than the average'.

It is important to provide feedback as promptly as possible. This highlights an important difference between formal learning and natural learning. Natural learning often involves trial and error, providing instant feedback on effort. Studies of accelerated learning have also stressed the import-ance of rapid feedback (for example Smith 1998). Indeed, it is unusual to have to wait a week or longer for feedback on informal learning and yet this is quite common with schoolwork (Sadler 1989). The ideal of rapid feedback is hard to achieve with large secondary classes and in subjects which entail a lot of written work. Nevertheless, when feed-back is delayed until pupils have moved on to new work, they usually ignore what no longer seems relevant. Some teachers address this prob-lem by doing an initial skim marking of pupils' work before assessing it fully so that pupils receive prompt feedback. Marking policies often specify time limits for returning marked work to pupils. Nevertheless, the need to minimize the gap between completing work and receiving feedback provides a further reason for a radical rethink of approaches to marking.

The challenge of improving marking is twofold: first, to make it more effective in terms of triggering the desired response from pupils; second, to make it more efficient so that teachers' throughput is improved. These are not separate aims. In fact, achieving the second is an important step towards attaining the first. Therefore, the following sections consider practical marking strategies, placing a dual emphasis on efficacy and efficiency. The strategies which are examined have the advantage of combining good professional practice with increased efficiency. There-fore, it is not a matter of cutting educational corners in order to improve marking turnover. A strength of these strategies is that sound educa-tional practice coincidentally results in a streamlined workload.

4.6 Focused marking

One of the first dilemmas facing a student teacher is what to mark. Should you attempt to mark everything that draws your attention? Should you confine your marking to the correction of errors and the identification of gaps and weaknesses or should you acknowledge strengths and achieve-ments too? To what extent is the technical accuracy of work (grammar, spelling and punctuation) your responsibility or should you focus exclus-ively on subject-specific matters? Implicit in all of these questions is the issue of a marking focus. In order to address these questions, it can be instructive to imagine yourself on the receiving end of various types of feedback. Imagine being in receipt of 'scattergun' marking which entails the teacher marking anything and everything that attracts attention. Returned work is likely to be covered in marking, drawing attention to positive features as well as a broad range of errors. The sheer range and quantity of the marking may distract, demoralize or overwhelm. Either way, you are unlikely to use it as a guide to future performance. A less extreme form of unfocused marking occurs 'when pupils attempt to respond to comments [but] teachers do not sufficiently acknowledge this when next marking their books' (Ofsted 1998a: 93). How helpful would you find it if a teacher had urged you to concentrate on particular aspects of your work but then provided feedback which was unrelated? Pupils will maximize their effort and concentration if they are able to focus on a limited number of aspects of their work and receive feedback directly related to these. Focused marking, therefore, helps to maintain a clear sense of purpose. It also requires teachers to resist the temptation to mark broader aspects of the work. There is, thus, sound justification for marking in a sharply focused way and markers who need not concern themselves with features of work beyond the foci make gains in speed and efficiency.

Ofsted (1998a: 92) has criticized teachers for a lack of clarity in the assessment criteria which are applied when marking pupils' work, arguing that the confusion is compounded when separate criteria are poorly differentiated. Therefore, the next question to address is how to choose a marking focus. The answer is, in fact, implicit in what has been said thus far about formative assessment. All pupils should be striving to achieve personal learning targets and all assessed tasks should have assessment criteria. The focus is thus determined by task-related assessment criteria, which should have been shared with pupils beforehand, and individual learning goals. This suggests that marking should have a dual focus: not only the assessment criteria for the task in hand (which may be common to all pupils), but also individuals' learning targets (which may be unique to them). A written record of these (for example on task instructions, on a feedback sheet, at the top of the piece of work or on a board) serves to reinforce their importance and provides a continuous reminder to pupils. If you have invited pupils to request feedback on an aspect of their work which concerns them, this provides a third focus.

The importance of complying with any marking policy which is in force has already been stressed. For instance, it is important to check your placement school's requirements with regard to feedback on ongoing features of work such as literacy. If you are free to develop a personal approach, it is important to explain the rationale of focused marking not only to pupils but also to other potential consumers, especially parents, some of whom check the marking of their children's work. They are likely to be familiar with traditional approaches to marking and a failure to mark what they regard as glaringly obvious errors may be misinterpreted as a sign of incompetence or laziness.

Task 4.1

Examine several sets of books/folders which have been marked by different teachers to compare their marking approaches.

Which assessment criteria seem to have been uppermost in each teacher's mind when the marking was completed?

Is there evidence that assessment criteria have been shared with pupils?

If there is a school/departmental marking policy, to what extent are different teachers' practices consistent with the policy and with each other?

4.7 Using referencing systems

Feedback typically takes the form of annotations made directly onto work and a grade and comment appended to it. Because pupils are usually being assessed against the same criteria (for example NC or GCSE criteria) and many display the same strengths and weaknesses, this approach entails a lot of repetition. Teachers find themselves making the same remark time and time again. Alternatively, the same point may apply at several points during a single piece (for example not explaining points) and if the teacher wishes to draw the author's attention to more than one example, the teacher is obliged to make the same remark repeatedly. So the next question to consider is whether there are ways of reducing the repetitive element of feedback while still providing pupils with the detailed guidance they have a right to expect.

If end comments are referenced (for example by using numbers), the teacher need make the comment once only while the reference number can be inserted onto the text or into the margin of the work any number of times to illustrate and clarify the point. For instance, a teacher may have inserted a 1 onto a script on three occasions. The end comment reads '1. You need to <u>explain</u> your point as well as describing'. A 2 has been added twice and the end comment reads: '2. Good attention to detail'. This tactic has a number of advantages beyond the obvious time saving. Pupils do need to have their attention drawn to specific examples of success and failure in their work to help them to emulate strengths and eliminate weaknesses. A referencing system allows a teacher to insert the relevant code repeatedly. In this way, pupils are likely to receive more detailed and better illustrated feedback than they would if a teacher had to annotate the text separately on each occasion. Another advantage of this approach is its lightness of touch. Although the marker makes very few marks on the work, its strengths and weaknesses are nevertheless clearly identified. The irony of teachers urging pupils to take pride in the appearance of their work only to deface it by writing all over it should not escape our notice! Marking systems which manage to leave the original piece virtually intact but nevertheless provide constructive feedback exemplify good practice.

This referencing strategy can be taken one stage further if the teacher prepares a class feedback sheet which is issued to each member of a group. Since the teacher makes each comment once only, they can afford to explain and illustrate it fully. Pupils must be given class time to read and reflect on the feedback sheet focusing on comments which apply to their own work. They should also be encouraged to respond – to complete corrections, to question comments which they don't understand or to justify their approach if the criticism seems unfair. Space could be provided on the sheet for identifying a personal target arising from the feedback for pupils' next piece of work.

It is also helpful to use a standard code for routine features of marking. For instance, most of us would know what was meant if we saw sp, // or ∧ on our work because the meaning of these symbols is well established. The rarely achieved ideal is when a whole school works to an agreed marking system (see Figure 5.1 on p. 99). Are there any regularly used criteria in your subject for which it would be useful to develop shorthand references? A code which is carefully defined, consistently used and understood by all also helps pupils who sometimes complain that they find it difficult to read their teacher's handwriting or to interpret their remarks. It alleviates this problem by cutting down on the amount of writing, reading and interpretation required. However, the whole point of developing a marking system can be defeated if it becomes overly complex so that using it is tantamount to learning a new language. Nevertheless, a few well-chosen symbols can replace frequently used narrative comments, enhancing communication and speeding up the feedback process. For instance, ✓ T could be used to signify points where a personal learning target has been achieved. In fact, the use of light ticks wherever criteria have been met represents a positive approach to marking which helps pupils to identify successful aspects of their work. It is even better if the tick can be qualified (as in ✓ T) to signify the nature of the success.

4.8 Using prepared feedback sheets

An alternative to individual comments written in longhand at the end of work is the use of feedback sheets. In some subjects, this is a necessity if a teacher wishes to provide written feedback in practical subjects such as drama and PE where work is ephemeral and provides no lasting record of performance for teachers to mark. Teachers of other subjects also require feedback sheets occasionally for oral activities such as role plays and presentations.

Even where feedback sheets are not a necessity, pupils and teachers can benefit from this approach. The initial investment of time in getting the format and contents right is repaid when it comes to marking individual pieces of work. For instance, standard items can be incorporated into the sheet avoiding the need for teachers to write them out repeatedly. Therefore, although initial effort is expended on the design and preparation of feedback sheets, the overall efficiency of the feedback process is increased. Pupils also benefit because they automatically receive the full complement of feedback in a standard form making it more intelligible.

4.9 Examples

This section provides examples of both approaches for your consideration. The first is an example of feedback written in longhand and appended to a piece of work by a Year 9 pupil (Figure 4.2). The second entails the use of a prepared feedback sheet (Figure 4.3).

Task 4.2

Consider the advantages and disadvantages of the approaches to marking, illustrated in Figures 4.2 and 4.3.

4.9a Points of interest in Figure 4.2

- The feedback is personalized; the teacher addresses the author by name and poses questions which invite a response. These features give the feedback a conversational feel. The comments represent the opening gambit in a dialogue, encouraging the pupil to engage with the feedback and respond to it.
- Although we do not know the purpose of the task or the associated assessment criteria, the feedback appears to be task focused. Positive comments focus on the piece's literary merits (the way in which drama and tension have been injected into the writing) not on Robert himself and corrective feedback centres on its linguistic defects.
- By acknowledging strengths of the work first, a positive tone is established at the outset and reinforced by emphatic diction (The story would 'sound tremendous' and it would make a '<u>very</u> good tape'). It is further reinforced at the end when the teacher expresses an interest in how the story ends rather than criticizing Robert for failing to finish it.
- Although the feedback is clear and constructive, no grade is provided and no marks have been made on the original text.
- The teacher does not shirk from stressing that the writing is error prone ('<u>lots</u> of mistakes') but places an emphasis on showing Robert

The Interrogation

"Come, come, Now Jackson Shorly you now
were frinton street is", 'No! I Dont', it's
the Road Next to the River oh' that
frinton Street NO I Was Not in frinton
I was at the Disco, Oh' No you
was not, you were in a house in frinton
Steet, Robbing Number 46, we have
Proth your frend John saw you
so, what have you got to say about
that. No I Was at the Disco,
who whit then I carnt Rememder.
Now. then were is the stuff were
DID you put it, "what stuff!"
Jackson shouted, the 10 grand stall
from the suth and you most have
had help from some one else,
then the sargent come in constable
the Results of the finger print's
Jackson's Dont mach. look. good
Lord, thay Dont

If you read this aloud, Robert, it would sound tremendous.
(It would make a <u>very</u> good tape.) You have made <u>lots</u> of
mistakes though, haven't you?
Try writing it again, looking for these three points:-

A new line for each new speaker →
"No, I don't."
"It's the road next to the river."
"Oh, <u>that</u> Frinton Street. No I was not in Frinton Street."

"Where did you put it?"
"What stuff?"

A question mark at the end of a question.

A full stop at the end of each sentence.

How does the story end?

Figure 4.2 An example of constructive written feedback
Source: Sutton 1981: 10–11

how to improve the technical accuracy of his work. The guidance is clearly illustrated and 'signposted' by the use of arrows.

- The feedback engenders a sense of 'mindfulness' by correcting each error once only and asking Robert to do the rest himself.
- The teacher has provided a model to scaffold Robert's redraft. It is unlikely that corrections made onto the original could have offered such clear guidance on how to correct faults.
- Although the work displays many grammatical imperfections, the teacher avoids overloading Robert with corrections by selecting three priorities for immediate attention.
- Overall, the appraisal is well balanced, setting weaknesses against strengths and giving due attention to each. The fact that the writing is error prone is reflected in the considerable attention devoted to this weakness in corrective feedback. However, this is offset by an enthusiastic opening response to the atmosphere the author has managed to create and by an expression of interest in the development of the story which revives the positive tone at the end.
- By opting to rewrite an extract for Robert to use as a model in correcting the piece, the teacher has invested considerable time in copying from the original. On the other hand, the teacher has saved time by making each corrective comment once only and by making no marks on the text. The identification of a marking focus (three features of the writing's technical accuracy) has allowed for many other imperfections to be ignored.

A recurring theme of this book is teachers' concern to provide positive, encouraging feedback. Sometimes this emphasis on the positive is enshrined in school policy which advises against references to weaknesses and difficulties. Truth is a frequent casualty of this approach, which results in an over-generous and misleading appraisal of the quality of work. It fails to provide clear guidance for pupils on what they need to do to improve and does not support their self-assessment. Ofsted (1998a: 92) reports that it is a common weakness of marking. Nevertheless, Ofsted acknowledges that a minority of teachers at all KSs manage to combine candour with constructive guidance (Ofsted 1995: 6). Figure 4.2 demonstrates such an approach, showing that an honest appraisal of a pupil's strengths and weaknesses need not undermine the positive and encouraging tone with which a teacher would wish to inject feedback.

The assessment record shown in Figure 4.3 was developed by Rosalind Hamson, Head of Humanities and Coordinator of ITT at Garendon High School, an 11–14 high school in Leicestershire. Originally it was a self-assessment checklist for pupils to complete and attach to their work before submission (that is, the top section only). Over time, it evolved to include other sections: a peer assessment section (optional); a teacher assessment record; and target-setting. The TA levels (Satisfactory to Very Good) link directly to NC levels for geography and pupils are aware of this. Pupils are given the relevant assessment sheet before they start a

RIVER OUSE FLOODING CHECKLIST

Self Assessment			Group Assessment
I			**You**
❏	1.	have described what flooding is	❏
❏	2.	have explained why rivers flood	❏
❏	3.	have described what effects flooding has	❏
❏	4.	have explained how flooding can change a place	❏
❏	5.	have described the effects of flooding on people	❏
❏	6.	have described and explained how flooding can be prevented	❏
❏	7.	have described and explained the effects of flood prevention	❏
❏	8.	have shown that flood prevention may have unintended effects	❏
❏	9.	have reached a conclusion	❏
❏	10.	have taken on the role	❏

ASSESSMENT CRITERIA	
S	You have described what happens when a river floods
S+	You have described flooding and flood prevention and how they can change the features of the place and affect the lives and activities of people in an area
G	You can describe and give reasons for river flooding and flood prevention. You give reasons for the ways that flooding and flood prevention change the environment. You explain your own views.
G+	You describe and explain flooding and flood prevention and the ways they change the environment of a place. You recognise that there are different ways to prevent flooding and that these may have different consequences. You reach a conclusion about the canal which fits the evidence.
VG	You describe and explain that many factors cause flooding and that flood prevention has many consequences including unintended ones. You explain that many factors will lead to the decision about whether to prevent flooding. You reach substantiated conclusions.

GRADES AWARDED BY THE GROUP

	Presentation Grade
	Effort Grade
	Content Grade

TARGETS

- To present the work more neatly
- To choose a more appropriate way to present the work
- To describe flooding or flood prevention
- To explain flooding, flood prevention or the consequences of flooding
- To explain the work in more detail
- To include more facts
- To reach a conclusion

Figure 4.3   An example of a prepared feedback sheet

new assessment task. They are also encouraged to look back at their most recent assessment record to remind themselves of previous results and their targets for the present task so that they approach it with a clear sense of what they need to do to progress. All tasks are self-assessed before submission. Most are then assessed by the teacher but about a quarter are peer assessed.

4.9b Points of interest in Figure 4.3

- By combining a number of functions on a single A4 sheet, Rosalind Hamson has created an economical, multipurpose assessment record. Assessment criteria are specified, a self-assessment checklist is provided (and optional peer assessment), teacher feedback is given and targets are set.
- The self-assessment checklist (top section) provides guidance on NC requirements, specifying an ideal towards which all pupils should aim, but without providing a model for pupils to copy. Pupils are thereby encouraged to think carefully about the level of match between their work and requirements.
- The criteria for TA (middle section) are based on NC level descriptions for geography but they have been translated into 'pupil-friendly' language to make them accessible.
- Feedback and target-setting processes have been made manageable because the need to write comments repeatedly has been eliminated.
- There is sufficient space in the TA section to individualize the assessment by modifying or adding to the specification. Teachers annotate the descriptors, crossing out bits which do not apply or adding comments to personalize the feedback, signalling to pupils that their work has been read carefully.
- Targets (final section) are related directly to assessment criteria (middle section). Therefore, the top section specifies an ideal towards which everyone should aim and the final section identifies targets tailored to individual needs. Because geography aims to develop generic skills and concepts which pertain regardless of the topic being covered (for example the ability to reach/substantiate a conclusion), it is possible for assessment tasks associated with one topic to suggest targets for the next.
- The target-setting section encompasses geography-specific and general targets. Therefore, assessment extends beyond academic requirements to encompass other aspects of performance such as effort and ability to work to deadlines.
- Marking is easier and more rewarding because faults which would otherwise have to be teacher-marked have already been eliminated through self-assessment.

Rosalind Hamson has found that when pupils are equipped to regulate their own performance, there is a measurable improvement in the quality of their work (Hamson and Sutton 2000).

Task 4.3

Consider your own marking practices.

● What kind of marks, if any, do you make on work? Where do you make them?
● Do you respond to errors in technique, factual mistakes or faulty understanding? If so, how?
● Do you respond to errors in grammar, spelling and punctuation?
● What form does feedback take, for example ticks and crosses, a written comment, a mark for quality, a grade for effort or a combination of approaches?
● How, if at all, do you expect pupils to follow up marking?

Task 4.4

(This task was suggested by Rosalind Hamson.)
Choose a NC topic which you expect to teach during placement. Use the relevant PoS and the NC level descriptions to devise a self-assessment checklist for pupils to monitor the quality of their work. Produce a set of TA criteria. Both the checklist and the assessment criteria should be couched in language which is accessible to the relevant age group.

Task 4.5

Devise a feedback sheet. It could be for general use or task specific. Make sure that you consider the following issues:

● What standard information should be included (for example space for pupil's name, date when work completed)?
● Will task requirements be specified? Itemized?
● In what detail will assessment criteria be specified (for example global criteria such as 'structure' and 'content' or elaborated criteria which provide more detailed guidance)?
● What methods will be used to indicate pupils' success in achieving criteria (for example written comments, ticklists, rating scales such as 'Excellent', 'Good', 'Satisfactory' or 'Unsatisfactory')?
● How will the feedback be used for feedforward purposes?
● How, if at all, will pupils be involved?

4.10 Further issues for assessment design

Traditional assessment is reliant on written tasks, generating a hefty workload for pupils and a corresponding mark load for teachers. It is, therefore, worth considering whether assessment objectives could sometimes be achieved just as effectively using tasks which reduce written requirements. Is the balance between written assignments and alternative approaches to assessment sensible? With a little imagination, it is possible to devise creative ways of achieving the same end, for instance oral presentations, role play exercises, class debates, creative or construction tasks, posters and displays as well as conventional end-of-unit tests and written assignments. A welcome bonus of diversification is that pupils actually enjoy assessed assignments!

Different types of tasks lend themselves to different marking approaches, thus role play and presentations lend themselves to peer assessment whereas self- or peer marking can be used with objective tests. A carefully thought out assessment programme which utilizes different approaches allows you to develop a marking regime in which self-assessment, peer assessment and self-marking can be used alongside TA in a balanced and judicious manner. It is also sensible to consider whether it is necessary always to mark at an even level. There may be occasions when light marking will suffice, for example, if your main purpose is to check that work has been completed, a tick may suffice. Even within a single piece, the approach may be varied with some sections earmarked for close marking while others are lightly marked.

Create and use opportunities for marking pupils' work alongside them in the classroom. A spoken commentary helps to elucidate the marking process and encourages pupils to ask assessment question. It is important to do this systematically so that not only the more visible children receive written plus oral feedback. Pupils are more likely to act upon immediate feedback and teachers benefit from the reduction in their 'cold marking' load.

Whatever strategies you employ, it is important to remember that the ultimate goal is high quality feedback provided as promptly as possible. It is, therefore, important to explain your objective to pupils and to ensure that the pupils appreciate the range of feedback strategies that will be used to achieve this end.

4.11 Marking reliably

This chapter has striven to achieve a better balance between the emphasis usually attributed to the grading function of marking and the provision of task-involving feedback, which is why grading has been consigned to this final section. However, it would be irresponsible to ignore the importance of assigning grades reliably in a system dominated by high stakes tests and examinations. You need to familiarize yourself with the standards of the NC, GCSE, Advanced Subsidiary (AS) levels, A levels and GNVQ. If Sadler (1989: 135) is right, and the ability to make complex, multicriterion judgements is '"caught" through experience', there are various strategies which will provide access to this 'guild knowledge of teachers'.

Task 4.6

- Study relevant grading criteria.
- Consult departmental portfolios containing samples of marked work where these are available. Ofsted (1998a) found that only a minority of schools had compiled exemplification material of this type. Alternatively, examine the marking of an experienced teacher such as your mentor. Once you feel that you are gaining a sense of relevant standards, conduct the exercise 'blind', that is decide the grade/level you would award *before* checking the teacher's mark.
- Examine exemplification material from awarding bodies and QCA.
- Arrange to do a paired marking exercise with your mentor using work you have set.
- Take part in departmental standardization/moderation exercises.

Part 2 | Managing assessment: the school context

School policies and procedures

5.1 Introduction

This chapter deals with assessment as a 'whole-school' concern for which there are cross-curricular and departmental requirements.

Objectives

By the end of it, you should have developed your understanding of two key ideas:

- the importance of familiarizing yourself with staff who have a coordinating role (for example the assessment coordinator and special educational needs coordinator (SENCO)) and with relevant policy statements (for example for MARRA, SEN and equal opportunities)
- an agreed policy and practices are prerequisites for good communication which is the bedrock of effective assessment.

At the start of a placement, students receive relevant documentation: staff/student handbook, school prospectus, lists of departmental resources and procedures, guidelines and policies for various aspects of the school's work. MARRA is among the topics on which there should be a whole-school written policy. In some schools, departments customize this to produce subject-specific guidelines. These documents may be your first indication that assessment is a corporate as well as an individual concern of teachers. Schools also appoint coordinators to manage cross-curricular aspects of their work. For instance, all maintained schools are required to have a SENCO (DfE 1994). The majority also have a designated assessment coordinator although this is not a requirement. Whereas schools usually introduce students to the SENCO, who may make an input to their training, a placement may pass without students ever knowing who the assessment coordinator is. This oversight is perhaps best explained by attitudes to assessment outlined in the Introduction to this book. This chapter identifies elements of MARRA in which the whole school has a stake and outlines how policies and designated personnel are deployed to meet requirements.

5.2 The assessment coordinator

Nowadays, the majority of schools appoint an assessment coordinator (Ofsted 1998a: 89) although the coordinator's remit varies from school to school. In some, it is combined with the role of examinations officer so that examination administration and assessment coordination are the responsibilities of one person. In others, a network of people assumes responsibility for different aspects of the coordinator's role such as records of achievement, data analysis and so on. Because of this variability in practice, this section cannot claim to typify the role. Instead, it is described in general terms and then a case study is provided to show how the role was developed in one school in response to circumstances.

The assessment coordinator maintains an overview of policy and practice within a school and of developments nationally and locally. Schools receive copious amounts of information associated with MARRA. Statutory requirements are issued by the DfEE in the form of education orders and circulars. Although non-statutory guidance does not have the force of law, it is designed to offer assistance to schools and, therefore, assessment coordinators also need to keep abreast of this and other information issuing from organizations such as QCA, their LEA and various awarding bodies. The assessment coordinator needs to be well informed, keeping up-to-date with new initiatives and disseminating information as appropriate. As well as ensuring that the school meets minimum obligations, a coordinator is also keen to promote good practice. Coordinators may offer CPD for colleagues, provide inductions for new staff and student teachers and ensure that when new staff bring expertise or innovative ideas to the school, these are effectively utilized. They may, therefore, take a lead in stimulating change, formulating action plans and overseeing their implementation.

The MARRA policy is a key tool for the assessment coordinator. When it is first formulated, the policy acts as a vehicle for drawing together the different strands of MARRA within a school. There may be a wide diversity of practices based on entrenched departmental positions and so the development of policy offers a focal point around which discussion and debate can be organized. This often entails thrashing out differences between departments and individuals and a willingness to compromise so that a consensus about aims, principles and practices may be achieved. The policy is the means by which all the different practices and systems operating across a school may be rationalized, coordinated and, where necessary, standardized. Once a policy has been finalized, it provides a formal record of the school's approach to which all staff, including student teachers, will be expected to conform. It is part of the evidence which schools submit to Ofsted during inspections of their work. Developing and maintaining a policy, and reviewing its working, are key responsibilities of an assessment coordinator who liaises with year heads and heads of department (HoD) to ensure that all staff understand and comply with requirements. Alternatively, they may adopt a quality control approach by sampling the work of staff and pupils to ensure compliance.

Developments in the mid-1990s shifted assessment coordinators' work towards an increased preoccupation with data collection and analysis so that targets for improving schools may be identified (Chapter 7). An important element of this work concerns the collection of information about pupils' progress and attainments in different subjects at different stages in their school careers. Statistical analyses then allow a school to scrutinize performance and compare it with that in similar institutions both nationally and locally. In this way, trends and patterns in performance, which suggest priorities for future development, are detected. For instance, a school's performance and assessment (PANDA) report (Section 7.2) may suggest that its GCSE results compare unfavourably with those of schools serving similar intakes (measured, for example, by the percentage of pupils eligible for free school meals or FSM). In particular, boys' grades for languages may be unsatisfactory when set against local and national benchmark information (Section 7.6). Improving boys' GCSE grades in languages may become a target for development in this school. Likewise, by analysing results at the end of KSs 2, 3 and 4, a school may discern an 'attainment dip' during KS3. This may prompt an investigation into arrangements for transition from primary schools to determine whether the receiving school does all it should to ensure continuity and progression in pupils' learning. Retrospective analyses of performance enable schools to build performance profiles which are used for evaluation purposes. Assessment data are also used prospectively to indicate potential and make predictions about future attainment. These two types of data, retrospective and prospective, allow performance targets to be set and pupils' current attainments to be monitored. These topics are revisited in detail in Chapter 7 which places these activities in the relevant statutory frameworks.

Roundhill Community College

Roundhill Community College, an 11–14 Leicestershire high school, was one of the first schools to be inspected by Ofsted in 1994. The ensuing report indicated that the debate on assessment within the school needed to be managed. A new vice-principal was subsequently appointed, with the development of MARRA as one of his key responsibilities. When Andy Morris arrived, he found that staff held a wide variety of views about assessment. Some adopted a narrow view, equating assessment with testing which was used mostly for summative purposes. Assessment policy, on the other hand, consisted of a single paragraph subsumed in other school documentation. Andy Morris drew up an action plan for the year which was designed to meet Ofsted's requirement and the school's own goal of developing policy and practice. An assessment specialist from the LEA was invited to initiate whole-school development work, examining the nature and purposes of assessment. Andy Morris believes that the staff-wide debate which this triggered was essential because it allowed staff to do some fundamental thinking about forms and uses of assessment, and to air and exchange views. Colleagues were also alerted to differences in perspective and practice between departments. An audit of current practices was subsequently carried out at departmental level and shared in meetings of curriculum managers (HoDs). Andy Morris was keen that existing practice should provide the basis for developing policy rather than attempting to introduce policy-led practice. Therefore, the audit was used to formulate a draft policy on which staff were consulted before it was finalized. The policy is accompanied by an action plan and both are reviewed annually which has allowed them to evolve in line with the school's development plan and changing circumstances. In this school, a systematic use of action planning and annual reviews has produced a dynamic policy that promotes continuing development.

Task 5.1

Investigate arrangements in your placement school. Does it have an assessment coordinator? To what extent are responsibilities similar to those outlined above?

5.3 Why bother about school policies?

I occasionally encounter students who regard school policies as an irrelevance. They are impatient to start teaching at the earliest opportunity and unconvinced by advice about the importance of familiarizing themselves with school policies and protocols by studying relevant documents and observing routines and procedures before they start to teach. One student stands out in my memory because she wrote a painfully honest account of learning the hard way that a student who fails to see the relevance of institutional norms and expectations will find it impossible to function competently during placement. She had been indifferent to advice about familiarizing oneself with a school at the start of a placement and described her irritation at the amount of paperwork she was given. She pressurized her mentor to allow her to start teaching quickly, regarding observation as a waste of time. Almost immediately she found herself faced with situations which she was uncertain how to handle: routine tasks for which she did not know the correct procedure; pupils seeking guidance; pupils 'sussing her out' by infringing behavioural norms. She found herself in the unenviable position of choosing between undermining her authority with pupils by showing that she did not know how to proceed or making snap decisions which might turn out to be in contravention of established procedure thereby jeopardizing her relationships with colleagues. Either way, she realized that she was steadily undermining her standing with teaching groups. Classes that had originally accepted her as a teacher were unnerved by her hesitant responses and the way her decisions did not conform to what they expected from 'proper' teachers. Members of the department started to complain to her mentor that requirements were being flouted and that their classes were becoming restive. There are, then, some matters on which a consistent, 'whole-school' approach is either desirable or necessary – matters such as acceptable standards of conduct, the use of rewards and sanctions, provision for pupils with SEN, equal opportunities and so on. Clearly, a school could not function as a well-ordered organization if teachers and pupils adopted personal standards and behaviour in relation to matters such as these.

MARRA is another area where schools have found it necessary to co-ordinate their work and introduce consistency into some practices. The value of a policy on MARRA is perhaps best illustrated by looking back to the 1970s and 1980s, a period when few schools possessed a written policy statement. The result – according to NFER (Clough *et al.* 1984) – was a bewildering variety of approaches to assessment within schools which complicated the teacher's role unnecessarily and mystified pupils and parents. Although there was increasing awareness of the need to rationalize practice, the formulation of policy was an issue which 'many schools have only just begun to consider' (Clough *et al.* 1984: 26). Dunsbee and Ford's (1980) slightly earlier study provides a graphic illustration of the difficulties which could arise from the absence of an agreed policy. They examined teachers' marking practices, uncovering wide discrepancies even among teachers working within a single school. One example concerns a single spelling error (dinorsour) where 'out of a total of twenty-seven, no fewer than sixteen teachers used perceptibly different symbols to correct it' (Dunsbee and Ford 1980: 45). This suggests that if pupils were to make use of written feedback to improve their work, they needed to be able to decipher a confusing variety of symbols and codes as they moved from one teacher to the next – almost like mastering a range of regional dialects. Although the variety of practices was in itself confusing, even more disconcerting was the 'inadequate symbolism' employed by some markers who failed to offer positive help to children in correcting their mistakes. Their marks and strokes ranged from the 'markedly idiosyncratic and strangely distracting' to the 'downright misleading' (Dunsbee and Ford 1980: 46). These examples highlight the importance of clarity and consistency of approach and the need for a policy which promotes best practice. At the heart of an effective assessment regime lie agreed practices and clear, consistently used systems of communication.

Task 5.2

Discuss your own experiences of assessment as a pupil with other students. What methods were used by different subjects? Were approaches to assessment clear and consistent?

5.4 Recent developments in MARRA policies

If one assumes that this emerging interest in assessment policies had culminated in better established practices by the 1990s, James's (1998) findings may come as a surprise. Having surveyed Ofsted reports on schools in 20 LEAs, she concluded:

> There was evidence that many of these policies were recently written and were more in the nature of 'statements of intent' than operational guidelines. Probably this was an indication of the flurry of policy-writing activity that has characterized many schools' preparations for Ofsted inspection.
>
> (James 1998: 10)

This seemingly surprising state of affairs may be symptomatic of the difficulties inherent in developing and maintaining policies, whatever their subject. In the rapidly changing world of education, policies date quickly and maintaining them requires an ongoing commitment. Unless a policy is reviewed regularly and updated in the light of new initiatives and changing circumstances, it will rapidly become a historical document which bears less and less resemblance to practice. A significant impediment to policy implementation, therefore, is that it is a high-maintenance activity – a difficulty which is compounded by the number of policies that schools have to maintain.

Once a policy has been agreed, the key challenge is to ensure that it is translated into practice consistently by all staff. Indeed, a recurring theme of all the Ofsted reports sampled by James (1998: 10) was inconsistency in implementation across, and sometimes within, departments: 'The most frequent criticism in all reports concerned the variability in teachers' assessment practices, particularly regarding marking'. These concerns echo those raised by Clough *et al.* (1984) and Dunsbee and Ford (1980) many years earlier. Clearly, ensuring that a policy remains current and relevant and that it informs the work of all teachers are key tasks for any school. Ofsted has found that where MARRA had been identified as a priority in a school's development plan, with initiatives overseen by a member of the senior management team (SMT), schools have been most successful. MARRA policies do not follow a set style or format and their contents and scope vary. Therefore, you should study the policy in each of your placement schools. Although it is unusual to find a comprehensive policy, and the detail of treatment varies (Ofsted 1998a: 89), the items which follow should be covered at either school or departmental level.

Most important of all, a policy should be consistent with a school's ethos and wider educational aims. These may be laid down in a mission statement or a general statement of goals and purposes. A policy should, of course, help a school to achieve its mission and this is more likely to happen if explicit links have been made between the two. When a policy is preoccupied with the mechanical details of MARRA, prescribing practice but neglecting the goals which underpin the school's work, there is a danger of a poor level of match. A policy statement needs, therefore, to be informed by a clear rationale. A well-developed policy addresses key questions on which it is useful for schools/departments to have identified a shared set of aims and purposes, shared principles for working towards their goals and common or coordinated practices

- Why?   A rationale which articulates the purposes of MARRA and the relationship between the school's aims and the policy statement.
- How?   The systems and procedures which have been developed to achieve those aims and purposes.
- What?   A specification of required or recommended practices.
- Who?   Roles and responsibilities of different staff.
- When? Key dates in the MARRA calendar.

Because it is essential for the policy to remain contemporary, procedures for review should also be outlined.

The level of detail which a policy should exhibit and the question of what needs to be specified at whole-school level and what can be left to the discretion of departments or individuals remain moot points. Many schools favour James's (1998) recommendation that school policy should be a succinct document which establishes a broad framework of aims and principles within which departments must work while enjoying discretion over the detail of what they do. Thus, although areas where consistency is essential are identified (for example information which subject reports to parents must provide), there are more where it is believed to be neither possible nor necessary to reach a consensus (for example whether feedback to pupils should take the form of marks, grades, levels, comments or a combination of these approaches). The consensus appears to be that styles of working and concerns in subjects as diverse as physics, religious education (RE) and PE are so subject-specific that it would be inappropriate to attempt to enforce uniform practice. Andy Morris conveyed the difficult line which assessment co-ordinators tread when he argued that a policy needs to be general enough to accommodate everyone but not so general as to allow too much inconsistency. Ofsted (1998a: 89) accepts this compromise, acknowledging that: 'High quality assessment of specific subjects requires specialist knowledge and expertise and perhaps for this reason senior managers generally leave it to subject departments to determine their own procedures'. On the other hand, Ofsted asserts that there are 'common elements' which should be determined at whole school level and, although the examples it cites are too vague to inform practice, it nevertheless singles out for praise a school where the assessment coordinator had produced a comprehensive policy which itemizes the roles and responsibilities of different staff such as year heads and HoDs, produces an assessment calendar for each year group, provides a checklist of requirements for staff plus information for pupils and parents. These are thorny issues for schools. Many content themselves with requiring internal consistency within a department but stop short of requiring uniformity across a school in all but a few designated areas. This pragmatic solution does not always address the range of subjects studied which exposes pupils to considerable variety of practice even when departments are internally consistent.

At Garendon High School, Loughborough, the assessment coordinator, Steve Roberts, has convinced staff of the merits of a whole-school marking policy which specifies a common grading system and indicates the symbols and strokes to be used when annotating pupils' work (see Figure 5.1). Prior to agreeing this policy, staff examined each other's marking practices during in-service training sessions. They were invited to imagine that they were pupils attempting to use the feedback. The message that greater consistency would have improved communication was further reinforced by parent and pupil surveys. Both groups expressed a desire for information to be conveyed using standard systems and formats.

Comparing the policy of one institution with that of another can be illuminating. As Ofsted (1998a: 89) noted: 'nearly all whole school assessment policies have weaknesses or gaps which are reflected in corresponding weaknesses in the assessment practice of teachers'. Therefore, a comparison can be informative, highlighting the relative strengths and weaknesses in different approaches.

GARENDON HIGH SCHOOL

MARKING POLICY

The school's marking policy is rooted in the aims, principles and practices outlined in the school's policy for the 'Assessment, Recording, Monitoring and Reporting of Student Achievement and Progress.'

Marking can be a central part of the assessment process if the comments and marks relate to intended or actual learning outcomes; also if the marking gives more structured feedback about what has been achieved, strengths and weaknesses and suggestions for improvement.

It is important that we do not try to mark everything in great detail <u>but</u> marking cannot contribute to assessment if it consists <u>purely</u> of ticks, crosses and unexplained numbers/grades. Making constructive comments less frequently but in more detail will be a more efficient use of our time.

The main aims of marking at Garendon High School are:

AIMS

1. To act as an aid to learning and help students improve their work.
2. To inform students, staff and parents about improving performance and help them monitor progress and achievement within and beyond the National Curriculum.
3. To reassure, guide, encourage and motivate students of all abilities.
4. To encourage students to be involved in taking increased responsibility for their own learning by helping them identify strengths and weaknesses while also identifying achievable targets to help improve performance.
5. To ensure students know their work and efforts are valued.
6. To ensure students know and understand the criteria used to judge/mark particular pieces of work.

PRINCIPLES AND PRACTICES

Marking is one of the significant ways in which achievement and progress is reviewed and recorded. It therefore has a key role to play in our Assessment, Recording and Reporting Policy.

The following principles and practices express and extend the aims set out above.

Marking at Garendon High School will:

- acknowledge the accuracy and/or completion of work by a tick and/or comment
- involve the writing of comments on some pieces of work. These comments will emphasise the positive but also identify weaknesses. Where appropriate, constructive suggestions/targets for further improvement will be made.
- acknowledge that different types of marking will be used to suit the task as and when appropriate for example brief comments, in depth analytical comments, scores, percentages, marks against specific criteria, the use of VG, G,S, W, H.D., U, N.I. etc.
- reflect an individual's progress against his/her own level of performance
- occur regularly at the most useful points in the scheme of work planned by the teacher
- consider the most appropriate style of marking applied to a particular task as part of the planning process
- acknowledge that not every piece of work will be marked in detail but certain important/key pieces will be marked thoroughly against shared criteria (where appropriate) in order to give effective feedback
- involve teachers, students and peers in the process on appropriate occasions
- where appropriate, involve students writing commentaries alongside their work which indicate difficulties they encountered, questions raised, needs or aspects of the work they feel required improvement

– avoid the over use of only one particular style of marking for example purely 'good work', ticks, grades, numbers. The question to ask is, how helpful is the marking to the student, parent, teacher?
– allow opportunities for students to review the marking. Parents and teachers should work to direct students to respond to points made through the marking process. This will help students to look at and learn from the marking process
– help provide information for staff to review and evaluate the success/effectiveness of a particular lesson/module i.e. (How appropriate were the objectives, resources, teaching methods, assessment methods, content etc.)
– provide examples of marked work for the departmental portfolio. These to be discussed at departmental meetings to help ensure consistency and standards
– address subject specific cognitive skills
– be helped by clear departmental guidelines regarding standards of presentation and layout of work
– help reinforce the importance of spelling, punctuation and grammar. These must be checked as part of the marking process. However, not every single mistake will be corrected as this could have a demotivating effect on the student. Better to focus on recurrent mistakes.

The following notation should be used on the line containing the mistake which will be O ringed or underlined to indicate something is wrong. The students should then make alterations as part of the review of teacher's marking or the teacher could write the correction out on the work.

Subject specific/specialist word lists will help this process.

– involve the use of numbers/percentages on some pieces of work where appropriate. However, it would help if they were set in context to let the individual know if 6/10 was a good performance for them. It would make sense to use VG, G, S, W, H.D., U, N.I., to help this process and also to indicate effort/application.
– not simply have a National Curriculum level number written on a student's piece of work. (How helpful will this be to learning?) However, this does not preclude reference to 'level description' statements written in language students can understand. These statements can be useful as an aid to marking as they can help teachers/students/parents/others see what the students know, understand and can do. In addition, the statements can help identify what the students need to do to improve their performance and assist the target setting process.

WHOLE SCHOOL MARKING GUIDELINES

It would make sense to use the following notation when correcting students' work.

Could be written
in margin

Sp	neumatic or neumatic	= spelling error
p	O or _____	= punctuation error
NP	//	= new paragraph needed
gr	O or _____	= grammatical error
cap or cl	O or _____	= capital letter needed
	∧	= word or letter missing
	(T)	= target/next step to improve your work

VG+ = an excellent/exceptional performance/piece of work which meets and/or goes beyond the objectives set for the piece of work
VG = a very good piece of work/performance which meets all of the objectives set for the piece of work with a high level of accuracy
G = a good piece of work/performance which in all but minor details meets the objectives set for the piece of work

S   = an acceptable piece of work/performance which meets over half of the objectives set for the piece and reveals steady progress. It also indicates the need for further improvement to some aspects of the work.

W   = an unacceptable piece or work/performance which meets few or none of the objectives set for the piece of work.

H.D. = you have found the work too difficult and the piece of work meets very few or none of the objectives set for the piece of work.

U   = you have met fewer than expected of the objectives set for the piece of work and you have shown in the past that you can produce work of a higher standard.

N.I. = you have made a real improvement in your performance and/or in the quality of your work.

A copy of these guidelines is to be found in each Student Planner to help parents and students understand what is meant by the above marks

Figure 5.1   Garendon High School marking policy

Task 5.3

Use the list below of gaps and weaknesses commonly found in MARRA policies (based on James 1998a; Ofsted 1998a) as a basis for analysing the strengths and weaknesses of the policies of your placement schools/ departments:

- policy restricted to marking – insufficient attention to assessment
- emphasis on recording strategies and on the assessment of externally examined courses – insufficient attention to the quality of day-to-day assessment and marking
- policy confined to prescriptions for practice – no sense of the school's underlying aims or of the principles and purposes which should inform practice
- insufficient attention to KS3 – emphasis on KS4 and post-16 requirements
- role of written feedback in raising standards of attainment not made explicit
- a norm-referenced grading system (typically a five-point A–E scale or a seven-point A–G scale) either recommended or required but its relationship to NC levels and criteria not specified
- little or no evidence that moderation procedures are used to develop consistency of judgements within and between departments
- little or no evidence that assessment is used to monitor pupils' progress or to inform planning
- limited evidence that assessment information transferred from primary schools is used to plan for progression in pupils' learning
- limited use of innovative strategies such as self- and peer assessment.

Examine the policy in the light of the school's mission statement or statement of aims. Does the policy seem well judged to support the school's goals?

   Talk to the assessment coordinator about when and how the policy was developed. Has it been updated? If so, how and why was it changed?

5.5 Using performance data to monitor progress

Monitoring 'involves the collection of information, on a regular basis, in order to check on progress . . . The intention is that significant departures from the expected should lead to appropriate corrective action' (Wilcox 1992: 8). Schools' responsibility for pupil progress has been given an added sense of urgency by successive governments' attempts to raise educational standards. Initiatives such as national testing at regular intervals throughout pupils' school careers, the publication of test and examination results in performance tables, the inspection of LEAs and schools by Ofsted, the publication of inspection results and the requirement that schools set and publish targets for improving their own performance are key elements in a package of measures designed to lever up educational standards by monitoring schools' performances and holding them publicly accountable for what they achieve. These pressures, coupled with a new emphasis on data analysis, are encouraging schools to adopt systematic, quantitative approaches to monitoring the progress of each child from entry to a school to exit.

The first stage entails collecting input data to establish a baseline for each child on entry to a school. Secondary schools cater for different age ranges and, although Year 7 represents the typical entry point, in some areas pupils transfer to new schools at other ages such as Year 8 or Year 10. Whatever the entry point, transition from one school to another creates challenges: how to ensure continuity and progression in learning and how to make effective use of information provided by a previous school in the receiving one. Research has focused on KS2/3, the most common transition point, identifying a disturbing hiatus in pupils' intellectual development, or even regression, following a change of school (for example Galton 1983: 93; Pringle and Cobb 1999: 70). Schools have been found to focus on the pastoral dimension to the move, introducing measures to help pupils to settle quickly into their new environment. However, curriculum continuity and progression have been neglected and secondary schools have been criticized for paying insufficient attention to the wealth of assessment information which accompanies children from primary schools. There are genuine difficulties here, such as when secondary schools receive pupils from large numbers of feeder schools. Nevertheless, Ofsted (1998a: 105) points to the 'considerable waste of pupils' time' when Year 7 subject teachers disregard pupils' prior attainments and the demands of KS2 PoS, preferring to treat pupils as 'clean sheets' and make a fresh start. Year 7 teachers have also been found to concentrate on identifying problems in new pupils' learning, not on promoting continuity (Galton, quoted in Pringle and Cobb 1999: 71). The accountability pressures described above are encouraging schools to adopt quantitative approaches to tackling these problems, using NC data available from KS2.

Given that it takes two years on average to pass from one NC level to the next, a level represents a very broad measure of attainment. Information about levels is, therefore, of limited use to receiving schools in meeting the needs of their new intake. Recognizing this, SCAA (1997) made additional information about pupils' attainments in Year 6 available:

- raw test scores for each child plus level thresholds for the tests
- age standardized scores showing pupils' performance in relation to others of their own age by month of birth (this information can be used in the same way that reading ages calculated from standardized reading tests can be used)
- separate test levels in English for reading and writing
- separate TA levels for each AT.

This plus any other input information which schools agree to share – for example standardized scores for reading ages, samples of pupils' work – are used to establish pupils' baselines on entry to a school. Some schools enrich their baseline data by conducting entry tests. These are usually commercially produced standardized tests such as NFER/Nelson's Cognitive Abilities Test (CAT), which is commonly used in Years 7 and 9 as an indicator of future attainment and to identify those who may be underachieving or exceeding expectations. The Curriculum, Evaluation and Management Centre at the University of Durham provides a commonly used alternative. The Middle Years Information System (MIDYIS), Year Eleven Information System (YELLIS) and Advanced Level Information System (ALIS) is a family of information systems which schools can use to monitor pupils' progress and self-esteem and the quality of school life. QCA has also introduced tests designed to monitor progress (Section 8.2). Figure 5.2 shows the profile of a Year 10 pupil on transfer from an 11–14 high school to a 14–19 upper school. Figure 5.3 shows a form used for tracking pupil progress across KS3 at Garendon High School.

Pupil performance data are useful in various ways. Prior attainment is widely regarded as the best indicator of future performance (Section 7.5) and so it is used to establish baselines, allowing performance targets to be set, subsequent progress to be monitored and the value added to children's education by a school to be 'measured'. It is also used to assign new pupils to appropriate teaching groups promptly after arrival, particularly in hierarchical subjects such as mathematics and science, which often set teaching groups. Close monitoring of pupils' progress, and the maintenance of records, means that schools are in a position to respond quickly should parents question their child's progress. Whereas teachers traditionally relied on their judgement of year groups, variously labelling them as 'weak' or 'able', they now generate statistics which bear out these impressions that year groups are better or weaker than those in previous years. Year group data assist in the annual setting of targets and year-on-year information can help a school to form a picture of its own development. Pupils' progress is also one of the criteria for crossing the performance threshold which gives mainstream teachers access to higher pay. Teachers, therefore, need pupil performance data to support their own career development. The following example illustrates one school's approach to establishing baselines and monitoring progress.

Cognitive Abilities Test

Student profiles with GCSE indicators

Name:

Sex:

High school:

Age: 14 years 5 months

Tutor Group:

	Raw Score	SAS 70–130	NPR 100%	Stanine 1–9
Verbal (100)	72	100	50	5
Quantitative (60)	39	97	42	5
Non-Verbal (80)	69	108	70	6

Overall mean SAS (−70 – 130+) 102

This is an average of the three SAS scores (Verbal, Quantitative and Non-Verbal) and is the score used for GCSE predictions.

Verbal: measures relational thinking when relationships are formulated in verbal terms
Quantitative: measures reasoning with quantitative symbols
Non-Verbal: measures flexibility in manipulating relationships expressed in symbols

Standard Age Score (SAS)
Normalised score scale in which the average score for each age group on each test is set at 100 and the standard deviation is set at 15, 130 being the top score and 70 is lowest.

Percentile Rank by Age (NPR)
Indicates the percentage of pupils in an age group that obtained scores below a particular score. For example, an NPR of 27 means 27% of pupils nationally scored less.

Standard Nine (Stanine)
Normalises the SAS into nine levels, 9 being highest.

SAT Scores (2–8)

English SAT: 6	English TA: 5
Maths SAT: 6	Maths TA: 5
Science SAT: 5	Science TA: 6

Standard Attainment Tests (SATs) are the national exams taken in the High schools and the Teacher Assessments (TAs) are the levels given by the High school teachers.

GCSE Indicators (80% Confidence)

A* to C grades:	6
A* to G grades:	9
Prob of 5 A* to C grades:	60%
Prob of 5 A* to G grades:	95%

Mean GCSE Point Score: 5

From numeric scale:
GCSE grade: A*=8, A=7, B=6, C=5, D=4, E=3, F=2, G=1

GCSE Grades (+/− one grade)

GCSE English:	C
GCSE Maths:	D
GCSE Science:	C

Reading and Spelling

Reading Age:	12.6
Spelling Age:	15.3

Figure 5.2 A Year 10 pupil's performance profile on the Cognitive Abilities Test

MONITORING OF ACHIEVEMENT AND PERSONAL PROGRESS

Tutor group 7 _____ 8 _____ 9 _____

Name: _____

KEY:

OA = Outstanding Achievement   OE = Outstanding Effort   VG = Very Good
G = Good   S = Steady Progress   NI = Notable Improvement   HD = Has Difficulty
W = Weak   U = Underachieving   Coop. = Cooperation + working with others
P.Org. = Personal organization including: remembering equipment and homework punctuality
Conc. = Concentration   Pres. = Presentation of work   N/A = Not applicable

Subject	Year	Teacher's initials	Set + move eg: 2 to 1	Effort	Coop.	P.Org.	Behaviour + attitude	Conc.	Speak. + listening	Pres.	Overall progress	Recom. for Cert. OA,OE,NI	1	2	3	4	Main target/Comment
French	7																
	8								N/A								
	9								N/A								
German	9								N/A								
Spanish	9								N/A								
PE	7		N/A			*				N/A							
	8		N/A			*				N/A							
	9		N/A			*				N/A							
RE	7		N/A											N/A	N/A	N/A	
	8		N/A											N/A	N/A	N/A	
Art	7		N/A												N/A	N/A	
	8		N/A												N/A	N/A	
	9		N/A												N/A	N/A	
Tech.	7		N/A												N/A	N/A	
	8		N/A												N/A	N/A	
	9		N/A												N/A	N/A	

Key to columns 1,2,3,4

French/ German/ Spanish
1 = Listening to a foreign language
2 = Speaking in a foreign language
3 = Reading in a foreign language
4 = Writing in a foreign language

PE
1 = Gymnastic activities
2 = Invasion games: hockey, soccer, basketball, netball, rugby
3 = Striking games: badminton, tennis, volleyball, cricket, rounders
4 = Athletic activities and swimming

*P.Org. includes remembering kit!

RE
YR 7 1 = Signs & symbols
YR 8 1 = World religions

Art
1 = Investigating & making
2 = Knowledge & understanding

Technology
1 = Designing
2 = Making

Figure 5.3 Example of a form used for monitoring pupil progress across Key Stage 3

Roundhill Community College

At Roundhill Community College, support staff do extra hours during the summer vacation to ensure that the KS2 database is ready for use with the new Year 7 cohort at the beginning of the school year. With over half of Year 7 arriving with level 4s in KS2 tests, this information was of limited use to the school in assigning pupils to teaching groups, in monitoring their progress or in judging the value added by their time at Roundhill. The school responded by manipulating these data to provide a more sensitive measure of performance. By obtaining level boundaries for KS2 tests and each child's raw scores, the school can determine whether a child simply scraped into level 4 or only just missed attaining level 5. The LEA has recommended qualifying levels thus: a = marks in the top third of the range; b = marks in the middle band; c = marks in the bottom third of the range. The school also administers MIDYIS to pupils one month after arrival to provide a measure of potential by the end of KS3. In the January of Year 8, a whole-school progress review is used to provide a current working level for each pupil in each subject, again qualified a, b or c. All of this information – qualified KS2 test results, qualified Year 8 current working levels and MIDYIS measures of end-of-KS potential – is entered onto the school's database. This enables the school to judge, half way through KS3, whether children are on target to achieve their academic potential as measured by MIDYIS. For instance, if a child arrived with a level 4 in the KS2 Maths test (qualified by the school to 4b) and MIDYIS had shown the child's potential to attain level 6 by the end of KS3, a current working level of 5b in the January of Year 8 would satisfy the school that the child was progressing satisfactorily. The progress review allows the school to identify and intervene in the case of children who are performing below expectation. These children are subsequently monitored closely by mentors from the SMT. The school has analysed this group of pupils in an attempt to identify common factors in under-performance. It considered various possibilities – a record of behavioural problems; unsatisfactory attendance; frequent lateness; summer born; on the SEN register; poor level of literacy. The analysis demonstrated that although pupils on the SEN register were under-performing relative to their peers, they were not under-performing relative to their potential as measured by MIDYIS. By far the most common factor which these children shared was a reading age below their chronological age in the year when KS2 tests were taken. The school responded by introducing an intensive reading course for which parents were required to provide support outside school hours. Pre- and post-course tests of literacy demonstrate that many children make dramatic gains in this way. For instance, one Year 8 child whose pre-course reading age was 8+ produced a score of 13+ in the post-course test. Although we often think of diagnostic assessment as focusing on individual children, this example shows that large-scale, quantitative data can also be treated as a diagnostic tool.

Similar approaches have been taken at departmental level.

Heart of England School

Bal Kaur, Head of Science at Heart of England School, an 11–18 compre-hensive in Solihull, was concerned about continuity and progression at KS2/3 (Kaur 1998). These issues were a particular concern in science be-cause of the conceptual difficulty of the subject and the variable levels of expertise in science teaching among primary staff. When KS2 data became available to the school in 1995, the department used these to establish individual baselines against which pupils' subsequent progress could be tracked. The department used pupils' raw scores in KS2 science tests to provide a more sensitive baseline than NC levels offered. Pupils' progress throughout KS3 is tracked using a series of differentiated end-of-topic tests devised by the department. Pupils decide, in negotiation with their sci-ence teacher, which tier of paper they will attempt. Results are recorded centrally in the department and performance at the end of each year is compared with previous results. The department distinguishes between half and whole NC levels which enables them to discriminate sensitively, identifying those whose performance is below expectations as well as those who are performing above average. Termly progress reviews allow the department to differentiate provision. Under-performing pupils are identi-fied and become the subject of action lists designed to target their diffi-culties. High achievers are given more challenging tasks to extend them. Pupils' value added scores are calculated at the end of each year in KS3. The results show that: 'as the pupils progress through the key stage there is an increase in their Value Added scores, and the number of pupils with negative scores decreases significantly' (Kaur 1998: 11). Although it is not possible to demonstrate a causal relationship between these improvements and the initiatives described above, Bal Kaur nevertheless believes that 'regular assessment is at the heart of any attempt to monitor pupil progress and promote achievement. The KS2 assessment data should be used con-structively in order to build on pupils' previous experiences' (Kaur 1998: 11).

Scrutiny of Year 7 data also showed that pupils were performing poorly on AT1 assessments (Scientific Enquiry) relative to their performance on the-ory ones. When this finding was shared with primary science coordinators at a liaison meeting, AT1 was identified as an area where primary teachers needed CPD. Staff from the secondary science department responded by offering workshops for primary science coordinators, showing again how trends apparent in large-scale, quantitative data can be treated diagnostically.

Similar approaches to monitoring are also adopted at KS4 and post-16. Data from the previous KS provide a prior attainment baseline and information systems such as CAT, YELLIS, ALIS and the Autumn Package of Pupil

Performance Information (Section 7.2) allow schools to project forward to the end of a KS and set targets. Entry point and end point data are fundamental requirements for these approaches to monitoring perform-ance and setting targets. Figure 5.4 shows the approach at Coundon Court, an 11–18 school with beacon school status in Coventry.

There are dangers inherent in systems designed to enhance perform-ance which rely heavily on a single performance indicator (PI) such as NC test levels (Section 7.7). Nevertheless, when quantitative analyses are used sensitively and recognized as investigative tools rather than ends in themselves, they offer a means of probing aspects of performance which might otherwise go unchallenged such as the performance of a subgroup of pupils. For instance, Ofsted (1998a: 49) cites the case of a school where comparison of internal data with LEA-generated *benchmarks* (Sec-tion 7.6) revealed that an apparently successful department where pupils achieved good results was actually performing below what might be

---

RSA, A. LEVEL & GNVQ

THE POST SIXTEEN SEQUENCE

- GCSE grades collected and recorded as students enrol for Post 16 A. Level and GNVQ courses.

- Average points scores from GCSE results are set against Alis predictions and "in house" previous performance data.

- These can then be used to set Minimum Target Grades for all A. Level and GNVQ students in each subject area.

- The information is refined on to a teaching group profile and distributed to staff...see Maths, GNVQ Adv. Business and GNVQ Intermediate Health profiles for Year 12 1999-2001.

- In the November of Year 12 an early Bromcom Review is taken to see how students have settled on to their courses and to inform discussion between tutor, student, teacher and parents. Targets are set and recorded in the Personal Organiser.

- The Bromcom Review is modified into an Interim Report that goes home to parents in December. Problems can be followed up by personal contact and congratulations given where appropriate. See exemplars.

- A full Bromcom Review of all students taking an Intermediate GNVQ course is completed in early March and an Interim Report sent home.

- A second review of A. Level and GNVQ Advanced students is taken in the Spring term of Year 12 to establish a P.P.G. (Present Performance Grade) and inform discussion at the Parents evening in mid March.

- Internal Year 12 / and external module exams take place during the Summer term followed by a Review meeting...Causes for concern are identified and parents consulted.

- Full Year 12 Report issued to parents in July.

- Year 12 modular exam results are collated and profiles updated see exemplars for GNVQ Advanced Business, Geography and Maths...these become...

- Year 13 Value Added profiles distributed to teaching staff...see previous exemplars.

- A Bromcom Review of Year 13 students is taken in October before half term. This review is also modified into an Interim profile and any problems can be quickly dealt with. See Exemplars.

- A similar pattern of reviews, monitoring and follow up meetings occurs in Year 13 together with tutor / student discussion and target setting...refer to Post 16 Role of Tutor.

- Year 13 Mock examinations take place immediately after the February half term and a full summative report is issued to parents in March.

- All A. Level and GNVQ results are collated and Value Added calculated for each teaching group. These are distributed to all Post 16 teaching and tutorial staff.

- Full Examination analysis is completed and Value Added ranked by subject area. See A. Level Exam results.

Figure 5.4 Example of an approach to target-setting and monitoring progress at Post 16

expected from it. Pupils studying the subject were predominantly more able and this was masking a degree of under-performance which was uncovered by the comparison.

5.6 The identification and assessment of pupils with SEN

About 90 per cent of pupils registered with SEN are educated in mainstream schools. You are, therefore, likely to find pupils at various stages on the *Code of Practice on the Identification and Assessment of Special Educational Needs* (DfE 1994) in your classes. Conditions which create a severe or permanent SEN (for example Attention Deficit Hyperactivity Disorder (ADHD) or Asperger Syndrome) are usually identified well before a child reaches secondary school. However, in the case of mild or temporary difficulties, a secondary teacher may well be the first person to raise concerns, placing subject specialists in the front line in the identification and assessment of SEN. Even during training, a student may be the first teacher to recognize and make provision for a child's need. For instance, a student teacher, who herself was partially sighted, developed an interest in visual impairment. She discovered that several of her pupils were colour blind and that they were helped by simple modifications to the use of colour in teaching resources. The pupils told her that she was the first teacher they had encountered who had taken care over this aspect of their teaching.

The Code of Practice details formal requirements (for example schools should appoint a SENCO and formulate a policy for SEN) and sets out a five-stage procedure for identifying and assessing SEN. You need to familiarize yourself with all of these stages, paying special attention to the early ones, for it is here that class teachers play a key role in recognizing and diagnosing difficulties and making an initial attempt to meet them as part of routine class teaching. At later stages, the SENCO, possibly in collaboration with outside agents such as educational psychologists, assumes lead responsibility although class teachers still play a vital role in implementing their recommendations. The code lays down some founding principles for good practice including the importance of early intervention so that needs are addressed before difficulties become compounded. This further underlines the fundamental role of the class teacher in making a prompt identification and assessment of needs at Stage 1.

SEN may seem a daunting aspect of your training because the range of needs which you might encounter is wide. SEN encompasses pupils who are exceptionally able as well as those who have learning difficulties and it includes emotional and behavioural difficulties as well as sensory and physical impairments. A pupil may, moreover, exhibit a combination of needs making each case uniquely challenging and complex. However, the principles of formative assessment are at the heart of practices required by the code: a careful diagnosis of individuals' learning needs; the use of this information to create individual education plans (IEPs) tailored to children's capabilities and requirements; plus the use of regular progress reviews involving consultations with learners and their parents. Thus, teachers who use assessment formatively are well placed to address the needs of pupils with SEN and many of the approaches which have been described in this book are pertinent to working with the Code of Practice.

- Plan flexibly, paying close attention to feedback on needs so that provision can be adapted to reduce or remove obstacles to learning.
- Vary tasks to accommodate different learning style preferences and avoid assessing using only one or a limited range of media which may disadvantage certain pupils.
- When diagnosing difficulties or monitoring progress, defer judgement until a body of evidence has been accumulated using various sources and assessment methods. Superficial judgements are particularly likely to be flawed in the case of SEN pupils where complex combinations of needs may be involved.
- Use focused observation and close questioning to gain insight into the nature of difficulties.
- Each subject has specific demands and characteristics which may challenge pupils with certain types of SEN. Planning needs to be differentiated not only to address the needs of individuals but also to accommodate subject-specific requirements. For instance, science is conceptually difficult and performing investigations requires pupils to follow detailed instructions, undertaking tasks in sequence. The teaching of MFL is often fast paced, moving rapidly through a series of activities with an emphasis on oral and aural skills and social collaboration. A lesson in English literature is likely to be a more deliberate occasion placing an emphasis on reflection and considered personal responses to a text. PE requires good physical coordination. Think hard about the nature of your subject. Does it entail cognitive, sensory, physical, behavioural or emotional demands which may create difficulties for pupils with SEN?

Although formative assessment is an excellent guide to general principles which should inform SEN work, seek specialized guidance from your placement school's SENCO on appropriate methods and resources for dealing with specific conditions such as dyslexia or dyspraxia.

Where SEN makes part(s) or the whole of a NC subject and/or its assessment inaccessible to a pupil, TA remains a statutory requirement although it is possible to have test requirements disapplied. However, test arrangements are intended to give as many children as possible access: modified large print and braille versions of tests are available. There are other adaptations which schools can make without seeking permission such as photocopying test papers onto coloured paper or shading diagrams to increase visual clarity or using readers or taped versions of the maths and science tests for children with reading difficulties. Teachers need to seek permission for some special arrangements such as allowing pupils extra time but a host of modifications may be permissible.

6 Record-keeping and reporting

6.1 Introduction

In an average week, a secondary teacher may encounter hundreds of pupils and make thousands of assessments. Although they may have a fair idea of each child's capabilities, it is impossible for teachers to carry in their heads comprehensive records of each pupil's progress, attainments and difficulties. Thus, the wealth of information which assessment provides must be sifted so that key details are recorded ready for subsequent use. Keeping records and reporting to others are complementary forms of action to the feedback and feedforward strategies described in Part 1 of this book. All teachers should maintain records for the pupils they teach and report the information to interested parties: learners themselves, other teachers, the next school, parents and so on. Records are also part of the evidence base used in preparing reports to parents which is the subject of the second half of this chapter.

Objectives

By the end of this chapter, you should have developed your understanding of two key ideas:

- keeping records should not be an inert, mechanical undertaking; active use should be made of the information to evaluate teaching and to manage pupils' progress and development
- effective reporting has a formative/feedforward function as well as serving summative purposes.

6.2 Record-keeping: lessons from past experience

When the NC was introduced (1989), many KS1 teachers devised exhaustive recording systems involving comprehensive ticklists which had to be completed for *each* child in *each* NC subject. Not only were teachers left reeling under the demands of these recording systems, but also they generated masses of performance data which were of questionable worth. The plethora of data obscured rather than illuminated key points in children's development and progress. Although these voluminous records were, in part, a knee jerk response to the detail and complexity of the original NC, they offer a useful reminder of the danger of record-keeping systems becoming unwieldy and burdensome. Onerous recording systems can distract teachers from their educative purpose: 'The collection of marks to fill up records is given greater priority than the analysis of pupils' work to discern learning needs' (Black and Wiliam 1998b: 6). Record-keeping may also reinforce the 'English obsession with . . . grading' (Hargreaves, quoted in Conner 1991: 127). Thus, record-keeping can become an end in itself with little value or purpose beyond the building of the record (Conner 1991: 131). Dense records are also offputting for potential users. A frequent criticism of transfer arrangements as pupils move through the education system is that teachers in receiving schools ignore the records carefully compiled by feeder schools, preferring instead to treat pupils as 'clean sheets' and make a fresh start. In responding to the criticism, teachers often plead the time which studying complicated transfer records would entail. At its worst, then, record-keeping is little more than a paper exercise with fulsome records, painstakingly compiled, but rarely consulted.

There are at least three lessons implicit in past experience:

- a clear sense of purpose(s) should determine the information to be collected – items surplus to requirements should be eschewed to avoid record-keeping for record-keeping's sake
- paramount among these purposes should be the formative function of the information such as using records to assist in evaluating the curriculum, setting targets, monitoring progress and diagnosing difficulties
- systems should be manageable, both for those producing records and for those using them: approaches should be concise, user-friendly and, where possible, consistent.

6.3 The main purposes of record-keeping

6.3a Fulfilling statutory requirements

Although written reports to parents are hedged around with statutory requirements, those for record-keeping are minimal. There is a requirement that schools maintain records on each child's academic progress and attainments, as well as documenting non-academic achievements, and that these records are updated annually but, beyond that, record-keeping is treated as a matter for professional decision-making. Schools, therefore, enjoy considerable discretion over their record-keeping and you should familiarize yourself with practice in each of your placement schools.

Task 6.1

Investigate record-keeping arrangements in your department/school. Where there is an established system in place, familiarize yourself with its requirements. If practice varies, acquaint yourself with approaches adopted by different teachers. By asking yourself the following questions, you should be able to devise an approach which meets your own needs and builds on the best of other teachers' practices

- Why record? A clear sense of purpose(s) will help to determine the type of records produced (for example informal, day-to-day records of pupils' learning for personal use in planning; formal records of work completed to hand over to the regular teacher at the end of a placement).
- Who is the target audience? This helps to determine the form of records and their contents (for example personal records should focus on significant or unexpected steps in pupils' learning. They may be in note form and need be intelligible only to you whereas records which will be read by others need to be explicit).
- What level of detail is required? (The experiences of those before you suggest that the attempt to record everything compromises manageability and intelligibility.)
- What types of records are needed? (Avoid maintaining overlapping records. Simple modifications could enable a single record to serve a common purpose.)
- How could IT assist your record-keeping?

6.3b Enhancing formative assessment

Ofsted (1998a: 93) found that although recording of pupils' progress had improved, 'the result are generally under-used'. This is unfortunate as records have a useful role to play in a formative assessment regime. Although work completed in the current year might seem like a natural starting point, records should also establish pupils' baselines when a teacher assumes responsibility for their learning. Information about their prior attainment and difficulties helps to smooth the transition from one year/KS to the next and enables teachers to provide for continuity and progression in teaching and learning. This information should include

NC test and TA results from the previous year/KS, the results of standardized tests, information from the school's internal monitoring system such as most recent 'effort' or 'personal organization' grades. A record should also be kept of details which will assist in adapting plans to meet individuals' learning needs, for instance key features of IEPs, ways of differentiating work for specific pupils, those who require extension work and so on.

Records which allow progress to be monitored are essential. The record should provide a visual check on rates of progress and therefore it is important to date entries so that it is easy to see those who are progressing as expected and those who are faring better or worse than expected. When the information for an entire class is held on a single record sheet, it is possible to take a whole-class overview as well as gaining a picture of individuals' progress. It is important to use this type of record to take stock of a situation, looking for long-term or large-scale patterns in performance which may not be apparent in smaller bodies of data. Class records can be useful for spotting problems which require further investigation, especially subtle trends in performance which may escape notice without scrutiny such as the under-performance of a subgroup of pupils. For instance, by studying data for an entire class, a teacher may discern that it was mostly girls who performed below expectation on a particular unit of work whereas boys' attainments were as anticipated. Likewise, by scrutinizing long-term data, a teacher may notice that a pupil made slower progress over the final two half terms than they did during the first four. The teacher may investigate this with the pupil with the aim of restoring progress in the following year. In both cases, records have captured patterns in performance which merit further investigation. The investigation may inform future curriculum planning, helping teachers to evaluate the merits of existing teaching approaches and so on. Good record systems, therefore, facilitate evaluation and planning of future work both for individuals and for entire groups. Just as schools maintain databases which allow performance to be monitored at a macrocosmic level (Chapter 7), it is useful for student teachers to treat their own records as a mini database which allows them to undertake similar analyses at a microcosmic level.

Task 6.2

Find out what information about pupils is routinely passed on to subject teachers and form tutors at the start of a year in your placement school. Draw up a list of information you will require when you assume responsibility for classes.

Well-maintained records are also a prerequisite for informing others.

6.3c Facilitating communication with parents

Records should provide the level of detail which is required to report meaningfully to parents. A written report which is so bland that it could apply to any number of individuals, without communicating anything of substance, is unacceptable. For instance, the admonition to 'try harder in this subject' contains no guidance for recipients on the behavioural changes that are needed. Without drawing on records, it is difficult for teachers to make comments which are sufficiently precise to guide future actions. Regularly updated records also enable schools to respond quickly and confidently whenever concerned parents make contact to question their child's progress.

6.3d Communicating with other professionals

You may need to report on pupils' progress to other professionals. For instance, your HoD will monitor the work of the department. The SENCO, or an educational psychologist, may require specific information about children on the school's SEN register. The assessment coordinator may maintain central records of all pupils' progress. Form tutors maintain an overview of the development of each child in a form. The next teacher/school needs to ensure continuity and progression on transfer. Supply and student teachers need to avoid gaps in the curriculum and unnecessary repetition. Maintaining appropriate records enables you to satisfy the demands of other professionals and facilitates the flow of information around the system, which is essential in complex organizations like schools. Many schools exploit the data-handling and retrieval capabilities of ICT to streamline their recording and reporting activities (Section 6.12). Investigate how ICT could support this aspect of your work.

6.3e Records as evidence

Although pupils' work is the teacher's primary evidence base, records provide an important secondary source. They offer a statement of what has happened, thereby demonstrating that statutory requirements have been met, such as coverage of NC PoS. Subject teachers are required to summarize their judgements of pupils' performance at KS3 in end-of-KS levels (Section 8.2d). They need to be able to demonstrate that these judgements have been arrived at by referring to appropriate evidence. A secure evidence base, therefore, strengthens the validity and reliability of summative judgements.

Written records provide the kind of 'hard-edged' evidence which it is useful for parents and pupils to consider during meetings. They offer a tangible focus for attention that is more easily grasped than abstract generalizations. Although records are useful for positive purposes, like reassuring anxious parents that progress is being made, they are particularly helpful where a teacher has identified a cause for concern which is liable to be disputed, for example, poor rates of work completion, punctuality and attendance. A written record, with dates and relevant figures, is more authoritative than the spoken word so that, while a child may refute a teacher's verbal claims, written records are hard to contest.

Career progression depends on the ability to produce evidence of quality in teaching. To pass over the performance-related payment threshold, teachers must demonstrate that their pupils make good progress. Samples of work are primary sources of evidence but records of attainment are an important secondary means of exemplifying quality. These data (especially test results) may be analysed to produce statistical evidence of pupils' rates of progress and the 'value added' (Section 7.6) by teaching.

6.4 What kind of records?

It is useful to distinguish between informal records retained for day-to-day use in planning and those which serve formal purposes. If it is assumed that most pupils will achieve short-term learning objectives, it is an unnecessary expenditure of energy to make an individual record of this for each pupil. Day-to-day records can, therefore, focus on unexpected progress or difficulties. Clarke (1998) suggests that the best way to capture this kind of ephemeral evidence is to provide space on lesson plans for assessment notes. Her advice may be particularly helpful to secondary teachers whose timetables provide little time between lessons for reflection, evaluation and recording. Assessment notes on lesson plans allow for rapid, informal recording of ephemeral evidence of progress/difficulties which may have faded from memory long before the teacher has an opportunity to make a formal record. Clarke (1998) argues that however informal these jottings may appear, they provide:

> formal assessment judgements, and form a continuous assessment record . . . To then transfer this information onto individual children's records would take an enormous amount of time, so notes made on short-term plans seem to be the most manageable record of children's attainment . . . This strategy appears to follow the statutory requirements for 'recording and retaining evidence' found in the QCA *Assessment and Reporting Arrangements* booklets:

> > In retaining evidence and keeping records, schools should be guided by what is both manageable and useful in planning future work. Ofsted inspectors will not require more detailed records.

> (Clarke 1998: 37)

Traditionally, the place for formal records has been the mark book with which teachers are issued each year. The conventional mark book reinforces the view that the main purpose of marking is to grade work. Its format – each page a grid of tiny squares – appears to be based on the assumption that record-keeping will take the form of digits and codes which can be inserted into confined spaces. Although many teachers still use mark books, others have dispensed with them in favour of more innovative approaches which better meet their needs, including electronic records.

The principle of 'fitness for purpose' is the key to devising an effective recording system. Vary the format of records as appropriate ensuring that entries are dated: ticklists for attendance and work satisfactorily completed, percentages for examination results, a written note of targets, special requirements and the key features of IEPs, a mark or level for attainment, a letter grade for effort and so on. When a record of personal details is kept in parallel with work and academic records, it provides a clear visual representation of the relationship between different aspects of performance; it may demonstrate a correlation between deteriorating rates of work completion and a decline in attendance or improved attainment levels may be traced back to improved effort grades.

6.5 Manageability

The benefits of record-keeping are easily undermined by systems which absorb inordinate amounts of time. Section 6.12 examines the potential of ICT to increase efficiency in record-keeping and reporting. Here, other ways of streamlining demands are considered.

One approach entails treating marked work as a marking record (Clarke 1998: 65; James 1998: 215) to eliminate duplication of effort at the recording stage. Marking and recording are typically treated as separate activities with one (marking pupils' work) leading to the other (the creation of marking records) whereas this approach conflates these processes so that marking serves a dual function, not only providing written feedback to pupils, but also providing a 'primary' (James 1998: 215) assessment record. As long as pupils' work (the primary record) is retained for the duration of the course, the teacher's record-keeping can be reduced. James (1998) suggests that it could be confined to ticklists for work completed and periodic, summative reviews of progress completed perhaps once a term or at the end of a unit of work.

Alternatively, some of the responsibility for record-keeping can be transferred to pupils. For instance, pupils could keep track of their progress on record cards or at the back/front of folders/exercise books. Pupils could also take charge of a portable target-setting record, attaching it to current work to remind themselves and their teacher of what their focus should be. This could take the form of a detachable card, Post-it® note or bookmark. Pupil-maintained records are, of course, natural complements to self-assessment (Chapter 3).

Task 6.3

Consider the importance of efficiency in record-keeping.

What are the advantages and disadvantages of using pupils' work as primary assessment records?

To what extent should teachers be prepared to share record-keeping responsibilities with pupils?

6.6 The National Record of Achievement and the Progress File

At the time of writing, trials are in progress to replace the National Record of Achievements (NRA) with the Progress File (PF) although DfEE will continue to make the NRA available to pupils in their final year of schooling until at least 2001. The NRA's short life span (1991–) is due to its limited success in schools and poor take-up by employers. In many schools, there has been a failure to integrate NRA with related processes such as progress reviews and career and personal development planning. Consequently, production of NRA has become an additional burden, completed hastily in Year 11, rather than the culmination of processes which have been going on throughout pupils' school careers. Very few pupils continue to use NRA after they have left school because employers who have their own training schemes have shown little interest in it. The Dearing (1996) *Review of Qualifications for 16–19 Year Olds* recommended that NRA should be restructured and relaunched under a new name.

There has been an attempt to learn from the failings of NRA so that similar weaknesses do not re-emerge in its successor. The move to PF represents a shift in emphasis, away from production of a glossy artefact for presentation to others (for example potential employers) and on to the processes which support personal and career development. PF is a package of interactive materials designed to support the processes of reviewing and recording achievements, decision-making, setting targets and planning career and personal development. It is essentially a tool designed to assist in managing own learning and making transitions between education, work and training. It is intended to support the development of generic, transferable skills, especially the key skills that are an essential feature of government's current educational policy.

PF is being launched via a series of regionally coordinated demonstration projects, one in each of the ten government regions in England. The aim is to develop and evaluate PF over the three-year life span of the projects (1999–2002). Therefore, it may be subject to revision following the demonstration phase. Each project is managed by a coordinator who is working to establish PF in colleges, training organizations and workplaces as well as in local schools. Each institution that is developing PF has an internal coordinator and local and national evaluations of the projects are being undertaken.

Pupils are introduced to PF in Year 9 to coincide with the selection of GCSE options, although from the outset they are encouraged to see education, training, personal and career development as lifelong processes for which they have personal responsibility. Teachers are most likely to become involved with it through work as form tutors and through personal, social and health education (PSHE) programmes. However, some local projects have recognized the importance of securing a place for PF in subject teaching as well. The importance of integrating PF into schools' existing systems for personal and academic progress reviews and action planning is being emphasized.

It remains to be seen whether PF can overcome the difficulties which caused the NRA to falter but progress reports in the project's magazine, ONFILE, suggest an encouraging response from the growing number of organizations that are adopting PF. For up-to-date information, consult the NRA (http://www.dfee.gov.uk/nra/index.htm) and PF (http://www.dfee.gov.uk/progfile/index.htm) websites.

6.7 Reporting to parents: statutory requirements

Each year, schools must issue a written report to parents on their child's achievements during that year. However, the annual report is a statutory minimum which many schools exceed by issuing reports on a half yearly or termly basis. Sometimes these additional reports take the form of interim progress reviews that are less full than the annual version, which must include the following information for Years 7, 8 and 9:

- a comment on progress in each subject and activity studied which highlights pupils' strengths and development needs
- a comment on general progress
- the pupil's attendance record
- arrangements for discussing the report with a teacher.

Schools have discretion over other aspects of report writing such as format and methods of describing progress. However, they are required to provide NC levels only at the end of KS3 when basic requirements are augmented to include the following statutory assessment results and norm-referenced data:

- pupils' levels for TA (mathematics, English, science, design and technology, geography, history, ICT, MFL, art and design, music and PE)
- pupils' levels for national tests (mathematics, English and science)
- a statement that levels have been arrived at by statutory assessment
- a statement where assessment regulations have been disapplied

- comparative whole-school data showing the percentage of pupils in each subject at each level for TA and tests
- a comment indicating what results show about a pupil's progress in each subject and in relation to the year group, drawing attention to individual strengths and weaknesses
- the previous year's national results in English, mathematics and science showing the percentage of pupils at each level in TA and test results.

Although RE is not part of the NC, it is a compulsory subject and must be reported to parents. From August 2002, citizenship joins the list of subjects on which schools must report to parents for pupils in Years 7, 8 and 9. Reports used in the annual review of pupils with statements of SEN may serve as the annual report to parents if a school wishes but they must contain the minimum information required by reporting regulations if they are to serve this dual purpose. There are no requirements associated with timing so most schools stage report writing to distribute the workload across a year and to coincide with key events in a child's education such as completing the first term in a new school or selecting GCSE options.

The intention behind end-of-KS requirements is to provide parents with a rounded picture which places their child against criterion-referenced, norm-referenced and ipsative-referenced data (that is against NC standards, standards within the school and nationally, and standards formerly achieved by the child). However, there is a danger that parents may be overwhelmed by the volume of data thus defeating the aim of keeping them well informed. Schools, therefore, have an important role in making the information accessible to parents.

6.8 Obstacles to effective communication with parents

The importance of clear communication has already been emphasized and nowhere is this more important than in reporting to parents. Keeping pace with the rate of educational change may be a daunting task for parents and the education their child receives may appear very different from the one they remember from their own school days. Reports, in particular, may have changed substantially. Nowadays most reporting systems are based on a loose leaf format with a page devoted to each subject plus a covering sheet for form tutors and/or pastoral heads/ headteachers to comment (see Figure 6.1). Pupils themselves usually play a part either through self-reporting or through an opportunity to respond to teachers' remarks. As well as making summative statements on progress, there is an emphasis on formative commentary, with reports treated as opportunities for diagnosis and target-setting. Activities and achievements beyond the scope of the curriculum are acknowledged. Parents are sometimes encouraged to record their responses in spaces provided for parental

Langley School

		ALWAYS	USUALLY	SOMETIMES	RARELY
SUBJECT: SCIENCE Name .... Form					
LEARNING	Can focus and concentrate in lessons.				
	Understands what needs to be done to progress.				
	Responds positively to advice.				
	Homework is done thoroughly.				
	Meets deadlines.				
WORKING WITH OTHERS	Co-operates with other pupils and adults.				
	Demonstrates reliability and responsibility within a group.				
	Demonstrates effective leadership skills within a group.				
DECISION MAKING	Understands and identifies the nature of the task.				
	Follows a set procedure to solve the problem.				
	Finds solutions to problems independently.				
	Responds imaginatively and creatively.				
ICT	Uses software effectively.				
	Uses ICT to present information appropriately.				
	Integrates ICT into experiments when required.				
COMMUNICATION	Makes oral contribution relevant to the audience situation.				
	Written content is relevant and presented clearly and accurately.				
	Reads with understanding and extracts relevant information.				
	Can use diagrams, graphs and number effectively.				

		ALWAYS	USUALLY	SOMETIMES	RARELY
SUBJECT STATEMENTS	Coursework deadlines are met.				
	Plans fair tests and identifies key factors.				
	Performs practical work safely / recognises hazards.				
	Makes accurate measurements and observations.				
	Represents results and observations in appropriate ways.				
	Explanations include detailed knowledge and understanding.				
	Considers whether evidence collected, or being considered, is sufficient or reliable to enable conclusions to be made.				
	Uses chemical symbols / formulae / equations.				
	Recalls / applies a wide range of information in – Biology				
	Chemistry				
	Physics				

COMMENTS & TARGETS	
	Estimated Grade based on current performance:
STAFF SIGNATURE:	DATE:

feedback on carbonized copies of the original report. Overall, reporting has become a more interactive process.

In contrast, traditional reports (mid- to late twentieth century) looked very different. A report was usually a single page of A4 on which figures

Langley School

SUBJECT: PASTORAL REPORT		
Name .... Form		
ATTENDANCE	**PUNCTUALITY**	**UNAUTHORISED ABSENCES**
........%	....	....
APPEARANCE	*Has difficulty in co-operating with school standards.* *Usually conforms to school standards.* *Conforms to school standards.* *Always smartly dressed in school uniform.*	
PERSONAL ORGANISATION	*Often needs support.* *Acceptable. Usually has correct equipment.* *Well-organised and has the required equipment.*	
RELATIONSHIPS WITH PEERS	*Needs encouragement to form relationships.* *Works well with others in self-chosen groups.* *Forms good relationships with other students.*	
RELATIONSHIPS WITH ADULTS	*Needs guidance in dealing with adults.* *Is gaining confidence in dealing with adults.* *Has established good relationships with adults.*	
PASTORAL ACTIVITIES	*Needs encouragement to work effectively.* *Usually works well and takes part in activities.* *Plays a full and constructive part in all activities.*	
EXTRA CURRICULAR ACTIVITIES & SERVICE TO THE SCHOOL:		
TUTOR COMMENT:		
PARENTAL COMMENT & SIGNATURE		
FORM TUTOR:	HEAD OF YEAR	HEADTEACHER
DATE:		

Figure 6.1 Examples of reporting format used by Langley School, Solihull

featured prominently. Reports gave prominence to 'measures' of performance – examination percentages, marks for coursework, position in the class rank order and so on. There was usually limited space for subject teachers to add cursory comments. Reports were essentially

Geography	Satisfactory progress.	Exam: 62% Position: 6/28
Chemistry	Valerie must try harder in this subject	39% 21/28

Figure 6.2 Extract from a report from the 1970s

summative documents which placed heavy emphasis on norm-referenced judgements. This normative information often revealed little about what children could and could not do, specific strengths, weaknesses and needs as Figure 6.2 shows. This style of reporting had not disappeared by the 1990s although it was unusual by then (Ofsted 1995).

Nowadays, reports strive to do much more than this but the complexity and lack of internal consistency in the NC represent obstacles to clear, concise communication. For instance, parents are given information in the form of *numerical* levels culminating in a *statement* of 'exceptional performance'. There are also technical terms and concepts to master, for example 'key stages', 'levels', 'attainment targets' and 'disapplications'. If they are not careful, schools can compound the difficulties, further complicating an inherently complex system. For instance, James (1998) found:

> evidence that many parents were receiving reports on subjects that included information in a confusing mix of reporting modes: National Curriculum levels for statutory tests and TA, predicted GCSE grades, percentages for internal examination results, letter grades for effort, rating scales for other aspects, and narratives and commentary from teachers and students. Moreover, within schools there was little evidence of consistency across subjects.
>
> (James 1998: 61)

The following example illustrates the potential for confusion which can be packed into even the briefest statement:

> Mathematics: NC level 5; attainment grade A.
> History: NC level 3; attainment grade A.
> (Y7 report queried at parents' evening)
>
> (Ofsted 1995: 7)

There is much here to baffle the uninitiated and expert alike! There is the use of acronyms (NC) and the technical concept of levels (what is a level and is 3 higher or lower than 5?) The report combines an internal system of lettered attainment grades with the numerical levels of the NC. What is the relationship between NC levels and attainment grades and why, when the attainment grades are the same, are the NC awards two levels apart? As James (1998: 62) warns: 'the parts will not be understood unless there is some attention to the whole'.

6.9 What kind of feedback do parents value?

There is evidence about the kind of information which parents value: 'parents have a strong desire for accurate and up-to-date information about how their children are getting on . . . In particular, they want to know about their children's strengths and weaknesses so they can provide help where necessary at home' (Hughes, *et al.* 1994, quoted in Headington 2000: 65). Parents, therefore, require a clear, informative account of how their child has progressed since the last report was written. Locating their child's performance within the class and year group is, for many parents, an essential component of a complete picture of how well the child is doing. Therefore, they value the type of normative information which is a statutory requirement at the end of KS3 although they would prefer to receive it more regularly. Parents also want an indication of potential so that they can help their child realize this. The Autumn Package of Pupil Performance Information (DfEE 1999: 41) advises schools to use graphs from Section 1C of the package to help with the identification of realistic but challenging targets (Section 7.6) and target grades for GCSE should be reported in Year 10. Targets are also set for NC levels to be achieved at the end of KS3.

Although academic learning is important to parents so too is personal and social development. Parents want to feel that their child is known and valued as an individual and reports should, therefore, be personalized to convey this. Some parents dislike computer-generated reports which rely on items selected from statement banks (Section 6.12) for this reason. Outside the formal reporting framework, personal approaches to parents pay dividends out of all proportion to the effort involved in making them when schools take the trouble to contact parents by letter or telephone to acknowledge something like a child's contribution to the life of a school. Most parents expect this kind of personal contact only when there has been a problem and are very grateful when personal achievements or contributions are acknowledged.

6.10 Some principles for good practice

6.10a Using plain English

Although some parents are familiar with the education system, it is safer to assume a lay audience. Therefore, reports need to be couched in unambiguous, jargon-free language. Where technical terms and concepts are unavoidable, they need to be explained. Any internal grading system, and its relationship to NC assessments, also needs to be clarified. Teachers sometimes adopt linguistic strategies aimed at softening criticism. They may use a convoluted or roundabout way of saying something or they may choose obscure terms and phrases instead of straightforward language. For instance, Ofsted (1995: 7) points out that: 'Uzma who can "concentrate for short periods of time" presumably cannot concentrate for very long but parents had not realized that a problem was being identified'. Because such tactics are as likely to conceal true meaning as they are to cushion the blow, these practices are self-defeating. A report should provide an accurate account of strengths and developmental needs in explicit language.

6.10b Providing a balanced appraisal of strengths and weaknesses

A recurring theme in this book is teachers' avoidance of 'negative' feedback such as a reluctance to reject or correct wrong answers to questions or to press pupils to improve partial ones (Chapter 3) and a preference for praising pupils for the effort they have put into work without drawing attention to how it might be improved (Chapter 4). There is clearly an assessment dilemma at the heart of teachers' work. Conscious of the ease with which fragile adolescent egos may be crushed, they are anxious to avoid anything which could undermine pupils' self-esteem and motivation. Criticism, even constructive criticism, is something they prefer to avoid. This same trait is apparent in report writing: 'Teachers feel uncomfortable in giving negative messages, albeit constructively, in writing; they find it even more difficult to do this in discussion with parents' (Ofsted 1995: 3). This difficulty has been compounded in report writing by mistaken beliefs about good practice. Many policies examined by Ofsted (1995) stated that reports should be positive and one assessment coordinator observed: 'A lot of our staff seem to think they are going against good practice if they mention weaknesses' (Ofsted 1995: 21). It is, unsurprising, therefore, that a key finding of the survey was that: 'Many reports are unduly positive and fail to make constructive criticism. Such reports give the impression that attainment is much better than it is' (Ofsted 1995: 2). It pointed out that: 'Pupils are not well-supported in developing skills of self-evaluation where teachers fail to report frank judgements about the quality of work' (Ofsted 1995: 6). Although statutory requirements have been introduced to combat this reluctance, recent inspections continue to identify this as a 'major weakness' (Ofsted 1998a: 73) underlining the persistence of the problem. Ofsted (1995: 6), nevertheless, acknowledged that a 'minority of teachers in all key stages manage to reconcile candour with supportive and sensitive reporting'.

A constructive report achieves a well-judged balance by setting weaknesses and difficulties against strengths and achievements without dwelling unduly on either. An emphasis on indicating the way forward gives a positive tone even to comments which draw attention to weaknesses. Most pupils *do* want to improve and deserve an honest appraisal of what they are doing wrong. As long as the emphasis is on suggesting strategies to improve performance and setting realistic targets, attention to weaknesses need not undermine motivation. Reports should also acknowledge pupils' contributions to wider aspects of school life (social and cultural), if they are to be regarded as fair and constructive.

6.10c Consistency in style and format

The issue of where to enforce a consistent, whole-school approach to MARRA is unresolved in many schools (Section 5.4). Approaches to reporting provide a case in point. Indeed, Ofsted (1995: 21) encountered a 'bewildering' range of reporting styles when it surveyed practices. Given that the end user is a lay person who will receive information from several departments, there is a strong case for schools to standardize reporting procedures. Ofsted (1998a: 73) confirms that this enhances accessibility.

6.10d Due attention to learning

A recurring criticism of ineffectual reporting is its preoccupation with behaviour, attitude and effort coupled with a neglect of academic progress and attainment. Just as feedback to pupils needs to focus firmly on knowledge, skills and concepts, reports to parents need to strike a balance between attention to learning and comments on other attributes.

6.10e Involving pupils

Although most schools involve pupils in report writing, requiring them to write a general comment often results in trite, superficial remarks which add little of substance to the reporting process. It is tempting to conclude that report writing is beyond the capabilities of the average adolescent but it may be that the task they are set encourages vagueness. When pupils are asked to provide subject-specific comments, the sharper focus enhances the quality of their contribution.

6.10f Achieving reliability

Reports should be as objective and reliable as possible. Ensure that comments are evidence based by consulting records and pupils' work rather than relying on impressions – which may or may not be accurate and unbiased!

6.11 Meetings with parents

So far, this book has presented the education of a child as a two-way partnership involving teachers and pupils. However, the potential for parents to support their children's education is best realized when parents are recognized as the third stakeholder in a three-way partnership. Recognizing parents as equal stakeholders has implications for the way they are treated during meetings.

Parental consultations are a disconcerting experience for many new teachers, requiring them to step outside their conventional role, which involves dealing with children and other professionals, to engage with an unfamiliar 'client group'. Unsure of the demands of this role, many resort to a traditional model of professional conduct. Elliott (1991: 311–12) has identified two models of professionalism based on studies of how various professional groups engage with their clients: 'the infallible expert' and 'the reflective practitioner'. Infallible experts:

- Expect clients to defer to their superior knowledge and wisdom in identifying, clarifying and resolving their problems.
- Engage in one-way communication. They tell and prescribe while the client listens and obeys. The client is allowed to ask questions from a position of deference but not to 'question' from a presumption of knowledge. There is little reciprocity in communication because the 'expert' is not concerned with developing a holistic view of the client's situation.

In contrast, reflective practitioners recognize the importance of:

- Collaboration with clients . . . in identifying, clarifying and resolving their problems.
- The importance of communication and empathy with clients as a means of understanding situations from their point of view.

New teachers often instinctively adopt the persona of infallible expert in consultations with parents. However, the role of reflective practitioner is usually more productive because pupils spend more time away from school than they do in it and a good deal of that time is spent with parents. Pupils sometimes behave quite differently in different contexts and they may be less guarded with their parents, revealing more to them than they do to teachers. Therefore, if teachers proceed on the tacit assumption that meetings with parents should be teacher-dominated occasions in which one-way communication enables them to deliver expert guidance to parents, they lose a valuable opportunity for a two-way exchange of insights and information about a child. Teachers can learn a great deal from parents if they are prepared to listen carefully as well as sharing their own views. By working in concert, parents and teachers can become a powerful force in helping children to improve. Therefore, parents should be involved in problem-solving and decision-making and not simply in giving or receiving information about their child. For instance, an action plan might be negotiated giving both parties a clear idea of how their concerted efforts will help the child to progress.

If you find the prospect of parents' meetings daunting, remember that they are formidable occasions for many parents too (Askew 2000).

Recognizing this, the DfEE has devoted an area of its parents' website (www.parents.dfee.gov.uk) to guidance on getting the best out of meetings. Diffident parents may need to be put at their ease if they are to participate. Although some parents assume the role of deferential client, listening respectfully, not all do. Some parents come armed with their own agenda and if teachers attempt to conduct meetings using a professional agenda, the outcome can be a clash of wills and expectations. It is, therefore, sensible to open a meeting by explaining the items you plan to cover during the consultation and checking whether this meets parents' requirements. If not, it may be easy to adapt your agenda at that stage so that it satisfies both parties. If it is inappropriate to discuss parents' concerns during the meeting, or time will not allow, it is always possible to offer a follow-up appointment or telephone call.

This meeting may be the only opportunity for face-to-face contact during the year and time should not be wasted figuring out what you want to say! Therefore, meetings need planning and preparation. Decide the key points you wish to discuss in advance and select the evidence which best illustrates them. It is sensible to have your records, a copy of the most recent report and samples of pupils' work available for examination. Attempting to discuss pupils' work without reference to examples makes the discussion abstract, and your meaning may be misconstrued, whereas work samples provide concrete illustrations. It is also sensible to go over the latest report beforehand because parents sometimes question the contents. Here again, pupils' work and records provide a focus for discussion, enabling parents to ask more probing questions than is possible when the exchange is conducted in an evidential vacuum. Creating the correct impression with parents may guarantee you a powerful ally in any future difficulties with the child!

If the notion of education as a triangulated partnership is accepted, it becomes inappropriate to exclude pupils from meetings. Pupils do attend parents' meetings at some schools and occasionally they are drawn into the reporting process to good effect. For instance, if pupils are involved in self-assessment, it makes sense for them to take responsibility for selecting work to illustrate their progress and needs. They can then take their parents through selected pieces, supported by their teacher. Action planning also works well when all three have been party to decisions so that children feel some ownership of the agreement but know they have the support of adults in overcoming their difficulties. Targets may have been negotiated with teachers in advance but these can be explained to parents during the meeting and this may lead to supporting targets being set between the child and parent for pursuit at home. 'Slippery' characters can also be tied down to definite undertakings such as meeting homework deadlines. Action planning and target-setting often work best when they are formalized, with a written record of who will do what with dates for review specified. Some schools use planning diaries for this purpose. In some schools, the timetable is suspended to provide an extended period of time for consultations. Just as the most effective assessment has a feedforward dimension, meeting parents should not be seen as an end in itself but as a way of stimulating change.

6.12 Using IT

Schools have been described as 'drowning in performance data. The problem is not storing it but making sense of it' (Haigh 1999: 46). This is an area where the data-handling capabilities of IT are becoming indispensable. IT is superior to paper-based systems in terms of the speed and efficiency with which data may be collected, stored, manipulated and retrieved. These attributes make it useful for monitoring, recording and reporting and a number of commercial organizations have exploited the potential of IT to assist schools with these aspects of their work. Commonly used management software packages which have assessment modules include Schools Information Management System (SIMS) (www.capitaes.co.uk), RM Management Solutions (www.rm.com) and Bromcom (www.bromcom.com). However, as the case study below shows, IT is a tool which has more far-reaching implications than gains in speed and efficiency of data handling.

Stoke Park

Stoke Park, an 11–18 Coventry school with community technology college status, was commended by the DfEE in a Busting Bureaucracy competition. It started to explore the potential of IT to make assessment data more accessible and intelligible in 1997. The school was already a 'data rich' environment but it did not always make most effective use of information because its paper-based systems lacked the data-handling capabilities of an electronic system. It wanted to be able to provide form tutors and subject departments with an overview of pupils' progress and to make this information readily accessible. Over a three-year period, Stoke Park used SIMS Assessment Manager to create a school-wide system which gives all staff access to regularly updated information on all pupils. However, information is not treated as an end in itself; its aim is to prompt action by raising issues associated with learning and raising achievement. The whole school now works to an agreed assessment profile at all key stages which is used to monitor individuals' progress on a termly basis. At KS3, attainment is rated using an A–E scale and Behaviour, Effort, Homework and Kit (where applicable) are rated 1–6. Pupils' scores for the previous term are shown in parentheses alongside current scores. This historical dimension to the records makes it possible for pupils, staff and parents to judge whether a child's performance is consistent, improving or regressing (Figure 6.3). As well as

Figure 6.3 Example of a pupil's performance profile on an interim progress review

STOKE **park**

Tutor Group: 09G

KS3 MARCH INTERIM REPORT

Name:

(Figures in brackets are marks from November Interim Report)

	Attainment	Effort	Behaviour	Homework
English	B (B)	5 (5)	5 (5)	6 ()
Mathematics	C (C)	3 (3)	4 (3)	5 (5)
Science	C (B)	3 (4)	4 (5)	4 (3)
Technology	C (B)	4 (4)	4 (4)	5 (5)
Geography	A (A)	5 (5)	5 (5)	6 (6)
History	B (B)	4 (4)	6 (6)	6 (6)
Religious Education	B (B)	5 (5)	5 (5)	5 (5)
French	D (B)	3 (5)	3 (6)	2 (5)
Art	C (C)	2 (3)	3 (4)	4 (4)
Music	C (B)	3 (4)	3 (4)	N/A
Drama	B (B)	5 (5)	5 (5)	N/A
Physical Education	B (C)	4 (4)	5 (5)	Kit: 6 (6)
Total		46 (51)	52 (57)	49 (51)

Attendance from 04.09.00 - 16.03.01

Percentage attendance: **94.02%**   Unauthorised absences: **0** centrally held records, there are satellite stations around the school so that each department and year team can enter its own data and view that of others. Different staff utilize the data for their own purposes. For instance, middle and senior managers can examine trends at whole-school and departmental level by plotting pupil performance against variables such as race, gender, subject and so on. In contrast, individual teachers may be interested to know whether pupils' performance profiles in their subject are consistent with profiles in other subjects.

IT is a tool which needs to be used flexibly and Stoke Park teachers decided that a more complex assessment profile was needed at KS4 to reflect the demands of GCSE courses. In Years 10 and 11, therefore, pupils are monitored for personal organization, use of class time, coursework on target, estimated grade and target grade. Again, it is possible for all staff to interrogate KS4 data.

Once information has been installed on the database, it can serve other purposes with minimal additional effort. For instance, Stoke Park uses it to produce information packs for subject staff and form tutors at the beginning of each year. The contents are negotiable according to what staff want to know but tend to include things like the last NC level in a subject and most recent effort review mark. Thus, new teachers are able to pitch work and expectations appropriately from the outset.

Research suggests that although parents appreciate the effort which teachers put into reporting, they would nevertheless like to receive more frequent reports. This is unlikely to be feasible in schools using paper-based systems because the workload associated with reporting is already hefty. Ofsted (1995) found that teachers at all KSs were spending between 30 and 100 hours per year on report-related activities. However, at Stoke Park the termly progress review has made more frequent reports possible because the same information can be used to generate interim reports to parents with minimal additional effort. Parents are pleased with this innovation because it conveys key information to them in a concise, consistent manner: 'The interesting thing is the way Stoke Park teachers used Assessment Manager to create a tool of clarity and simplicity that was accessible and intelligible to staff, pupils and parents' (Haigh 2000: 71). Online records mean that, technically, the school is capable of reporting progress 24 hours a day, 365 days of the year. Previously, when a concerned parent contacted the school about their child's progress, there was a delay while a round robin was circulated to relevant staff but now records of current progress, plus a recent history, can be called up on screen at a moment's notice.

The school also uses IT to produce its annual written report to parents. Subject reports, which specify attainment and targets for development, are compiled by selecting statements from computer-generated item banks. It is, however, possible to differentiate statements to reflect individual differences. The KS3 orders express reservations about this approach, noting that parents are unhappy when it leads to reports becoming impersonal (QCA 1999: 61). Ofsted (1995: 34) was similarly guarded, noting the 'indifferent quality' of some computer-generated reports which were characterized by weaknesses in fluency, bland, unhelpful generalizations and/or inaccessible jargon. However, it acknowledged that good software which allows reports of 'outstanding quality' (1995: 34) to be produced is available. Jane Freshwater, Deputy Head at Stoke Park, insists that schools need to think carefully about their statement banks, refining and adding to them on a regular basis if they are to avoid these pitfalls. Teachers at Stoke Park have been freed to focus on this task by the employment of an assessment clerk who administers the reporting system, collecting data from satellite stations, checking it for omissions and inaccuracies, printing and collating reports. Teachers, relieved of clerical aspects of report production, are able to focus on improving the quality of their statement banks.

Using IT has had unforeseen consequences for the way the school works, according to Jane Freshwater. For instance, access to comparative information stimulated increased dialogue between tutors and pupils about progress and attainment – just one sign that the system was prompting action around the school which might not have happened otherwise. The school responded by introducing periods of whole-school review during which the timetable is collapsed so that pupils can discuss progress with tutors and negotiate targets. The school has rethought its attitudes to assessment and IT has been instrumental in this change. The introduction of three key assessment points during the year has tightened up the school's assessment calendar resulting in a clearer definition of roles and responsibilities. The school now has a clear specification of who needs to know what and who needs to take action when. The school has also been able to augment the role of middle managers. Key stage coordinators are now required to analyse performance data and decide on action to meet issues arising from their findings. They meet regularly to scrutinize performance data and share ideas, concerns and solutions to problems.

Jane Freshwater has been struck by the fact that although conventional wisdom suggests that it is important to get the philosophy right and then find a system to fit it, Stoke Park's experience of experimenting with the capacity of software has produced many benefits some of which were unforeseen:

- Developing the system has been valuable for focusing teachers on fundamental issues, obliging them to think hard about what it is essential to assess at different KSs.
- Information is instantly accessible to anyone who might need it; trends in performance are identified promptly and corrective action can be taken.
- It has been possible to enhance the roles of various staff – pastoral (form tutors and year heads) and academic (key stage coordinators) – who have become more proactive in managing pupils' learning.

- The same information is used to generate termly reports to parents but with no extra commitment of teaching staff's time.
- Although the initial investment of time was considerable because systems needed to be installed and staff needed training, there have been longer term gains in efficiency and a reduction in teachers' administrative loads. Time taken by the mechanical aspects of recording and reporting has been reduced.
- Because teachers no longer maintain time-consuming paper systems, their energies can be properly channelled into challenging professional issues such as identifying and addressing causes of underachievement. More time is spent with pupils and there is an increased emphasis on raising attainment.
- The school has a more comprehensive picture of categories of pupil need so that it can plan its learning programmes accordingly, quickly guiding pupils into relevant programmes.

Part 3 | Assessment: the wider context

Assessment, accountability and standards

7.1 Introduction

This chapter considers assessment in relation to educational standards and the responsibilities of different stakeholders for their achievement.

Objectives

By the end of this chapter, you should have developed your understanding of two key ideas:

- processes which take place at departmental and school level are also relevant for individual teachers
- this influences the types of information teachers seek, the records they retain and data analysis and target-setting at classroom level.

In the mid-1990s a 'new role for assessment' (Stobart and Gipps 1997: 24) emerged. It entails using assessment data to manage the performance of pupils, teachers, schools and LEAs. It is 'currently the most public use of assessment' (Stobart and Gipps 1997: 24) because individual performances are evaluated against internal, local and national data so that targets for improvement may be set and published. This monitoring and comparing of performances takes place within a target-setting hierarchy. Requirements at each level are influenced by, and influence, those at adjacent levels but all are subject to national targets, determined by government, which permeate the system:

- The government sets national targets and monitors standards achieved by LEAs and schools which are required to contribute to the attainment of national targets.
- LEAs monitor achievement at local level, negotiating performance targets with schools which will enable the LEAs to meet targets set for them by government.

- A school's SMT analyses the performance of departments, teachers and pupils and compares them with trends in local and national data. Priorities for development are thereby identified and converted into clear, measurable targets. The school's development plan is modified to allow targets to be achieved.
- Heads of department collect information about performance in their subject and set it against performance throughout the school and standards within the subject locally and nationally. Departmental action plans, aimed at raising performance within subjects, contribute to the achievement of whole-school targets.
- Teachers compare the progress of groups and individuals for whom they are responsible with parallel school and external data to determine group and individual targets.
- Pupils are encouraged to engage with processes of self-review and target-setting, viewing their performance in the light of data which show the difference between their predicted and potential results.

Although this interconnecting chain of accountability involves different stakeholders operating at various levels, it all hinges on changes being made in the way that teachers teach and pupils learn. Thus, although the learning targets negotiated by teachers and pupils occupy the lowest echelons in this target-setting hierarchy, the efficacy of the entire structure rests upon them. Therefore, individual learning targets, developed as part of a formative assessment regime (Section 3.7), are the cornerstone of the current school improvement movement.

Regardless of the level at which it takes place, the essential components of this school improvement system are the same:

- the data-handling capacity of IT is used to build databases that allow performance to be anatomized; users interrogate the data to achieve a better understanding of the components of performance (for example prior attainment, social class, gender and race) and how they interact with one another
- information is set against relevant data sets (for example parallel classes, comparable schools locally and nationally) to highlight strengths and weaknesses in performance
- existing data are used to generate performance profiles which allow users to project forward and specify *predicted* and *potential* performance by the end of the phase for any new cohort (for example Year 7's likely NC test levels at the end of KS3 based on input/output data for previous cohorts) or subgroup (for example boys or ethnic minority pupils)
- information is gathered about the prior/current attainment of any new cohort to establish a baseline which will be used to measure progress during the current phase (for example the year or KS)
- an emphasis is placed on setting *challenging* targets which aim to take performance (for example of a school, LEA, teacher or pupil) beyond projected to potential outcome (for example a teacher could use the

GCSE results of previous cohorts to help Year 10 pupils to recognize what they are likely to achieve at the end of Year 11 based on their performance at KS3 and what they could achieve by adopting personally challenging targets)

- progress is monitored regularly to ensure that the pupil/teacher/ department/school is on track to achieve its targets
- underachievers are identified and become the subject of close monitoring and action plans aimed at boosting progress
- final results are used to refresh the database
- an end-of-phase review provides the starting point for the next phase of target-setting and development planning.

Since 2001 schools have also been required to set targets for the percentage of pupils achieving level 5+ in English, mathematics and science, at the end of KS3.

This approach entails establishing performance norms and setting individual performances against them. In this sense, it is norm-referenced. The research to which this book refers condemns norm-referencing, especially the pernicious effects of encouraging pupils to compare themselves with one another. This raises the question: will norm-referencing prove to be a fundamental weakness in this school improvement initiative? There may, however, be an important difference in the *purpose* of norm-referencing here. Traditionally, it has been used for ranking purposes to aid sifting, selection and certification. For instance the rank order established by the 11-plus test enables grammar and secondary modern school places to be allocated. It allows grade boundaries to be fixed in public examinations, pupils' positions within a class to be determined and so on. In school improvement, however, norm-referenced data are used to set individually challenging attainment targets. In this way, norm-referencing may be said to serve ipsative purposes which may temper some of its negative potential. Furthermore, since target-setting requires users to think SMART (Section 3.7) targets are likely to be criterion-referenced, that is related to precise criteria for reaching a higher level in NC, GCSE, A level or GNVQ. Thus, school improvement requires a complex amalgam of approaches. Nevertheless, the deleterious effects of norm-referencing are largely due to its use in high stakes activities and school improvement is undoubtedly a high stakes activity. Because this approach is new, its longer term impact on the system as a whole, and on individual components of the system, can only be determined with the passage of time. However, experts are already questioning the sustainability of the current approach to raising educational standards (for example Black 1998: 146; James 2000: 361).

The measurement of performance requires the use of appropriate PIs. Wilcox (1992) notes that:

> PIs are frequently derived from an *input-process-output* model of organisations. Such a model may be very appropriate to describe the

functioning of factories, where inputs are the raw materials which are transformed by successive processes into outputs or products. Each of these three phases can be unambiguously identified and the conversion of raw materials into products confidently controlled.

(Wilcox 1992: 67)

This business model applies less neatly in schools where the raw materials are unstable and unpredictable and final products are less amenable to control. Nevertheless, it is the model which has been adopted for use in schools where targets focus on processes and outputs and where measurements of progress are made by relating inputs to outputs. In a school context, pupils, staffing and financial resources are among the relevant *inputs*. Related indicators might include pupil ability as measured by NC and commercially produced tests, staff–pupil ratios, proportion of pupils registered with SEN, proportion of pupils known to be eligible for FSM and so on. *Processes* include school policies and procedures, the curricular and extracurricular activities offered as well as a school's style of management. Related indicators might focus on teacher behaviours or the proportion of time devoted to different activities. *Outputs* are the results and achievements of a school, the most widely used indicator being test and examination results. Other possible indicators, which relate to pupil outcomes rather than schooling processes, include measures of unauthorized absence, rates of staying on into the sixth form, pupil destinations at 18-plus and rates of involvement in extracurricular activities.

The following sections explain the statutory framework for these activities in more detail. First, though, it is helpful to know something of the political agenda that has shaped this new role for assessment.

7.2 The recent political context

Successive governments have seen educational assessment – especially summative tests and examinations – as the key to raising measured standards of attainment in schools. This quest has been fuelled by international comparability studies that have presented the UK in an unflattering light in some areas when the achievements of its pupils are set against those of countries which are its economic competitors. The Conservative government (1979–97) introduced a programme of educational reform designed to raise standards in state-run schools and centralize control of education. This culminated in the introduction of a National Curriculum (1989) specifying what should be taught at each KS in maintained schools. The NC was complemented by a programme of testing every child in mainstream education (except those for whom tests had been disapplied) at ages 7, 11 and 14 to check what had been learnt. However, even before the Conservatives embarked on this ambitious reform programme, moves to make schools more accountable for educational standards were already afoot.

Many commentators (for example Gann 1999; Shorrocks-Taylor 1999) trace this curbing of the professional autonomy of teachers to a speech made in 1976 by the Labour Prime Minister, James Callaghan. Callaghan launched a 'Great Debate', calling for schools to become more accountable to the communities they served and for the debate about quality in education to be opened to those who were not professionally involved. This Ruskin College speech is often seen as a watershed in public attitudes to – and expectations of – schooling. It was made at a time when there were few constraints on what teachers taught and few checks on the standards achieved in schools. When a Conservative government replaced the Labour administration in 1979, it acted quickly passing the 1980 Education Act which required all secondary schools to publish their results in examinations at 16-plus and 18-plus. This represented an important step in making schools more publicly accountable for the quality of their work as measured by examination successes. This was followed, a decade later (1992–), by the publication of national performance tables showing, among other things, the percentage of pupils gaining five GCSE grades A–C and A–G by LEA and by school. These were dubbed 'school league tables', largely due to the media's use of the information to rank schools according to the percentage of their pupils achieving five GCSEs at grades A–C.

Some educationalists responded, arguing that it was unfair and misleading to rank schools on the basis of raw results in examinations. Some research has suggested that as much as 92 per cent of the variation in pupil performance could be attributed to the socio-economic background of a school's intake (Gann 1999: 30). While other studies have produced less dramatic results (for example Saunders 1998), they confirm that background levels of poverty and social disadvantage are key factors in poor performance. Therefore, little could be learnt by drawing direct comparisons between the results of selective independent schools and inner city comprehensives no matter how close together these schools happened to be situated. What was needed, it was argued, was not a comparison of raw results but some method of measuring the improvement children made as a result of attending one school rather than another. Thus, the quest was launched to develop a simple means of measuring the 'value added' to a child's education by attending a school. At first, statisticians struggled to find a suitable technique for measuring value added – one which was powerful enough to adjust for the different variables known to affect achievement while producing results which were accessible to a non-specialist audience. Methods must not be so complicated that their use was limited to a small band of experts.

Throughout the 1980s and much of the 1990s, a crude combination of testing plus publication of results was meant to act as a lever for raising standards of attainment in schools. Simply naming and shaming schools that produced poor results was assumed to provide sufficient impetus for them to try harder and do better in the future even though results alone provide little guidance on what a school needs to do to improve. An influential development that has supported the quest to make a more sophisticated use of performance data is the school improvement movement. Although publication of results has not been abandoned, performance data are now treated as a tool in the service of school improvement. Now that national testing of pupils takes place at ages 5, 7, 11 and 14, alongside already established public examinations at 16-plus and 18-plus, and results are collected centrally by the national data collection agency, the UK generates more performance data than ever before. This mass of data about pupils' performances at different ages and in different subjects is capable of an enormous variety of statistical analyses and interpretations. Data can be manipulated to investigate topics as diverse as performance by subject, by age, by date of birth, by sex, by racial group, by socio-economic group, by prior attainment, by school, by school type and by LEA and these variables can be investigated separately or in combination. Simple procedures for estimating the value added to a child's education by attending a school have been introduced. Studies have also scrutinized the effects of Ofsted inspections on schools' performances in subsequent years. Coupled with the mass of performance information now available to schools, the focus of Ofsted inspections has shifted towards schools' self-evaluation of the quality of their own work (Ofsted 1998b). Schools need to be self-monitoring organizations, capable of identifying their own strengths and weaknesses and responding accordingly. Currently, schools devote a great deal of effort to generating internal data so that performance can be monitored and set against data provided by external agencies such as DfEE, QCA and Ofsted.

7.3 Target-setting: the national framework

The government sets national *foundation targets* for young people by the ages of 19 and 21. There are also national *lifetime targets* which focus on lifelong learning through further education, training and the workplace. An Ofsted (1996a) survey of target-setting found that a weakness of the prevailing system was its fragmentation across the various sectors of the educational service. Different stakeholders were not answerable to one another and might even be ignorant of national targets. Often, 'members of a school's senior management team were well aware of the Targets, but did not see them as being very relevant . . . Many classroom teachers were not even aware of them' (Ofsted 1996a: 35). It concluded that 'very few schools [were] either aware of or able to make maximum use of the [national] Targets' (Ofsted 1996a: 8). The Labour government which came to power in 1997 introduced legislation to strengthen the accountability of schools and LEAs for the achievement of national targets and to forge firm links between different echelons in the target-setting hierarchy. The Labour government's foundation targets for 2002 include the following:

- by age 19, 85 per cent of young people to achieve five GCSEs at grade C or above, an intermediate GNVQ or an NVQ level 2
- by age 19, 75 per cent of young people to achieve level 2 competence in communication, numeracy and IT.

Since 1998, governing bodies of maintained secondary schools have been required to set and publish annual targets for the achievement of their pupils in GCSE and equivalent vocational qualifications at the end of KS4 (DfEE 1998b). Target-setting for KS3 NC levels was subsequently introduced. To help with these tasks, schools have received an Autumn Package of Pupil Performance Information produced jointly by the DfEE, QCA and Ofsted since 1998. There are separate packages for each KS containing:

- national summary results for the relevant KS
- national benchmark information for the previous academic year
- national value added information.

Electronic versions of the Autumn Package are available at www.standards. dfee.gov.uk/performance. Ofsted also provides PANDA reports which place a school's inspection and test/examination results in their social context by providing information about the school's background level of poverty and how it compares with other schools in similar circumstances as well as with national averages. Inspection results, attendance rates, test and examination results are set against poverty indicators for the electoral wards surrounding the school, for instance the proportion of children living in overcrowded households and the proportion of adults with higher education. The percentage of pupils known to be eligible for FSM is another indicator of the socio-economic status of a school's intake. LEAs provide additional analyses of local information. The purposes of this cornucopia of information are to enable schools to place facets of their own performance in relevant contexts and to identify priorities for development which are translated into targets and an action plan.

Schools are required to work within a three-year time frame. Each autumn they must:

- carry out a review of performance based on their previous year's results
- review progress towards targets for the current year
- set targets for the following academic year (giving five terms to achieve them).

For instance, in autumn 2002, a school must review its GCSE/GNVQ results for 2002, evaluate its progress towards targets for 2003 and set targets for 2004. The target-setting required of schools is intended to enable government to meet national targets and, therefore, it focuses on outputs as measured by performance in GCSE and equivalent vocational qualifications. Schools must specify the percentages of pupils to achieve:

- grades A*–C in five or more GCSE subjects, equivalent vocational qualifications or a combination of both
- grades A*–G in one or more GCSE subjects, equivalent vocational
  qualifications or a combination of both
- the average points score for the school using a rising scale where GCSE
  grade G=1 and A*=8.

There are various types of targets (Tabberer *et al.* 1996) and the statutory requirements for schools exemplify two of these. *Threshold targets*
identify a qualifying baseline which must be achieved or surpassed for a
target to be met. Five or more GCSE passes at grades A*–C is an example
of a threshold target whereas the requirement that schools specify the
improvement to be achieved in their average points score is an example
of a *cohort target* because it applies to the whole pupil cohort. By requiring different types of target, the government is attempting to pre-empt
some of the negative consequences that have already emerged as a result
of publishing school league tables.

There is a well-documented link between high stakes assessment activities and their attendant backwash effect on the behaviour of teachers
and pupils (Section 1.4). Evidence shows how behaviour is influenced
(distorted?) by raising the stakes in assessment. For instance, the league
tables' emphasis on the achievement of GCSE grades A*–C has been
criticized for encouraging schools to lavish special attention on pupils
expected to achieve D grades in the hope of raising them into the A*–C
category. Schools are thereby helped to achieve this particular measure
of success but at the expense of certain pupils, particularly low attainers
who have no hope of achieving GCSE at grades A*–C. By raising the
stakes associated with attaining grades A*–C, the league tables encouraged a skewing of school resources to concentrate on a select group of
pupils rather than deploying them equitably across the ability range.
Fitz-Gibbon and Tymms (1997) have described this effect as 'measure-
fixation'. Threshold targets can also produce this discriminatory effect,
concentrating time and resources on pupils who are performing just
below the threshold for a target. The current requirements that schools
also set targets for pupils achieving one or more GCSEs at A*–G (a very
low threshold) and for the school's average points score represent attempts to make target-setting more equitable for those below the top and
middle of the ability range.

The statutory targets focus on outputs as measured by performance in tests
and examinations. Headington (2000: 90) has noted that since the introduction of NC levels to demonstrate attainment, 'numbers have become the
currency of education'. They are indeed a common currency that can be
used throughout the compulsory years of schooling as a standard PI. This
may reinforce the tendency towards measure-fixation. As Gann (1999) notes:

> All the targets required by the DfEE are *quantity* targets – they come about
> through counting current outputs and projecting future, hoped-for,

numerical scores. The measurement that happens involves counting some result that can have numbers attached to it, even when the counting may be of something that is subjective and comparatively unscientific.

(Gann 1999: 38)

Schools are, however, able to set targets beyond these quantity output targets. Indeed, Tabberer *et al.* (1996: 8) have argued that, because process targets set the conditions for output targets to be realized, 'Successful target-setting requires a balance of not too many outcome targets linked to a larger number of *related* process targets.' For instance, if a school set an output target to increase the percentage of pupils achieving level 6 in KS3 English tests, it would also need to identify a range of process targets focused on strategies for developing pupils' literacy: 'each process target and each outcome target will need its own action plan, i.e. the combination of responsibilities, tasks and timetable needed to make changes happen' (Tabberer *et al.* 1996: 8). Therefore, it is unwise for schools to adopt too many output targets because 'they will set themselves a whole raft of simultaneous process targets too. A likely consequence will be confused rather than concerted effort' (Tabberer *et al.* 1996: 8).

From 2000, a school's statutory targets must be published, alongside performance information, in a governing body's annual report to parents. Each target must be published for four consecutive years, the first two years as targets only and against actual performance in the third and fourth years. This requirement to publish targets and performance over a four-year time scale is intended to address the concern that it is difficult to draw meaningful conclusions from data for a single year whereas figures for several years allow trends in performance to emerge. The government also publishes schools' results against their targets each year in the School and College Performance Tables. These requirements make all schools publicly accountable each year.

Legislation in the 1990s has also locked LEAs into the target-setting hierarchy, giving them a stake in the process. LEAs have been given exacting targets to meet in the drive towards national targets. Just as schools have to consider how individual departments will contribute to the achievement of whole-school targets, so too LEAs must determine the part each school will play in enabling them to meet LEA targets. Schools' statutory targets must be agreed with the LEA and are subsequently published in the authority's education development plan.

7.4 The target-setting timetable

Schools have been advised to treat target-setting as a five-stage cycle with a carefully phased timetable. (Words in italics are from DfEE 1997: 7. Explanatory comments are added in parentheses.)

- *Stage 1*   *analyses its current performance:*
  'How well are we doing?'
  Looking critically at pupils' current achievements is an essential first step towards improvement.

(This stage should be completed during the first half of the autumn term. The focus is on interrogating school-specific data to make a critical analysis of current outcomes as measured by pupils' performances in national tests, GCSE, GNVQ and A level.)

- *Stage 2*   *compares its results with those of similar schools*
  'How well should we be doing?'
  By comparing current and previous results, and those from similar schools, a school can better judge performance.

(This stage should also be completed during the autumn term. Here the focus is broadened to encompass local and national data provided by the LEA, Ofsted and the Autumn Package. Judgements made at Stage 1 are sharpened by setting internal data against relevant external data, especially benchmark information for similar schools. This may signal a school's strengths as well as triggering the diagnosis of weaknesses.)

- *Stage 3*   *sets itself clear and measurable targets*
  'What more can we aim to achieve?'
  With good information, a school can set itself realistic and challenging targets for improvement.

(Target-setting is expected to start in November and should be completed by 31 December. Priorities for improvement identified at Stage 2 must be converted into clear, specific and measurable targets for raising standards of attainment.)

- *Stage 4*   *revises its development plan to highlight action to achieve the targets*
  'What must we do to make it happen?'
  Once it has set its targets, the school must then take determined action to improve.

(Targets are unlikely to yield success if they are treated as 'bolt-on' extras. It is essential to identify actions that need to be taken and their resource implications. Targets must, therefore, be integrated with the school's development plan.)

- *Stage 5*   *takes action, reviews success, and starts the cycle again.*
  A school must monitor and evaluate its actions in terms of improved pupil performance.

(It is impossible to carry on the same as before if challenging targets are to be met. Changes must be made and actions need to be taken and both need time to take effect. Therefore, the SMT must ensure that stages 1–4 are completed promptly to maximise the time available for Stage 5.)

7.5 Approaches to target-setting in schools

Schools have received varied advice on this matter. For instance, the DfEE (1997) refers to practice in Birmingham LEA where schools were encouraged to set targets in pairs: one modest and one ambitious. A modest target represented the minimum that a school would hope to achieve in a given area whereas the ambitious alternative represented better progress. The DfEE itself advised schools to think in terms of four zones (Figure 7.1).

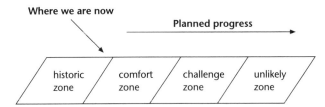

Figure 7.1 Target zones
Source: DfEE 1997: 14

The historic zone is below current levels of attainment and represents a depression of expectations. The comfort zone specifies an attainment range where success should be readily achievable. It is recommended for areas of low priority for schools where heads and governors are content with small steps forward. In areas of high priority, schools are expected to adopt targets in the challenging zone 'where they will represent a marked difference' (DfEE 1997: 15) in achieving pupils' full potential. Target-setting in the unlikely zone is presented as suitable only in exceptional circumstances such as when a new head seeks to turn round a failing school but not for routine use. Pringle and Cobb (1999: 32) advise teachers to treat target-setting as a way of adding challenge to predictions:

Targets = prediction + challenge.
A prediction says 'This is what you are likely to achieve if you carry on as you are now'.
A target says 'This is what you could achieve IF . . .'

Whether the decision is made by a class teacher or a school's SMT, deciding what is 'challenging', 'modest', 'ambitious', 'unlikely' or 'comfortable' remains a matter of judgement. The task of pitching targets so that they offer an appropriate level of challenge, yet remain realistic, is a demanding one. Pringle and Cobb (1999: 9) point out that predicting future performance can never be an exact science. Indeed, the varying fortunes of sports professionals remind us that performance varies from occasion to occasion and not all of the factors which might affect it can be anticipated. Nevertheless, some commentators argue that what at first might seem like best guesses quickly develop into a skill which teachers practise with increasing assurance and accuracy (DfEE 1997: 16; Pringle and Cobb 1999: 9). Thus, although there will always be an element of uncertainty in target-setting, the inherent capriciousness of the exercise can be reduced by making a systematic study of relevant data and using it as a guide to future attainment. Therefore, target-setting is a matter of making professional judgements informed by hard evidence and this is where a school's internal statistics plus information supplied by the LEA, QCA, DfEE and Ofsted are essential.

7.6 How performance data are used to make target-setting more scientific

Although there is debate over the relative importance of variables known to affect attainment, socio-economic status, race, gender, date of birth and prior attainment are generally agreed to be key factors. The strength of the correlation between social class and academic attainment has been recognized for many years, with some research suggesting that over 90 per cent of differences in achievement may be explained in this way (Gann 1999: 30). Saunders (1998: 2) claims that: 'Typically, pupils' prior attainment plus the overall level of social disadvantage in the school (as measured by free school meals) can account for as much as 80 per cent of the apparent difference between schools'. James (1998: 241) argues that since prior attainment is influenced by other contributory factors, such as race and gender, it can be seen as subsuming them and therefore it is convenient to regard it as the key determinant of future performance. Hedger and Jesson (1999: 37) agree. The Autumn Package is predicated on similar findings. For instance, the KS4 package (DfEE 1999: 15) quotes the findings of the *Value-added National Project: Final Report* that average scores in tests/examinations at the end of KS3 and KS4 provide 'the best single predictor of subsequent success' and claims that 'prior attainment is by far the best predictor of pupils' ultimate performance'. This provides the rationale for approaches recommended by the Autumn Package. Illustrations used in the following paragraphs are taken from the KS4 package which focuses on KS3 and KS4 data. The KS3 version contains broadly similar information but for KS2 and KS3.

Section 1A of the Autumn Package presents performance information globally to give an overview of how all pupils performed at the end of KS4. This summary information is then differentiated for boys and girls as shown in Table 7.1.

This information is further analysed by subject to provide a breakdown of results for boys and girls in different subjects. This allows schools to examine their own results in relation to broad trends apparent in national data.

Table 7.1 Results for all pupils, boys and girls in England in 2000

	Entered for 5+ GCSEs or GNVQ equivalent	Achieving 5+ grades A*–C at GCSE or GNVQ equivalent	Achieving 5+ grades A*–G at GCSE or GNVQ equivalent	Entered for 1+ GCSEs or GNVQ equivalent	Achieving 1+ grades A*–G at GCSE or GNVQ equivalent	Achieving no passes	Average GCSE/ GNVQ point score
All pupils	90.7	49.0	88.8	95.5	94.4	5.6	38.7
Boys	89.0	43.8	86.9	94.7	93.4	6.5	36.1
Girls	92.5	54.4	90.8	96.2	95.3	4.7	41.5

Source: DfEE 2000: 3

Section 1B of the Autumn Package provides benchmark information.

Benchmarks are national 'reference points' which can provide an initial like-for-like context into which a school's results can be set. These benchmarks are constructed by looking at the pattern of results in a large national grouping of schools of a similar type.

(Hedger and Jesson 1999: 13)

The package has done this by dividing schools into seven categories based on one readily available measure of the socio-economic status of a school's intake: the percentage of pupils known to be eligible for FSM. The first category is for schools where up to and including 5 per cent of pupils are known to be eligible for FSM and the final category is for schools where over 50 per cent of pupils are known to be eligible for FSM. There are two further categories for grammar and secondary modern schools. Schools evaluate their results by selecting the relevant category and studying the associated table showing the range of performances for schools which share broadly similar characteristics (as measured by eligibility for FSM). These benchmark tables show the standards achieved by the best and worst members of the group as well as those in between. For instance, Table 7.2 shows benchmark information for schools in the first category where very few pupils are eligible for FSM. The blank columns are for schools to plot their own data.

Tables such as this may suggest sizeable disparities in achievement among pupils attending schools that accept cohorts with broadly similar socio-economic characteristics. Indeed, when the benchmark tables were launched, a QCA official remarked: 'For too long schools have been in the dark about how others like them are performing nationally', arguing that the tables would 'puncture complacency' (*Times Educational Supplement* (*TES*) 30 January 1998: 9).

Whereas Section 1B of the Autumn Package attempts to consider 'school effects' by placing results into categories defined by FSM, Section 1C of

Table 7.2 Non-selective schools with up to and including 5% of pupils known to be eligible for FSM

Percentage of pupils achieving

	95%	UQ	60%	Median	40%	LQ	5%
English GCSE A*–C	88	78	73	70	68	63	51
Maths GCSE A*–C	83	68	64	61	59	55	42
Science GCSE A*–C	82	71	66	63	60	56	44
5+ GCSE/GNVQ A*–C	85	73	69	66	64	59	48
5+ GCSE/GNVQ A*–G	100	98	97	97	96	95	92
1+ GCSE/GNVQ A*–C	100	99	99	98	98	97	95

Average point score achieved

	95%	UQ	60%	Median	40%	LQ	5%
GCSE/GNVQ PS	55.1	49.2	47.2	46.2	44.7	43.1	38.1

(Number of schools: 273)

Source: DfEE 1999: 19
Note: Median refers to 'the score/level for which half of the relevant pupils or schools achieved a higher result and half achieved a lower result'. Upper quartile (UQ) 'is the score/level for which 25% of the relevant pupils or schools achieved a higher result' and lower quartile (LQ) 'is the score/level for which 25% of the relevant pupils or schools achieved a lower result' (DfEE 1999: 69).

the package focuses on the relationship between input and output by setting KS4 results against attainment at the end of KS3. These value-added measures are intended to allow schools to compare progress made by their own pupils with progress made by pupils nationally. The information is presented in two ways: value-added line graphs (Figure 7.2) and chance graphs (Figure 7.3).

The upward trend of the line graph shows that as one score increases so does the other, demonstrating a clear relationship between KS3 average points scores and GCSE/GNVQ total points scores. In fact, the correlation between KS3 test results and GCSE performance has been found to be as high as 0.8 (James 1998: 242). The chance graphs present the same information in a different form. Each graph shows the distribution of attainment in GCSE/GNVQ for a group of pupils with similar attainment in KS3 tests.

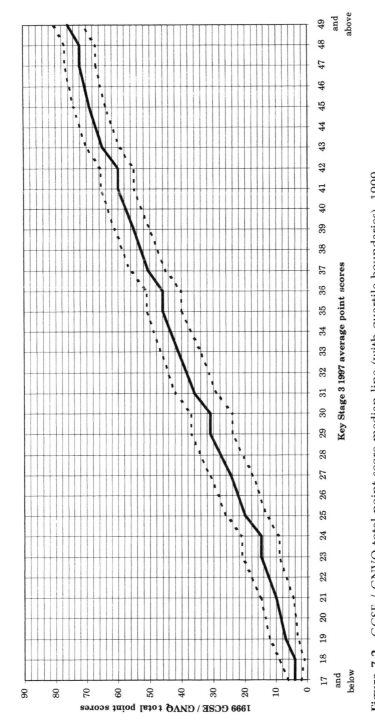

Figure 7.2 GCSE / GNVQ total point score median line (with quartile boundaries), 1999
Source: www.standards.dfee.gov.uk/performance

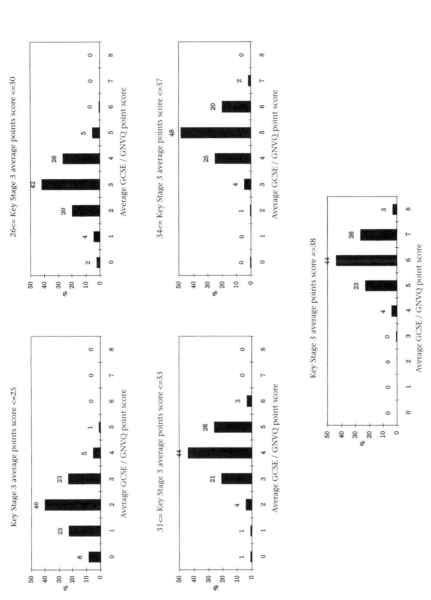

Figure 7.3 Chances graphs for GCSE / GNVQ average point score, 1999
Source: www.standards.dfee.gov.uk/performance

Schools are urged to use information in Section 1C of the Autumn Package with pupils and parents because it provides a clear visual representation of the relationship between prior attainment and future performance and can be used to engage them in the process of setting personally challenging targets.

Task 7.1

Find out how national and local performance data are used in your placement school.

How is pupils' progress monitored? How are targets set at departmental/whole-school level?

Talk to different teachers about their responsibilities: the assessment coordinator, your HoD and a form tutor.

7.7 But the science remains inexact . . .

Although these techniques represent an improvement on the use of raw results, considerable care needs to be exercised when analysing and interpreting data of this kind for there are pitfalls inherent in it. For instance, the Autumn Package itself (DfEE 1999: 2) warns teachers to take care over the significance they attribute to scores generated for small year groups and small schools. When raw numbers are converted into percentages, the resulting scores have the potential to mislead when the original figures were small and the addition or subtraction of a single pupil's results may have a disproportionate effect on resulting percentages. Academic researchers have pointed to more fundamental considerations:

> Quantitative analyses usually contain a degree of statistical 'uncertainty': this is because calculations based on differences from the average or norm may be the consequence of pure chance rather than of something more 'real', such as the quality of education. Statisticians use tests of significance to assess the degree of chance in particular sets of results. These tests typically reveal that only a few schools can be said – with a reasonable degree of certainty – to be performing above (or below) the average. This is true for either raw or 'value added' results.
>
> (Saunders 1998: 8)

Gray (1996, in Stobart and Gipps 1997: 33) agrees that: 'The majority of schools achieve precisely the sort of results one would predict from their intakes'. Moreover, although the graphs in the Autumn Package demonstrate correlations, a correlation is not the same as a cause. For instance, entitlement to FSM is not a cause of below-average performance, although there is a correlation between the two. Although this point seems obvious in the case of FSM, there are instances where it is tempting to assume that a correlation confirms a causal relationship.

Stobart and Gipps (1997: 32) recommend caution in interpreting the results of the kind of ranking exercise attempted in Section 1B of the Autumn Package, pointing out that 'changing or modifying criteria for ranking' can result in 'quite different rankings' so that results 'can vary considerably and apparently haphazardly by making trivial modifications to the adjustment procedures'. They also point out that rank orders can change quite considerably from one year to the next. Other research suggests that differences *within* schools (between departments, for instance) may be greater than differences *between* schools (Saunders 1998: 8) which further questions the usefulness of ranking schools. Harvey Goldstein and Desmond Nuttall (cited in Stobart and Gipps 1997: 26) found that only schools in the top and bottom 25 per cent of a rank order could be reliably compared because the overlap in the middle 50 per cent of schools was so great that small changes in a few results could reverse schools' positions.

It is still early days for the ground-breaking techniques required to measure value added. Unpublished research from NFER (Schagen undated; *TES* 15 January 1999: 8) questions whether the simple model of value added which has been adopted, based on comparing pupils' results with their previous achievements, is sophisticated enough to take proper account of all the factors associated with poor performance especially the effects of a school's socio-economic background. Saunders (1998: 10) asserts that: 'the notion of a value added measure which tells you – and everyone else – how well your school or department or class is doing, and is also simple to calculate, understand and use, is a non-starter!'

These caveats underline the need for caution in analysing performance information, offering a reminder of the sheer complexity of what is being attempted and the limitations in current procedures. The use of assessment data as a diagnostic tool to achieve a better understanding of performance and to probe the causes of poor performance remain worthwhile activities. But recognition of the inexactness of the underlying science emphasizes the need for a tentative approach to interpreting significance and drawing conclusions. This provides a timely reminder of how slippery and elusive the concept of 'standards' is!

7.8 Measuring educational standards

One of the few aspects of measuring educational standards which is uncontentious is successive generations' belief that they are witness to a decline. This 'wistful' tendency to look back and lament the falling of standards is neatly illustrated by the Bullock Report (DES 1975: 3) which documents concerns over deteriorating standards going back almost a century. Despite the conventional wisdom that 'Things ain't what they used to be' (Black 1998: 146), the attempt to measure educational standards is, in reality, fraught with difficulties.

At the fundamental level of meaning, discussions of 'educational standards' often lack conceptual clarity (Butterfield 1995: 154). Frequently, educational standards are equated with performance in tests and examinations but the problem with such a restricted definition of the term is illustrated by an international study of performance in science. Japanese pupils were among the highest scoring in written tests but produced one of the lowest proportions of pupils who said they enjoyed the subject (Black 1998: 145). How satisfactory are 'standards' when a high level of performance is not accompanied by an enthusiasm for the subject? Likewise, one of the highest performing primary schools in KS2 league tables was found by an Ofsted inspection to be failing its pupils in important respects, offering poor quality teaching ill-matched to pupils' potential (Shorrocks-Taylor 1999: 173). This suggests that high standards in NC test performance offer no guarantee of similar standards in teaching and learning.

Beyond the difficulty in reaching a consensus over what constitutes educational standards, the quest to measure them is beset with technical challenges which can be offset in scientific experiments by working under controlled conditions. Science measures the effects of specific variables by controlling or randomizing the effects of others but education is conducted in the real world where it is not possible to exercise the control that is feasible in a laboratory. This makes it difficult to isolate and measure educational standards, either on a single occasion or over time. Indeed, the range of factors found to correlate with academic performance is expanding as interest in this subject intensifies. For instance, a study by the British Education, Communication and Technology Agency has identified a relationship between the resourcing of primary schools with computers and KS2 results in English, mathematics and science: the better resourced the school, the higher the results (*TES* 12 January 2001: 8).

Measuring standards over time is equally problematic. If it were possible to use the same measuring instrument year after year – that is the same test – there would be an unchanging yardstick against which standards could be assessed. However, in the high stakes setting of national testing and results publication, pupils often receive intensive coaching, making it impossible to use the same test items repeatedly. Even if this were possible, further problems would remain because test content dates so that the level of match between it and current educational practice (the curriculum, teaching approaches and assessment techniques) diminishes with time. In 1999, BBC Radio 4's *Today* programme made a light-hearted excursion into the field of measuring how educational standards are changing by pitting one of its journalists, who had taken O level geography many years before, against a 16-year-old who was about to sit geography GCSE. For the purposes of the experiment, the journalist took that year's GCSE paper and the 16-year-old sat the relevant O level paper in addition to his GCSE. This was, of course, no more than an entertaining media event but it did illustrate serious underlying difficulties in trying to determine what is happening to educational standards with the passage of time. The papers concentrated on different attributes – factual knowledge was placed at a premium by the O level examination whereas GCSE was more concerned with assessing skills and the ability to apply knowledge. As each candidate had been prepared for the demands of the paper he actually sat, it is unsurprising that each was less well equipped for tasks which emphasized different abilities. The experiment was not comparing like with like and therefore it was impossible to use the results to demonstrate falling/rising standards. The experiment confirmed that standards had *altered* – different abilities were highly rated at different times – but it was not possible to assert that standards were higher or lower. They were simply different.

Because each testing occasion requires new items, it is hard to maintain consistent levels of difficulty despite the fact that questions are trialled to determine their ease. For instance, many primary teachers believe that the improvement in boys' KS2 reading test results in 1999 was explained by the use of more accessible reading material. An experiment in one school where pupils took both the 1998 and 1999 tests seemed to bear out this view (*TES* 29 October 1999: 4). The measurement of standards is further compromised if a test demonstrates a bias in favour of one subgroup or against another. It is difficult to provide test content which is neutral in terms of equality of opportunity for pupils of different sexes, races, social and cultural backgrounds. This may introduce bias into the measurement (Gipps and Murphy 1994). In the case of the 1999 KS2 reading test, the use of a short, large-type poem on the subject of spiders, illustrated with cartoons, was felt to be more to boys' tastes than the 1998 material, an extended piece of writing where the main character was a girl. Although examiners can adjust grade boundaries to allow for unanticipated differences, where cut scores are finally set remains a matter of judgement rather than an objective exercise.

The way in which high stakes systems are 'incentivized' may further undermine the attempt to measure standards by encouraging schools to play the system. For instance, KS1 schools are delaying teaching their new intake until baseline assessment is finalized. This tactic is intended to depress pupils' baselines on entry to create more favourable value added measures at the end of KS1. Likewise, research has shown that it is easier to gain a grade C on foundation tier GCSE than on the higher tier (Section 8.4). This offers an incentive to schools to 'play safe' by entering pupils for the less demanding foundation tier even where they would benefit from the challenge of studying for the higher tier.

Some commentators (for example James 1998: 239) are concerned that the use of NC test levels and GCSE/GNVQ grades as the key indicators in the current school improvement regime places too great a burden on a single series of PIs. These PIs form the basis for

- setting targets at national and local level as well as providing the main test of whether targets are being met
- judging progress made by individual schools
- measuring value added by attending particular schools
- assessing individual pupils' attainments.

This 'sets up a potentially very narrow and circular view of standards, only engaging with a single dimension of the complex work of schools' (Butterfield 1995: 171). Moreover, it requires a high level of confidence in the validity and reliability of these tests and examinations, that is that they actually measure what they purport to measure and that they do so with a good level of consistency and accuracy. Both of these fundamental requirements have been questioned by research into NC assessment arrangements (for example Gann 1999; Shorrocks-Taylor 1999).

Many experts (for example Butterfield 1995: 63; Stobart and Gipps 1997: 108) argue that a sensible, cost-effective alternative to blanket testing for all 5-, 7-, 11- and 14-year-olds is a system of anonymized testing of light samples designed to represent the national cohort. Although anonymous, light sampling would remove the high stakes which distort current measurements, this approach has not found political favour. This being so, experts agree that confidence in current approaches to measuring educational standards could be strengthened by using sophisticated statistical techniques which provide subtle, complex results. Unfortunately, this, too, may be politically unacceptable because politicians favour measures which are 'few, straightforward and intelligible to parents' (DfE cited in Stobart and Gipps 1997: 32).

It is important to remember that data collection and analysis should not become ends in themselves. The true measure of their worth is the extent to which they contribute to the quality of teaching and learning in schools.

| 8 | Recent developments in testing and examinations |

8.1 Introduction

Testing has become a high profile aspect of teachers' work, exercising an increasingly powerful influence over what is taught and ways in which it is taught (Section 1.4). In an article tellingly entitled 'Measured lives', James (2000) points out that:

> many children starting school in 2000 should expect to take some form of external test or examination every year with the sole exception of Year 8, although even here some new tests are planned for the most able . . . England has now achieved the dubious distinction of subjecting its school students to more external tests than any other country in the world and spending more money on doing so.
>
> (James 2000: 351)

It has been estimated that testing costs £150 million each year in England alone (Carver 2000: 5). Even if only testing at the end of KS2 and KS3 is taken into account, around 1.8 million pupils and 7.2 million scripts are involved (*Guardian Education* 9 May 2000: 6). Changes to the qualifications framework for 14–19-year-olds have prompted QCA (2000b) to issue a leaflet entitled *Finding Your Way Around* and a former chairman of examiners has enquired 'Has the examination system got out of hand?' (Lloyd 1999: 130). Trainee teachers have not been immune to the spread of a testing culture, experiencing the introduction of a numeracy test in 2000 followed by a literacy test in 2001 with a test in ICT to follow. The effects of this 'testamania' (Iven 1992, quoted in Shorrocks-Taylor 1999: 150) have been felt even in the best-sellers lists, with sample papers for tests for 11-year-olds ranked among the top 15 non-fiction best-sellers and GCSE revision guides outselling even fiction! Clearly, testing looms large in the lives of pupils and their teachers. Therefore, it may seem surprising that it has been reserved until this final chapter. However, within this book, there has been an attempt to redress the balance, elevating formative assessment to counter the importance which will inevitably be attributed to testing in schools and the understandable pressures to neglect other kinds of assessment.

Gipps (1994) attributes the current relish for testing to 'the symbolic power of tests in the minds of policymakers and the public' arguing that:

> By requiring testing to take place, policymakers can be seen to be addressing critical reform issues. So a high-stakes testing programme is often a symbolic solution to a real educational problem. It offers the appearance of a solution, and indeed, as test scores rise over time, because of teaching to the test, policymakers can point to the wisdom of their action. However, the reality is that the testing programme may not be a cure for the educational problem.
>
> (Gipps 1994: 35)

There is little doubt that high stakes tests raise standards of test per-formance. As teachers become familiar with the demands of new tests, they become skilled at preparing pupils for them. Even at KS2, where the stakes are arguably lower than at KS4, Year 6 teachers and pupils devote enormous effort to test preparation. For instance, teachers report that 'SAT revision' has become the focus of the 12 weeks leading up to the tests and that some parents arrange for private tuition (Carver 2000: 5). Schools even provide last-minute intensive coaching at weekends and during Easter vacations. Whether this activity also raises wider educa-tional standards is questionable whereas there is now 'hard' evidence that formative assessment does yield learning gains (Black and Wiliam 1998a). This also explains the positioning of tests and examinations in the final chapter of this book.

Although secondary school assessment is often 'construed as taking examinations' (Stobart and Gipps 1997: 78), high stakes tests and exam-inations are the aspects of assessment which are most likely to have a pernicious effect on teaching and learning. This is not to suggest that all tests and examinations are 'bad' or that all their effects are negative but simply to recognize that summative testing, especially when it involves 'high stakes', is associated with deleterious consequences (Section 1.4). Stobart and Gipps (1997) contend that 'good' examinations display cer-tain qualities:

- a mix of examination and coursework is determined by fitness for purpose
- they encourage teachers to innovate and respect professional judgements
- they motivate pupils through imaginative and flexible syllabuses and assessment techniques, especially the use of coursework
- where subjects require it, papers are differentiated to meet the needs of candidates with different levels of ability so that all pupils are provided with opportunities to show what they know, understand and can do thereby demonstrating positive achievement.

First, this chapter outlines current arrangements for external testing and examinations and end-of-KS3 TA. Although many schools use tests developed by independent organizations (Section 5.5), QCA is responsible for approving and overseeing nationally mandated awards which are the focus of this chapter. A chronological approach is used to provide a year-by-year account of compulsory and optional testing activities. Testing opportunities are currently expanding and so website addresses where up-to-date information may be obtained are provided. Later in the chapter, some of the technical requirements of assessment are considered. Although these requirements are important in all assessment, they are especially significant in the context of high stakes, public assessment which is why they are dealt with in this chapter.

Objectives

By the end of this chapter, you should have developed the following:

- familiarity with the key tests and examinations approved by QCA (http://www.qca.org.uk/) and how they fit into the qualifications framework
- awareness that although assessment is an inexact science fraught with technical difficulties, these are thrown into sharp relief by the requirements of high stakes tests and examinations.

8.2 Testing at KS3

The dip in attainment which characterizes the start of KS3 has been recognized for many years (Section 5.5). It became the focus of renewed attention in the 1990s when the drive to raise educational standards and the use of test data to monitor progress highlighted the phenomenon. Policy-makers' belief that there is a direct relationship between testing and improved educational standards is stated explicitly in the KS3 assessment and reporting orders for 2001 which introduced two new tests: Year 7 progress tests and Year 7 and 8 optional tests. 'These new tests form a significant part of the Government's strategy to raise standards at key stage 3' (QCA 2000a: 46). These tests also illustrate an important development in testing policy in that previously national testing was an end-of-KS3 activity whereas now it is encouraged throughout.

8.2a Year 7 progress tests

These tests are for two categories of pupils: those who did not take tests at the end of KS2 (either because of absence or because the tests were disapplied) and those who did not reach level 4. Although the tests are not compulsory, they are designed to measure the progress which pupils in these categories made during their first year of secondary schooling and schools are strongly encouraged to administer them. The tests are offered in two of the three core subjects (English and mathematics) and are intended to complement the drive to raise standards of literacy and numeracy through the national literacy and numeracy strategies.

8.2b Year 7 and 8 optional tests

Available in English and mathematics, these tests are also designed to assist in monitoring progress and in setting and achieving targets for the end of KS3. At Year 7, they are available for those who achieved level 4 or higher at KS2 and for Year 8 they are for those working within levels 4–6.

8.2c Year 8: world class tests (www.qca.org.uk/world-class-test/wct-9-13.htm)

As well as tests for average and underachieving pupils, tests are also being deployed to extend the most able. The so-called 'world class' tests derive from the gifted and talented strand of the Excellence in Cities initiative and are aimed principally at gifted and talented children in inner cities. However, the ambitions of this project extend far beyond its immediate target group. The tests are intended to help England to keep up with the highest standards globally. Therefore, QCA is benchmarking them against standards internationally, focusing on the best performing countries as identified in international surveys. QCA hopes that these countries will become involved in developing and using subsequent tests. So as well as measuring pupils' performances against those in schools locally and nationally, world class tests will enable schools to compare their most able children with the 'best' from around the world! These optional tests are aimed at the top 10 per cent of the ability range in Years 5 and 8 and focus on mathematics and problem-solving. They will be administered electronically to allow for more innovative approaches to assessment than conventional paper and pencil tests allow. Test development started in 1999 and the first tests became available in November 2001.

8.2d End-of-KS3 statutory requirements

KS3 statutory requirements are set out in Education Orders which are published annually by QCA in association with the DfEE. They are available from QCA Publications (tel: 01787 884444) or can be downloaded from QCA's website (www.qca.org.uk/). These arrangements apply to all pupils in maintained schools who are in the final year of KS3 except those for whom they have been disapplied because of SEN. Independent schools may participate in these arrangements but are not obliged to do so.

There are two types of statutory assessment: end-of-KS tests in the core subjects – mathematics, English and science – and TA. National tests are taken by all Year 9 pupils who are assessed by their teachers to have a current working level of 3 or above in mathematics and science and 4 or above in English unless they have been disapplied. For pupils working below these levels, TA is the sole statutory requirement. Tests are taken during a week in May and in all three subjects they follow the same format: two compulsory written papers of between one and one and a half hours duration plus an optional extension paper. In mathematics and science, the compulsory papers are tiered (science: levels 3–6 and 5–7; mathematics: levels 3–5, 4–6, 5–7 and 6–8) and pupils must take both papers from the same tier. Pupils who are entered for extension papers are expected to take the highest tier in the relevant subject. There is also a 20-minute mental arithmetic test and pupils must be entered for the appropriate tier here too (higher or lower). In English, the undifferentiated compulsory papers cater for levels 4–7. The extension papers cover level 8 and exceptional performance in English and science and exceptional performance in mathematics.

TA is required in all NC subjects and RE and for all pupils, even those for whom parts of the NC have been disapplied. Whereas tests provide snapshots of performance, TA should offer a summing up of what has been achieved throughout the KS and across the entire PoS, taking into account the full range of pupils' work and the full range of performance contexts. However, practice is known to be restricted. For instance, Ofsted (1998a: 89) observed: 'a greater variety of assessment approaches in English than in other core subjects' at KS3. English teachers also favour 'continuous assessment', using written and oral assignments undertaken as a regular feature of class and homework to inform judgements. Mathematics and science, on the other hand, prefer end-of-unit tests and examinations using scores in these to calculate aggregated results (James 1998). Furthermore, student teachers 'use only a limited number of the assessment . . . strategies that are available to teachers. They do not, in general, show the confidence to use the full range of techniques necessary if pupils' levels of attainment and learning difficulties are to be fully appreciated' (Ofsted 1999: 16). It is, therefore, important to develop a range of assessment strategies and guard against falling in with narrowly defined, subject-specific preferences.

All NC subjects are composed of ATs which form the basis of TA. ATs define subject-specific skill and content areas and each subject has between one and four of them. For instance, English has three: 'Speaking and Listening', 'Reading' and 'Writing'. A teacher must provide a level for each AT, where there is more than one, plus an overall subject level. Overall subject levels are calculated by aggregating the AT levels which are equally weighted unless otherwise specified:

English	3 ATs
Mathematics	4 ATs weighted 4:9:4:3
Science	4 ATs
History	single AT
Geography	single AT
Design and technology	single AT
ICT	single AT
Modern foreign languages	4 ATs
Art and design	single AT
Music	single AT
Physical education	single AT

Level descriptions specify requirements at each level, helping teachers with the task of assigning levels for ATs. Teachers are required to work with the principle of 'best fit', selecting the level which in their judgement best matches a pupil's attainments during the KS and then checking adjacent level descriptions to ensure that the chosen level provides the best fit. However, assigning pupils to levels is not an objective exercise and it is rarely straightforward. Something as multifaceted as performance across a subject often fails to fit neatly into a category. Pupils display uneven profiles, even within an AT, performing well against certain criteria but less well against others. Therefore, strengths and weaknesses have to be weighed against one another and finalizing levels is a matter of professional judgement. Compensation is the technical term for the process by which strengths in certain areas are allowed to offset weaknesses in others and it is often necessary to apply this principle to assign pupils to levels. This pragmatic solution to the difficulty of assigning pupils to levels compromises the spirit of strict criterion-referencing (Section 3.4) which requires candidates to satisfy all relevant criteria for the award of a level.

8.3 The 14–19 age phase

8.3a The qualifications framework

Traditionally, KS4 and post-16 have been treated as separate educational phases. However, the advantages of treating the 14–19 age group holistically have been recognized increasingly. It helps to rationalize and give coherence to what has been the most disparate and fragmented phase in education: the bridging point between compulsory academic education, elective academic education, vocational education and training. James (1998: 71–2) argues that trying to make sense of this complex system of award-bearing courses is 'akin to negotiating Spaghetti Junction!' and notes the prevalence of the language of travel in describing the task – talk of 'routes', 'pathways', 'finding your way around', 'journeys' and 'destinations'. The Dearing (1996) review of 16–19 qualifications recommended

Level of qualification	General		Vocationally related		Occupational
5	Higher-level qualifications				Level 5 NVQ
4					Level 4 NVQ
3 advanced level	A level		Free-standing mathematics units level 3	Vocational A level (Advanced GNVQ)	Level 3 NVQ
2 intermediate level	GCSE grade A*–C	Free-standing maths units level 2	Intermediate GNVQ		Level 2 NVQ
1 foundation level	GCSE grade D–G	Free-standing maths units level 1	Foundation GNVQ		Level 1 NVQ
Entry level	Certificate of (educational) achievement				

Figure 8.1   The qualifications framework
Source: http://www.qca.org.uk/nq/framework/

the establishment of a national framework encompassing all the main qualifications and this has been established for England, Wales and Northern Ireland. Relationships are clarified by dividing qualifications into three main types:

- *general qualifications* such as GCSEs and A levels
- *vocationally related qualifications* such as vocational A levels and GNVQs
- *occupational qualifications* such as NVQs.

Equivalences have been established by assigning each qualification to one of six levels. Figure 8.1 shows how entry level is used as a stepping stone, allowing pupils with SEN to access the qualifications hierarchy which extends to encompass professional qualifications at levels 4 and 5.

8.3b Awarding bodies

This rationalization also entailed reducing the number of examining bodies and the number of syllabuses available. Prior to this reform (1997), there were over 600 syllabuses on offer at A level and 1110 were examined at GCSE by six separate boards (Stobart and Gipps 1997: 91). With so many syllabuses available in the same subjects, it was difficult to ensure consistency of standards across and within awarding bodies. The 'system' was further complicated by the existence of thousands of occupational and vocationally related qualifications offered by separate organizations working to their own idiosyncratic requirements. The reforms required the main academic and vocational awarding bodies to amalgamate to form three new 'super boards': Oxford, Cambridge and Royal Society of Arts (OCR), the Assessment and Qualifications Alliance (AQA) and Educational Excellence (Edexcel). Each offers a streamlined set of syllabuses across the range of qualifications types. The work of these bodies is overseen by QCA, which exercises control over standards attempting to ensure that they are consistently high. QCA has core content requirements and quality standards which must be satisfied if awarding bodies are to gain approval for their syllabuses. The government had several aims in undertaking these reforms:

- to create awarding bodies which can offer a full examinations service for schools and colleges
- to improve choice
- to create a coherent and manageable system characterized by high and comparable standards
- to reduce variability to a point where standards can be monitored effectively.

However, Lines (2000: 17) takes a different view, arguing that the reforms have created an oligopolistic industry (one with very few large providers). Their salient characteristics are as follows:

- producers cannot compete on price
- there is almost no product differentiation
- what competition there is comes through marketing.

He argues that the new awarding bodies display all three characteristics and that this encourages them to find alternative ways of competing for market share: 'by making textbooks "official" and, though this can only be whispered . . . lower standards' (Lines 2000: 17). Others (Brooks 1993; Stobart and Gipps 1997) are concerned that, traditionally, experimental syllabuses, developed at local level, have gone on to become mainstream options. The current system inhibits this type of professionally led innovation and examination reform.

In so far as it is possible to separate what there has been an attempt to integrate, Sections 8.4 and 8.5 deal with general qualifications and Section 8.6 considers vocationally related and occupational qualifications.

8.4 KS4

Following its introduction in 1988, GCSE became the recognized school-leaving qualification for 16-year-olds. Stobart and Gipps (1997: 82) argue that GCSE proved remarkably successful at the outset because it embodied characteristics of a 'good' examination (Section 8.1) but that subsequent impositions (a ceiling on coursework and the reduction of syllabuses and teacher freedom) 'have weakened the model' (Stobart and Gipps 1997: 85). Since the 1980s, the tendency towards central control has intensified and the combination of regulations and options governing the KS4 curriculum have made it bewilderingly complex. The detail of what is compulsory and what is optional would probably cloud more than it clarifies the salient characteristics of assessment at KS4. Furthermore, requirements are sure to change with time. Therefore, this section provides an overview of the principal features of KS4 awards whereas up-to-date detail is best sought on relevant websites: http://www.qca.org.uk/, www.aqa.org.uk, www.edexcel.org.uk and www.ocr.org.uk

At KS4, the NC consists of an extended compulsory core comprising English, mathematics, science, design and technology, ICT, MFL and PE. Citizenship will join the list in 2002. The core is expected to occupy roughly two-thirds of curriculum time leaving space for individual choice in the remaining time. James (1998: 74) notes that: 'The list is remarkable for the way in which it underwrites an "employers' curriculum" with clear emphasis on subjects deemed to be necessary for economic activity in global markets'. Although the arts and humanities continue to be offered as options in schools, 'these no longer have a protected place or a prescribed programme of study for this key stage'. Most KS4 subjects are tied to award-bearing courses. However, the range of awards has expanded considerably and GCSE is no longer the only recognized qualification. In 2000, it became possible for certain pupils to omit GCSEs in some subjects and move straight to vocationally related courses or Advanced Subsidiary (AS) level. Although GCSE remains the principal qualification, Figure 8.2 (DfEE 2000: 94–5) shows the main qualifications and how they compare.

8.4a GCSE

GCSE is available as a full and a short course. The full course is the only GCSE option for English, mathematics and science and most pupils are expected to take full courses in these subjects. Other compulsory subjects may be studied as short courses which are designed to take half the time of a full GCSE and count as half a GCSE for accreditation purposes. Full courses usually take two years to complete whereas short courses are sometimes completed in Year 10. Vocational GCSE is due for introduction in autumn 2002, replacing foundation, intermediate and Part One GNVQs. It will be based on Part One GNVQ making it equivalent to two GCSEs. This new qualification is intended to parallel the introduction of a vocational A level and to make vocationally related education more widely available at KS4.

Differentiation is a characteristic of 'good' examinations according to Stobart and Gipps (1997). Just as KS3 mathematics and science tests are tiered, so too are some GCSEs. With the exception of mathematics (which has three tiers), tiered GCSEs are divided into higher (grades A*–D) and

	Year 10 (age 14–15) September	January	June	Year 11 (age 15–16) September	January	June	Assessment	Grading system	Equivalent to
GCSE	Coursework		Exams (some courses)			Exams	The final grade can depend upon exams and coursework or just exams	A*–G	One GCSE
GCSE Short Course	Coursework		Exams	(Some pupils take a GCSE short course over two years, with the exam at the end of Year 11)					Half a GCSE
Vocational GCSE from autumn 2002	Coursework	Test Opportunity	Test Opportunity		Test Opportunity	Test Opportunity	Portfolio of coursework and tests	A*–G	Two GCSEs
Part One GNVQ foundation or intermediate	Coursework	Test Opportunity	Test Opportunity		Test Opportunity	Test Opportunity	Two-thirds of the final grade depends on a portfolio of coursework, the rest on three tests	Distinction, Merit, Pass	**Intermediate:** two GCSEs at grades A*–C **or foundation:** two GCSEs at grades D–G
Six-unit GNVQ foundation or intermediate	Coursework	Test Opportunity	Test Opportunity		Test Opportunity	Test Opportunity	Two-thirds of the final grade depends on a portfolio of coursework, the rest on two tests	Distinction, Merit, Pass	**Intermediate:** four GCSEs at grades A*–C **or foundation:** four GCSEs at grades D–G
GNVQ units foundation or intermediate or advanced	Coursework	Test Opportunity	Test Opportunity		Test Opportunity	Test Opportunity	Each unit is assessed either by a portfolio of coursework or a test	Distinction, Merit, Pass	Single units have no GCSE equivalent
NVQ Level 1 or Level 2	Coursework					Exams (some courses)	Pupils are tested by an assessor when they are ready	Pass or fail	**Level 2:** GCSE grades A*–C **Level 1:** GCSE grades D–G

Figure 8.2 The main qualifications at Key Stage 4 and how they compare

foundation (grades C–G) alternatives. The two-grade overlap is intended to aid choice for 'borderline' candidates, avoiding a situation where the achievements of middle-of-the-range candidates are capped at too low a level if teachers play safe and enter them for the foundation tier. This arrangement also accommodates higher tier candidates who perform below expectation, avoiding a situation where they simply 'fall out' of the tier and receive an 'unclassified' result. A further safeguard is the provision for higher tier candidates to go down one grade and still qualify for an E grade if they do badly in the examination. In subjects where it is possible to differentiate by outcome alone, and it is deemed unnecessary to differentiate content, papers are untiered.

When GCSE was first introduced, the opportunity for coursework to count towards the final grade was one of its most successful features. Some pupils found this highly motivating, lavishing great care on coursework. No restrictions governed the percentage of marks which could be allocated in this way and so some syllabuses were examined entirely by coursework. However, teacher-assessed coursework is viewed with suspicion in some quarters where it is believed to compromise the fairness and reliability which external examinations are assumed to possess. In 1991 the then Prime Minister, John Major, announced unexpectedly that he was attracted to the idea of limiting GCSE coursework to 20 per cent of the final mark. This personal preference subsequently found its way into government policy, although advice that it would be difficult to impose this limit in all subjects was accepted (Daugherty 1995: 136–7). The nature of subjects was taken into account in fixing limits with academic subjects typically allowed a coursework component of between 20 and 30 per cent (for example history, mathematics and geography). Subjects involving the acquisition of practical skills were allowed to allocate up to 60 per cent of marks for coursework (for example art, music and IT) but only PE was granted a limit as high as 70 per cent (SCAA 1995: 4).

8.4b Entry level certificates

These certificates are designed to motivate and recognize the achievements of pupils with SEN. Entry level certificates are intended as a stepping stone to give pupils who are not yet ready access to the qualifications framework. They are available in NC subjects and in broad vocational areas. Awards are made at three levels corresponding approximately to NC levels 1–3. Candidates are assessed on spoken, practical and written tasks.

8.5 Post-16 general qualifications

Despite the reform of the qualifications framework, the 16–19 landscape is still dominated by A level, an examination introduced in the middle of the twentieth century to cater for the top 20 per cent of the ability range in preparation for university study or entry to the professions. This pedigree has invested A level with symbolic significance as an 'academic gold standard' with which successive governments have been reluctant to meddle. This helps to explain the longevity of A level. Introduced in 1951, it has survived longer than any other school-leaving qualification and changed only incrementally over the next half century. Until the 1990s, it was the only post-16 award available in many sixth forms. However, this should not be taken as a sign of widespread contentment with A level. Longstanding concerns include the following:

- A conventional course of study centred on two or three subjects, often in related areas, encouraged early specialization.
- A level is too narrow and academic, and insufficiently applied and practical. In particular it neglects the key skills (Section 8.6c) which employers' organizations regard as essential to the UK's economic well-being.
- Traditionally, there has been a sharp divide in status between academic and vocational qualifications. The failure to achieve parity of esteem for vocational qualifications led to A level becoming the aspiration of the many irrespective of how well it suited their abilities and needs.

These concerns suggested that a reform programme should

- seek to balance depth with breadth in the post-16 curriculum
- create flexible qualifications in which the academic and vocational are equally esteemed and pupils are encouraged to mix and match elements from each.

A review of 16–19 qualifications was eventually carried out (Dearing 1996). However, the potential for a radical overhaul of the system was written out of the remit which specified the government's desire to maintain the rigour of A level and further develop GNVQ and NVQ. In effect, Dearing was asked to reform the system while preserving its main features intact which curtailed his room for manoeuvre. Notwithstanding these restrictions, he was to advise on how greater coherence and breadth could be injected into the post-16 curriculum and how greater participation and the minimizing of waste could be achieved. The framework for national qualifications (Figure 8.1) is one outcome of the Dearing Review. By specifying equivalences between academic, vocationally related and occupational qualifications, and by ensuring that all three are represented at the highest levels in the framework, the reforms have gone some way to addressing the issues of parity of esteem and flexible routes through the qualifications hierarchy.

The most far-reaching reform of A level ever attempted has led to its reformulation as a two-phase qualification (2000). The initial phase, AS level, has introduced a new qualification halfway between GCSE and A

Qualification	Level	No. of units	Equivalences
Part One GNVQ (foundation)	1	Three specified units	2 GCSEs at grades D–G NVQ level 1
Part One GNVQ (intermediate)	2	Three specified units	2 GCSEs at grades A*–C NVQ level 2
Foundation GNVQ	1	Six units, three of them specified	4 GCSEs at grades D–G NVQ level 1
Intermediate GNVQ	2	Six units, three of them specified	4 GCSEs at grades A*–C NVQ level 2
Advanced GNVQ (three-unit award)	3	Three specified units	AS level NVQ level 3
Advanced GNVQ (six-unit award)	3	Six units, three or four of them specified	A level NVQ level 3

Figure 8.3 GNVQ and the qualifications framework

level. AS level was designed as a one-year qualification which would provide better progression between GCSE and A level so that fewer pupils would drop out, finding the gap between the two unacceptably wide. For those who abandon their studies, a one-year qualification was intended to reduce the number who left with nothing to show for their efforts. The reform also addressed the issue of breadth by encouraging pupils to take five subjects in their first year of post-16 study, dropping to three in the A2 year. Flexibility was achieved by making a 'unit' the common currency across qualifications. The reformed A level has six units, the first three of which are studied at AS level. Equivalent qualifications are shown in Figure 8.3. It was hoped that this arrangement would encourage pupils to study a broad programme combining vocationally related and academic elements.

8.5a Advanced Subsidiary Levels

AS is the successor to another form of AS level – the Advanced Supplementary level introduced in 1989. This earlier AS level was intended to cover half the content of an A level but at full A level standards. The theory that it was possible to achieve A level standards while covering only half the content did not convince many teachers and Advanced Supplementary failed to become established as a viable alternative to A level. The revised qualification takes an alternative approach, treating AS level as a staging post between GCSE and A level. Its predecessor's problem with disappointing take-up has been pre-empted by making AS level the first compulsory half of an A level course, worth half the final marks, and ensuring that there are no free-standing A levels independent of it. While this measure may have solved certain problems, it may have simultaneously created others! The key challenge, according to Stobart and Gipps (1997: 89) 'is how a new "standard", equivalent to the first year of A levels, is to be created so that it is both reliable and comparable across subjects'. Lloyd (1999) has also considered the potential impact of these new arrangements on standards. He concedes that the most obvious conclusion is that A level standards will be diluted by awarding half of the marks for units studied at a standard appropriate for the first year of A level. However, he argues that it is a nonsense to assume that all A level topics and questions ever did exhibit a uniform standard, acknowledging that levels of difficulty are intricate, subject-specific issues, perhaps only fully appreciated by those who are expert in a subject. His own view is that 'top grades will become easier to get as half of the assessment contributing to them will be less demanding' (Lloyd 1999: 124). The usual retort to this criticism is that mark schemes and grade boundaries can be adjusted to maintain standards. However, Lloyd maintains that a fundamental flaw in these new arrangements is that awards are based on two standards, one lower than the other:

> One would not contemplate allowing candidates to carry GCSE marks forward to contribute to A-Level assessment, let alone to take GCSE papers in their A-Level year and use marks gained in them in that way. The flaws in allowing AS to be used in this way are less obvious, since we are accustomed to a system in which AS has been of a full A-Level standard.
>
> (Lloyd 1999: 125)

The extent to which AS level will succeed in broadening post-16 studies is also questionable. At the sharp end of the depth versus breadth tension are the resourcing difficulties for schools, which must find the staff and time to teach an expanded AS level programme. Schools have reported considerable difficulties in accommodating five AS levels within their existing timetables. Extending the school day, restricting the number of AS subjects to four and squeezing the time available for general studies and extracurricular activities are some of the responses that are being tried. AS level also generated a sharp increase in the volume of examination entries. The logistical implications of this increase became apparent in the summer of 2001 when the first cohort sat AS level examinations. Schools struggled to cope with the resource demands: more invigilators, larger rooms, more desks and more examinations officers were required. There was an unprecedented number of examination clashes that were resolved by providing overnight supervision for candidates or by allowing them to take several papers on the same day. Schools also found that their examinations costs had soared. These practical difficulties confirmed that sandwiching a new award between the GCSE and A2 years had resulted in an examinations overload. This may also have deleterious consequences for the quality of teaching and learning at A level. At the time of writing, a review of AS level has been announced. Therefore, arrangements described here will be subject to change.

8.5b A level

The reformed A level is normally a six-unit qualification available in traditional linear format with examinations coming at the end of a course of study or as a modular option with staged assessments. Although modular courses are agreed to be good for motivation, conventional wisdom casts them as soft options which lower standards. Requirements have been built into the reforms to counter this criticism and safeguard the rigour of A level standards. Individual units can be retaken once only. Whichever assessment option is chosen, a significant element of A2 (normally 20 per cent) must be by external, synoptic assessment. Synoptic assessment is designed to test understanding of the syllabus as a whole and the ability to make connections between different aspects of a subject. There has also been a modest increase in coursework limits with up to 30 per cent of the marks being allocated in this way in most subjects. Just as Part One GNVQ is being replaced by a vocational GCSE, so too Advanced GNVQ and A level have been aligned with a six-unit vocational A level graded A–E replacing Advanced GNVQ.

8.5c Advanced Extension Awards (AEAs)

AEAs will replace Special level (S level) in 2002. They are intended to complement the world class tests being developed for the most able 9- and 13-year-olds and are aimed at those who are expected comfortably to achieve A grades at A level. Whereas very few centres enter candidates for S level, AEAs are designed to widen participation by making their content accessible to able pupils irrespective of the A level specification they have followed or the institution in which they have studied. QCA claims that no additional teaching or resources need be committed to preparing pupils for AEAs, which will focus on depth of understanding rather than breadth of coverage, the ability to think critically and creatively and to understand the connections between different elements of a subject. Trials have experimented with innovative approaches to assessment including pre-released case studies and investigations, extended essays and the use of computers as an examining medium. However, feedback from trial centres has indicated a preference for conventional examinations because candidates were ill prepared for unfamiliar styles of assessment despite the claim that no additional teaching and practice would be required (*TES* 2 February 2001: 11). Given the overloading of the post-16 curriculum, trial centres suggested that they would be hard pressed to divert resources into preparation for AEAs.

8.6 Occupational and vocationally related qualifications

GNVQs and NVQs percolated from further education to the post-16 curriculum and then to KS4 in the 1990s to address the need for alternatives to GCSE and A level for the thousands of pupils who left school with no academic qualifications.

8.6a NVQ

NVQs are job-specific qualifications which assess the ability to perform occupational roles against the standards required for employment during work placements. Although they are not widely used at KS4, schools are able to set aside certain KS4 curriculum requirements if an NVQ at level 1 or 2 is deemed to be the best way to meet pupils' needs. This option is particularly suited to non-academic pupils who are in danger of dropping out of the education system. These pupils follow a reduced NC programme alongside a regular work placement and/or course provided by a local further education college or other training provider.

8.6b GNVQ

GNVQs are work-related qualifications but they do not train pupils for specific jobs. They involve studying broad vocational areas such as health and social care, leisure and tourism or business. This study often involves time in the workplace where pupils can interact with adults although they do not do the work themselves. Thus, GNVQ offers a broad preparation for work, equipping pupils with relevant knowledge and skills. GNVQ was introduced in 1992 at foundation, intermediate and advanced level but, because foundation and intermediate GNVQs were equivalent to four GCSEs, few schools could find time to offer them as part of the KS4 curriculum. However, the introduction of GNVQ Part One (1999), a two-year course equivalent to two GCSEs, enabled GNVQ to become an option at KS4. GCSE-equivalent GNVQs will be replaced by Vocational GCSE in 2002.

GNVQ seeks to provide alternative styles of teaching, learning and assessment to those offered by conventional academic courses. There is an emphasis on active, experiential learning through projects, research assignments and other investigative activities. Pupils learn independently, taking considerable responsibility for planning their own work, seeing it through and evaluating their achievements. GNVQ often involves group work and collaboration, placing an emphasis on the *application* of knowledge and skills. External testing is a late addition to GNVQ assessment requirements. It accounts for one-third of final marks and was introduced to enhance the public credibility and reliability (Section 8.7a) of the qualification. Two-thirds of the final award is based on a portfolio of evidence which pupils compile to demonstrate their attainments.

GNVQ is a unit-based qualification comprising mandatory, optional and key skills units ('communication', 'application of number' and 'ICT'). Figure 8.3 shows the different 'sizes' and levels available and their academic and vocational equivalences (see p. 172).

As well as being an award in its own right, GNVQ is a bridging mechanism in the qualifications framework. It offers access to further and higher education and allows pupils to switch pathways to focus on vocationally specific NVQs and employment.

8.6c Key skills qualifications

Although key skills units were always part of GNVQ, pressure from employers for the key skills of 'communication', 'application of number' and 'IT' to become a *compulsory* part of the post-16 curriculum led to the introduction of a new Key Skills award in 2000. Key Skills units remain an integral part of GNVQ although they are now separately certificated. Other young people over 16 are being encouraged to take the optional key skills award whatever their main programme. The award has been aligned with the qualifications framework and is available at levels 1–4. The three units (communication, application of number and IT) do not have to be at the same level so candidates receive a profile showing what level they have reached in each. Assessment is on a pass/fail basis using a portfolio of evidence and externally set and marked tests. No grades are awarded. So far, take-up has been poor because the expectation that pupils will study up to five subjects for AS level has expanded their workload, forcing them to prioritize demands on their time. Since universities have not made key skills qualifications a compulsory part of their entry requirements, this has further weakened the incentive to take another qualification (*TES* 9 February 2001: 11). 'Working with others', 'problem-solving' and 'improving own learning and performance' – often described as the 'wider key skills' – are also available, assessed by portfolio only.

8.7 Technical aspects of assessment

Although technical requirements are usually overlooked in the low stakes setting of day-to-day assessment, validity and reliability are important considerations for all assessment. Any assessment, however informal, which fails to measure what it is intended to measure, or where there can be little confidence in the accuracy of results, is futile. The higher the stakes, the more important it becomes that the validity and reliability of an assessment procedure command confidence. Where results determine pupils' life chances acting as passports to further and higher education and employment and where they are used as key performance indicators for judging the success of schools, the importance of procedures which combine high levels of validity with optimum reliability cannot be overestimated.

8.7a Validity, reliability and dependability

A valid assessment measures the knowledge, skills and/or concepts which it purports to measure. Although there are different ways of estimating validity (Wiliam 1992), content validity (the extent to which a test adequately samples the content of the relevant PoS) is the principal consideration for the purposes of this text. It may seem unlikely that anyone would set a test which failed to measure what it set out to measure but there are, in fact, many ways in which assessments can be invalidated. Tests are invariably short and this immediately raises questions about the extent to which they compromise content validity. NC tests provide a case in point. Originally conceived as 'Standard Assessment Tasks', which would be barely distinguishable from good classroom practice (DES 1988), a series of revisions transformed SATs into 'conventional examinations . . . a long way from the lofty hopes of the TGAT [Task Group on Assessment and Testing] report which initiated national curriculum assessment' (Stobart and Gipps 1997: 81). In all three subjects, KS3 tests last less than three hours, raising questions about their adequacy as samples of broad PoS (Shorrocks-Taylor 1999: 150). The content validity of the tests was further weakened by an early decision (1991) to exclude the 'process' AT, AT1, because 'Speaking and Listening' in English, 'Using and Applying Mathematics' and 'Scientific Enquiry' proved difficult to assess under test conditions. Validity can be undermined in other ways. For instance, the literacy demands of some KS2 science and mathematics tests have prompted questions about the extent to which their validity is undermined by their language and format. Validity should be the paramount consideration for any assessment procedure (Crooks *et al.* 1996: 265). However, it is invariably marginalized when the stakes are high. Stobart and Gipps (1997: 92) note that whenever 'assessment is high-stakes . . . the emphasis shifts to the *reliability* and *comparability* of qualifications'. Wood (1991, quoted in Black 1998: 53) agrees that 'The examining boards have been lucky not to have been engaged in a validity argument . . . [They] know so little about what they are assessing'.

Test results should be reliable which means they must be consistent, accurate and capable of being replicated. Thus, whereas the test *per se* should be valid, it is the *results* of a test that should be reliable. There are four components of testing which can introduce variability, thereby affecting the reliability of results:

The candidate	Performance varies from task to task making 'the interaction of student with task . . . by far the greatest source of variation' (Satterly 1994: 63).

	Therefore, one-off snapshots may offer an unreliable representation of 'true' performance.
The marker	Inter-rater reliability indicates the extent to which different markers marking on the same occasion agree. Mark re-mark reliability indicates the extent to which results can be replicated if an assessment is repeated. Variations within and between markers are important sources of unreliability.
The test	Different procedures are associated with more or less reliable results, for example objective tests have an in-built level of reliability which is greater than that associated with tests 'where subjectivity plays a part' (Satterly 1994: 62)
Test administration	The standardization of test-taking conditions is usually seen as one of the greatest assets of a test, for instance candidates take the same paper with access to the same resources and the same amount of time in which to complete it. However, test administration is occasionally a confounding variable. For instance, at KS1, the immaturity of the candidates has made it impossible to standardize test conditions.

A perfectly reliable test would give identical results regardless of when or how the assessment was made. However, in practice 'a significant proportion [of candidates] are given the wrong grade' (Black 1998: 41). For instance, at KS3, using one measure of reliability only 'about 30 per cent of pupils would be placed in the wrong level – there is no way of knowing how much worse this figure might be if all of the other factors could be taken into account' (Black 1998: 41). Moderation is one of the procedures employed by awarding bodies to offset threats to the reliability of their awards. Nevertheless, although external examinations command the confidence of policy-makers and the public, there is no evidence that awards made in this way yield more reliable results than those produced by externally moderated TA.

Validity and reliability are, to some extent, interdependent in that the absence of one requirement compromises the other. For instance, there would be little merit in an assessment which carefully sampled course content if it proved impossible to achieve consensus among assessors on how to grade it. Likewise, it is a hollow achievement to construct a test which produces high levels of agreement between markers if it neglects Key Skills/concepts from the PoS. Thus, a very poor level of validity automatically devalues the reliability of an assessment and vice versa. For this reason, experts favour an overarching notion of dependability to the separate notions of validity and reliability because it captures the symbiotic relationship that should exist between them. In practice, the demands of validity are usually in tension with the requirements of reliability so that enhancing one has the effect of weakening the other. Therefore, dependability is about creating a balanced relationship between validity and reliability in which each is maximized. Gipps (1994: 173) defines it as the extent to which an assessment 'is both content valid and reliable'.

One approach to examination reform which has aimed to improve the validity and reliability of traditional norm-referenced systems is criterion-referencing (Section 3.4). Many awards introduced since the 1980s have adopted a criterion-referenced approach to assessment.

8.7b Criterion-referencing and competence-based assessment

Although criterion-referencing is an essential component of formative/ ipsative assessment, where it confers many benefits on pupils and teachers (section 3.4), its use in public examinations has proved to be much more problematic. The assessment of both GCSE and the NC were originally intended to be criterion-referenced but neither managed to produce a workable system. These high-profile failures are instructive, offering insights into some of the limitations of criterion-referencing. Gipps and Stobart (1993: 75) argue that criterion-referencing is 'ideal for simply defined competencies ("*can swim 50 metres*")' whereas in complex, elaborated systems its use is fraught with difficulties. Ironically, it is a feature of criterion-referencing which was described as a strength in Chapter 3 which provides the stumbling block here.

The attempt to make assessment transparent simultaneously makes criterion-referencing unmanageable in an external examination context because it encourages the formulation of comprehensive specifications of assessment criteria for each grade, level or award available and for each domain into which a subject is divided. Time and time again, the result has been bewildering lists of assessment criteria characterized by exhaustive detail and complexity. For instance, when GCSE was introduced, subject working parties were set the task of producing grade-related criteria.

> In history . . . there were ten sub-elements across three domains and criteria were given for four levels of performance within each sub-element (and in GCSE there are seven levels, i.e. grades), adding up to 40 statements of performance . . . The maths group produced *eighty* detailed criteria for *one domain* at a *single grade* level.
>
> (Gipps and Stobart 1993: 77–8)

Before GCSE was launched, the attempt to produce grade criteria was abandoned as 'largely unworkable' (Gipps and Stobart 1993: 78) and with it went the prospect of creating a criterion-referenced examination.

These difficulties did not deter the attempt to criterion-reference NC assessments but the experience turned out to be depressingly familiar.

For instance, in the original subject orders for KS1, mathematics and science accounted for no less than 31 separate ATs (17 in science and 14 in mathematics). These ATs were further subdivided into separate statements of attainment (the criteria for assessment). There were sometimes several statements of attainment at each level in each AT. Overall, there were 296 for mathematics and 407 in science (Wiliam and Black 1996). By December 1990, the seven subjects on stream had between them over 1400 statements of attainment (Stobart and Gipps 1997: 48). Each infant had to be assessed against each statement and the resulting levels had to be put through complicated aggregation systems to arrive at final NC levels. Unsurprisingly, the NC collapsed under the weight of its own assessment apparatus, culminating in a teacher boycott of the 1993 tests. Statements of attainment were jettisoned in the revised NC and replaced by broad level descriptions operating on a principle of 'best fit' (Section 8.2d). The demise of the statements of attainment also marked the end of the attempt to criterion-reference the NC.

Criterion-referencing is a more enduring feature of occupational and vocationally related qualifications where it takes the form of competence-based assessment. However, the same tendencies are also manifest there:

> This ever-receding goal of total clarity derives not from bad luck or incompetence, but is actually inherent in the methodology adopted. The more serious and rigorous the attempts to specify the domain being assessed, the narrower and narrower the domain itself becomes, without, in fact, becoming fully transparent. The attempt to map out free-standing content and standards leads, time and time again, to a never ending spiral of specification.
>
> (Wolf 1995: 55)

Task 8.1

Evaluate the lists you formulated in response to Task I.1.

References

Arnot, M., Gray, J., James, M., Rudduck, J. and Duveen, G. (1998) *Recent Research on Gender and Educational Performance*. London: The Stationery Office.

Askew, S. (ed.) (2000) *Feedback for Learning*. London: RoutledgeFalmer.

Ausubel, D. (1968) *Educational Psychology: A Cognitive View*. New York: Holt, Rinehart and Winston.

Ausubel, D. (1987) Learning as constructing meaning, in N. Entwistle (ed.) *New Directions in Educational Psychology: Learning and Teaching*. London: Falmer.

Best, B. (1992) *The Rationality of Feeling*. London: Falmer Press.

Black, P. (1998) *Testing: Friend or Foe? Theory and Practice of Assessment and Testing*. London: Falmer.

Black, P. and Wiliam, D. (1998a) Assessment and classroom learning, *Assessment in Education*, 5(1): 7–78.

Black, P. and Wiliam, D. (1998b) *Inside the Black Box: Raising Standards through Classroom Assessment*. London: King's College.

Board of Education (1939) *Secondary Education with Special Reference to Grammar Schools and Technical High Schools: Report of the Consultative Committee on Secondary Education* (Spens Report). London: HMSO.

Broadfoot, P., James, M., McMeeking, S., Nuttall, D. and Stierer, S. (1988) *Records of Achievement: Report of the National Evaluation of Pilot Schemes*. London: HMSO.

Brooks, V. (1993) The resurgence of external examining in Britain: a historical review, *British Journal of Educational Studies*, 41(1): 59–72.

Brooks, V. and Little, V. (1995) *'I'm Still Using GRASP': Independent Evaluation of the Dudley/Comino GRASP® Project*. Coventry: University of Warwick.

Brooks, V. and Little, V. (1997) GRASPing for development, *Teacher Development: An International Journal of Teachers' Professional Development*, 1(2): 219–30.

Brooks, V. and Sikes, P. (1997) *The Good Mentor Guide: Initial Teacher Education in Secondary Schools*. Buckingham: Open University Press.

Bruner, J. (1983) *Child's Talk: Learning to Use Language*. Oxford: Oxford University Press.

Butterfield, S. (1995) *Educational Objectives and National Assessment*. Buckingham: Open University Press.

Butterfield, S., Williams, A. and Marr, A. (1999) Talking about assessment: mentor–student dialogues about pupil assessment in initial teacher training, *Assessment in Education*, 6(2): 225–46.

Capel, S., Leask, M. and Turner, T. (1999) *Learning to Teach in the Secondary School: A Companion to School Experience.* London: Routledge.

Carver, G. (2000) *Tested to Destruction? A Survey of Examination Stress in Teenagers* (www.pat.org.uk Professional Association of Teachers).

Child, D. (1997) *Psychology and the Teacher.* London: Cassell.

Clark, C. (1989) Asking the right questions about teacher education: contributions of research on teacher thinking, in J. Lowyck and C. Clark (eds) *Teacher Thinking and Professional Action.* Leuven: Leuven University Press.

Clarke, S. (1998) *Targeting Assessment in the Primary Classroom.* London: Hodder and Stoughton.

Claxton, G. (1984) The psychology of teacher training: inaccuracies and improvements, *Educational Psychologist,* 4(2): 167–74.

Clough, E. and Davis, P. with Sumner, R. (1984) *Assessing Pupils: A Study of Policy and Practice.* Windsor: NFER-Nelson.

Cohen, L., Manion, L. and Morrison, K. (1996) *A Guide to Teaching Practice.* London: Routledge.

Conner, C. (1991) *Assessment and Testing in the Primary School.* London: Falmer.

Conner, C. (ed.) (1999) *Assessment in Action in the Primary School.* London: Falmer.

Crooks, T. J., Kane, M. T. and Cohen, A. S. (1996) Threats to the valid uses of assessments, *Assessment in Education,* 3(3): 265–85.

Daugherty, R. (1995) *National Curriculum Assessment: A Review of Policy 1987–1994.* London: Falmer.

Dean, J. (1990) *Organizing Learning in the Primary School.* London: Routledge.

Dearing, R. (1996) *Review of Qualifications for 16–19 Year Olds.* London: SCAA.

Department of Education and Science (DES) (1975) *A Language for Life: Report of a Committee of Inquiry* (Bullock Report). London: HMSO.

DES (1988) *National Curriculum Task Group on Assessment and Testing: A Report.* London: DES.

Department for Education (DfE) (1992) *The New Requirements for Initial Teacher Training: Circular 9/92.* London: DfE.

DfE (1994) *Code of Practice on the Identification and Assessment of Special Educational Needs.* London: DfE.

Department for Education and Employment (DfEE) (1997) *From Targets to Action: Guidance to Support Effective Target-setting in Schools.* London: DfEE.

DfEE (1998a) *Teaching: High Status, High Standards: Requirements for Courses of Initial Teacher Training: Circular 4/98.* London: DfEE.

DfEE (1998b) *Target-setting in Schools: Circular 11/98.* London: DfEE.

DfEE (1999) *The Autumn Package 1999: Pupil Performance Information GCSE/GNVQ.* London: DfEE.

DfEE (2000) *Learning Journey: Ages 11–16.* London: DfEE.

Dickinson, C. and Wright, J. (1993) *Differentiation: A Practical Handbook of Classroom Strategies.* Coventry: National Council for Educational Technology.

Dunsbee, T. and Ford, T. (1980) *Mark my Words: A Study of Teachers as Correctors of Children's Writing.* Sydney: Ashton Scholastic.

Elliott, J. (1991) A model of professionalism and its implications for teacher education, *British Educational Research Journal,* 17(4): 309–18.

English, M. (1981) Talking: does it help?, in C. Sutton (ed.) *Communicating in the Classroom.* London: Hodder and Stoughton.

Fitz-Gibbon, C. and Tymms, P. (1997) *The Value-Added National Project: Final Report.* London: SCAA.

Freeman, R. and Lewis, R. (1998) *Planning and Implementing Assessment*. London: Kogan Page.

Furlong, J. and Maynard, T. (1995) *Mentoring Student Teachers: The Growth of Professional Knowledge*. London: Routledge.

Galton, M. (1983) *Moving from the Primary Classroom*. London: Routledge and Kegan Paul.

Gann, N. (1999) *Targets for Tomorrow's Schools: A Guide to Whole School Target-setting for Governors and Headteachers*. London: Falmer.

Gardner, H. (1983) *Frames of Mind*. London: Fontana.

Gardner, H. (1993) *The Unschooled Mind*. London: Fontana.

Gipps, C. (1994) *Beyond Testing: Towards a Theory of Educational Assessment*. London: Falmer.

Gipps, C. and Murphy, P. (1994) *A Fair Test? Assessment, Achievement and Equity*. Buckingham: Open University Press.

Gipps, C. and Stobart, G. (1993) *Assessment: A Teachers' Guide to the Issues*. London: Hodder and Stoughton.

Gipps, C., Brown, M., McCallum, B. and McAlister, S. (1995) *Intuition or Evidence?* Buckingham: Open University Press.

Gray, J. (1996) The use of assessment to compare institutions, in H. Goldstein and T. Lewis (eds) *Assessment: Problems, Developments and Statistical Issues*. London: Wiley.

Haigh, G. (1999) How to focus pupils on making the grade, *Times Educational Supplement Online*, 8 January.

Haigh, G. (2000) Modern day cures to banish those testing time troubles, *Times Educational Supplement Online*, 7 January.

Hamson, R. and Sutton, A. (2000) Target setting at Key Stage 3, *Teaching Geography*, January: 8–11.

Hargreaves, D. (1990) Assessing the alternatives, *Times Educational Supplement*, 15 April.

Harlen, W. (1977) *Match and Mismatch*. Edinburgh: Oliver and Boyd.

Harris, A. (1998) Effective teaching: a review of the literature, *School Leadership and Management*, 18(2): 169–83.

Headington, R. (2000) *Monitoring, Assessment, Recording, Reporting and Accountability: Meeting the Standards*. London: David Fulton.

Hedger, K. and Jesson, D. (1999) *Numbers Game: The Use of Assessment Data in Primary and Secondary Schools and by OFSTED Inspectors*. Shrewsbury: Shropshire Education Publications.

Her Majesty's Inspectorate (HMI) (1992) *The Implementation of the Curricular Requirements of ERA*. London: HMSO.

Honey, P. and Mumford, A. (1992) *The Manual of Learning Styles*, 3rd edn. Maidenhead: Peter Honey.

Hook, C. (1985) *Studying Classrooms*. Deakin: Deakin University Press.

Hughes, M., Wikeley, F. and Nash, T. (1994) *Parents and their Children's Schools*. Oxford: Blackwell.

Husbands, C. (1996) *What is History Teaching?* Buckingham: Open University Press.

Husbands, C. (1999) *PGCE Secondary Course Core Programme Study Guide 1999–2000*. Unpublished, University of Warwick.

Iven, H. (1992) Testamania: the proposed Key Stage 3 pilot tests, *Education 3–13*(3): 30–3.

James, M. (1998) *Using Assessment for School Improvement*. Oxford: Heinemann.

James, M. (2000) Measured lives: the rise of assessment as the engine of change in English schools, *The Curriculum Journal*, 11(3): 343–64.

John, P. (1993) *Lesson Planning for Teachers*. London: Cassell.

Kaur, B. (1998) Primary/secondary liaison in science and value added from Key Stage 2 to 3, *Education in Science*, 179: 9–11.

Kolb, D. (1984) *Experiential Learning: Experience as the Source of Learning and Development*. Englewood Cliffs, NJ: Prentice Hall.

Kounin, J. S. (1970) *Discipline and Group Management in Classrooms*. New York: Holt, Rinehart and Winston.

Kyriacou, C. (1992) *Essential Teaching Skills*. Hemel Hempstead: Simon and Schuster.

Lawley, P. (1999) *Target Setting and Bench Marking*. Dunstable: Folens Framework.

Lines, D. (2000) A disaster waiting to happen, *Times Educational Supplement*, 17 April.

Lloyd, J. G. (1999) *How Exams Really Work: Guide to GCSEs, AS and A Levels*. London: Cassell.

Lodge, C. and Watkins, C. (1999) *Targeting Strategies – Hit AND Miss*. Coventry: National Association for Pastoral Care in Education.

Lucas, P. (1995) A neglected source for reflection in the supervision of student teachers, in T. Kerry and A. Shelton Mayes (eds) *Issues in Mentoring*. London: Routledge.

Madaus, G. (1988) The influence of testing on the curriculum, in L. Tanner (ed.) *Critical Issues in Curriculum*, 87th Yearbook of NSSE Part 1. Chicago: University of Chicago Press.

McIntyre, D. and Cooper, P. (1996) The classroom expertise of Year 7 teachers and pupils, *Education 3 to 13*, March.

Morgan, N. and Saxton, J. (1993) *Asking Better Questions*. Ontario: Pembroke.

Munby, S. with Phillips, P. and Collinson, R. (1989) *Assessing and Recording Achievement*. Oxford: Blackwell.

National Foundation for Educational Research (NFER) (1998) *Learning from Differentiation: A Review of Practice in Primary and Secondary Schools*. Slough: NFER.

Ofsted (1995) *Reporting Pupils' Achievements*. London: HMSO.

Ofsted (1996a) *Setting Targets to Raise Standards: A Survey of Good Practice*. London: HMSO.

Ofsted (1996b) *The Annual Report of Her Majesty's Chief Inspector of Schools*. London: HMSO.

Ofsted (1998a) *Secondary Education 1993–1997: A Review of Secondary Schools in England*. London: The Stationery Office.

Ofsted (1998b) *School Evaluation Matters*. London: The Stationery Office.

Ofsted (1999) *Secondary Initial Teacher Training: Secondary Subject Inspections 1996–1998 Overview Report*. London: The Stationery Office.

Pidgeon, S. (1992) Assessment at Key Stage 1: teacher assessment through record keeping, in G. M. Blenkin and A. V. Kelly (eds) *Assessment in Early Childhood Education*. London: Paul Chapman.

Pringle, M. and Cobb, T. (1999) *Making Pupil Data Powerful: A Guide for Classroom Teachers*. Stafford: Network Educational Press.

Pryor, J. and Torrance, H. (1996) Teacher–pupil interaction in formative assessment: assessing the work or protecting the child?, *The Curriculum Journal*, 7(2): 205–26.

Qualifications and Curriculum Authority (QCA) (1999) *Key Stage 3 Assessment and Reporting Arrangements*. London: QCA.

QCA (2000a) *Key Stage 3 Assessment and Reporting Arrangements*. London: QCA.

QCA (2000b) *Finding Your Way Around: A Leaflet about the National Qualifications Framework.* London: QCA.

Riding, R. (1998) *Cognitive Styles and Learning Strategies.* London: David Fulton.

Rudduck, J. and Sigsworth, A. (1985) Partnership supervision, in D. Hopkins and K. Reid (eds) *Rethinking Teacher Education.* Beckenham: Croom Helm.

Rudduck, J., Chaplain, R. and Wallace, G. (1996) *School Improvement: What can Pupils Tell Us?* London: David Fulton.

Sadler, D. R. (1989) Formative assessment and the design of instructional systems, *Instructional Science*, 18: 119–44.

Satterly, D. (1994) Quality in external assessment, in W. Harlen (ed.) *Enhancing Quality in Assessment.* London: Paul Chapman.

Saunders, L. (1998) *'Value Added' Measurement of School Effectiveness: An Overview.* Slough: National Foundation for Educational Research.

Schagen, I. (undated) Exploring school effectiveness and 'value-added quadrants' via GCSE performance data (unpublished research).

School Curriculum and Assessment Authority (SCAA) (1995) *Key Stage 4 Update.* London: SCAA.

SCAA (1997) *Making Effective Use of Key Stage 2 Assessments at the Transfer between Key Stage 2 and Key Stage 3 to Support Teaching of Pupils in Year 7.* London: SCAA.

Shorrocks-Taylor, D. (1999) *National Testing: Past, Present and Future.* Leicester: British Psychological Society.

Simpson, M. (1990) Why criterion-referenced assessment is unlikely to improve learning, *The Curriculum Journal*, 1(2): 171–83.

Smith, A. (1998) *Accelerated Learning in Practice: Brain-based Methods for Accelerating Motivation and Achievement.* Stafford: Network Educational Press.

Smith, R. and Alred, G. (1994) The impersonation of wisdom, in D. McIntyre, H. Hagger and M. Wilkin (eds) *Mentoring: Perspectives on School-based Teacher Education.* London: Kogan Page.

Somers, J. (2000) Knowing the shadow or knowing the bird, in J. Sefton-Green and R. Sinker (eds) *Evaluating Creativity.* London: Routledge.

Stobart, G. and Gipps, C. (1997) *Assessment: A Teacher's Guide to the Issues.* London: Hodder and Stoughton.

Sutton, C. (1981) *Communicating in the Classroom.* London: Hodder and Stoughton.

Sutton, R. (1992) *Assessment: A Framework for Teachers.* London: Routledge.

Sutton, R. (1995) *Assessment for Learning.* Salford: RS Publications.

Tabberer, R., Hine, T. and Gallacher, S. (1996) Seven obstacles to effective target-setting, *Education Journal*, 7: 8–9.

Torrance, H. and Pryor, J. (1998) *Investigating Formative Assessment: Teaching, Learning and Assessment in the Classroom.* Buckingham: Open University Press.

Valentine, C. (1932) *The Reliability of Examinations: An Enquiry.* London: University of London Press.

Wilcox, B. (1992) *Time-constrained Evaluation: A Practical Approach for LEAs and Schools.* London: Routledge.

Wiliam, D. (1992) Some technical issues in assessment: a user's guide, *British Journal of Curriculum and Assessment*, 2(3): 11–20.

Wiliam, D. and Black, P. (1996) Meanings and consequences: a basis for distinguishing formative and summative functions of assessment?, *British Educational Research Journal*, 22(5): 537–48.

Wolf, A. (1995) *Competence-Based Assessment.* Buckingham: Open University Press.

Wood, D. (1998) *How Children Think and Learn.* Oxford: Blackwell.

Wood, R. (1991) *Assessment and Testing.* Cambridge: Cambridge University Press.

Wragg, E. C. (1984) *Classroom Teaching Skills.* London: Croom Helm.

Wragg, E. C. (1997) *Assessment and Learning.* London: Routledge.

Wragg, E. C. (1999) *An Introduction to Classroom Observation.* London: Routledge.

Wragg, E. C., Wikely, F. J., Wragg, C. M. and Haynes, G. S. (1996) *Teacher Appraisal Observed.* London: Routledge.

Index